Daughters of Independence

Gender, Caste and Class in India

Joanna Liddle and Rama Joshi

kali for women

Zed Books Ltd

Daughters of Independence was first published in 1986

In the United Kingdom
Zed Books Ltd.
57 Caledonian Road,
London N1 9BU

In India
Kali for Women
N84 Panchshila Park
New Delhi 110 017

Copyright © Joanna Liddle and Rama Joshi

Cover design by Lee Robinson
Printed by The Bath Press, Avon

British Library Cataloguing in Publication Data
Liddle, Joanna
  Daughters of independence : gender, caste & class
  in India.
  1. Feminism — India — History
  I. Title   II. Joshi, Rama
  305.4'2'0954   HQ1742

  ISBN 0-86232-405-X
  ISBN 0-86232-406-8 Pb

US Distributor
Biblio Distribution Center, 81 Adams Drive,
Totowa, New Jersey, 07512

Contents

Glossary   vii
Foreword by Dr Ursula Sharma   1
Preface   3
Introduction   5
The Problem   5
The Fieldwork   7
The Women   8
The Method   10
The Researchers   11
The Objectives   11

PART I: WOMEN'S ORGANISATION   15

1. The women rise . . .   17

2. . . . and not for the first time   19
    Men's Organisation   19
    Women's Organisation   20

3. The Main Enemy: Imperialism   24
    Britain's Financial Interests in India   24
    The Impact of Colonial Rule on Women   25
    Sati   27
    Matriliny   28
    Britain's Approach to the Women's Question   30

4. The Freedom Alliance   33
    Women and the Nationalist Movement   33
    Women's Suffrage   35
    Personal Law   36
    The Approach of the Nationalist Movement to the
        Women's Question   37

5. Freedom for India, and Women?   39

PART II: GENDER AND HIERARCHY   47

6. **Roots of Women's Resistance**   49

7. **Patriarchy and the Matriarchal Heritage**   51
    Matrilinial Family Organisation   52
    Matriarchal Religious Tradition   53
    Women's Heritage   55

8. **Women and Caste**   57
    Features of the Caste System   58
    The Impact of Caste on Women   59
    The Aryan Impact on Women   61
    Challenge and Response   62
    Resistance and Integration   66

9. **The New Middle Class**   70
    Creation of the Middle Class   71
    The Impact on Women   72

10. **The Problems Remain, So Does the Struggle**   74
    The Movement Disappears, the Ideas Remain   75

    PART III: EMERGENCE FROM SECLUSION   85

11. **Experiences of Orthodoxy**   87

12. **The Significance of Seclusion**   89

13. **Forces for Change**   94
    Social Movements against Caste, Class and Imperialism   95
    The System of Male Domination   96

14. **The Urge to Fly**   100
    Caste and Women's Work   100
    Class and Women's Work   106

15. **The Basis of Women's Subordination**   109
    Women's Resistance   109
    Women's Subordination and Social Hierarchy   109

    PART IV: LIMITS TO FREEDOM   113

16. **Class Privilege and Male Supremacy**   115

17. **Education: The Path to Emancipation**   117
    Effects of Economic Resources   117

Effects of Imperialism 118
Effects of Gender 121

18. **Employment: Women's Professional Work** 124
Class Privileges over Non-professional Women 126
Gender Privileges over Professional Men 128
Gender Discrimination 131
Physical Mobility 136
Social Interaction 138

19. **Family: Women's Domestic Work** 142
Women's Work in the Joint Family 143
Women's Work in the Nuclear Family 147
Women's Work in Alternative Forms of Family Organisation 148
Men's Domestic Work 149
Domestic Work and Class 150
Paid Work and the Family 151
Paid Work and Class 154

20. **Winning and Losing** 157
Mechanisms of Male Control 157
Men's Material Benefits 158
Connections between Gender and Class 158
The Social Processes of Gender and Social Hierarchy 159

PART V: WOMEN'S CONSCIOUSNESS 167

21. **Conflicts and Contradictions** 169

22. **Woman's Place in a Man's World** 174

23. **Creating Gender** 177
Inferiority 177
Subservience 180
Domesticity 182

24. **The Context of Gender** 186
The Cultural Context 187
The Context of Imperialism 188

25. **Exposing the Myths** 191
The Attitudes in Context 192
Changing Attitudes 193

PART VI: MECHANISMS OF STRUGGLE   195

26. **Working for Change**   197

27. **Sacrifice**   200

28. **Compromise**   206

29. **Resistance**   215

30. **A New Beginning**   225
    Mechanisms of Resistance   225
    Changes achieved   226
    The Character of the Changes   227

PART VII: CONCLUSIONS   231

31. **Understanding Women's Oppression and Resistance**   233
    Is Women's Subordination Related to Men's Position in the
        Social Hierarchy?   233
    Is Women's Liberation Related to the Influence of the West?   235
    What Social Processes Link the Structures Together?   237

    Statistical Tables   241
    Bibliography   252
    Index   261

Glossary

Ahimsa	Non-violence
Aryan	Indo-European language group who migrated to India around 1500 BC
Ayah	Nursemaid
Bhakti	Devotion
Brahmin	Priests; first caste in the Hindu social hierarchy
Devi	Goddess
Dharma	Righteousness, a general moral ideal, or law
Diwani	Revenue collection rights
Dravidian	Family of languages spoken in south India
Jati	Sub-caste or kin group in the local caste system (literally 'birth')
Karanavan	Head of Nayar taravad, i.e. the eldest brother
Karma	Action
Kayasth	Scribes; a caste inferior to brahmins but superior to vaishyas in the Hindu social hierarchy
Kshatriya	Warriors and princes; second caste in the Hindu social hierarchy
Lathi	Baton
Mata	Mother
Maiya khana	Room where a woman is secluded prior to marriage
Manushi	Woman
Pativrata	Husband worshipper
Purdah	Female seclusion
Raj	Rule
Sannyasi	Wandering holy man
Sati	Widow-burning (literally 'true one')
Satyagraha	Passive resistance or civil disobedience (literally 'hold fast to truth')

Satyagrahi	Passive resister
Shakti	Female power; the active force in Hindu religion
Smriti	Codes of Hindu law (literally 'remembered')
Sudra	Menial workers; fourth caste in the Hindu social hierarchy
Swadeshi	Indian-made goods (literally 'of our own country')
Swaraj	Self-rule
Tali	Pendant
Tantra	Hindu cults and sects often worshipping the goddesses with magical ceremonies
Taravad	Extended family of the matrilineal Nayars
Vaishya	Traders and artisans; third caste in the Hindu social hierarchy
Varna	Caste, referring to the four major castes in the national caste system (literally 'colour')
Vedas	Earliest books of Hindu religious scripture, written by the Aryan-speaking people
Zamindar	Revenue collector in Muslim times; landlord in British times
Zamindari	Revenue collection rights

Foreword

by Ursula Sharma

This is a book in which the subjects speak – yet it is more than just a record of conversations. There is both an ethnographic rhythm and a theoretical rhythm to the exposition of the interview material collected by the authors. At one level the experience and consciousness of particular women is described in depth, while at another, a more general argument about the relationship between class and gender is developed. It is, therefore, possible to see the professional women who form the subject of the study both as individuals, each with her own peculiar life story, and as products of general social conditions at a particular point in India's history.

Joanna Liddle and Rama Joshi contend that it has been possible for educated middle-class women in India to move into the professions, albeit to a limited extent, because the social groups to which they belong are moving from caste-oriented to class-oriented strategies for maintaining power and status. In a society dominated by caste organization and values, the seclusion of women brought prestige. Class society builds upon the gender hierarchy established by the caste system. In certain social strata, class privilege can be better maintained if some of the considerations which restricted the activities of women under the caste order are relaxed somewhat. Hence, the educated daughters of the old privileged castes begin to enter those areas of professional work deemed compatible with notions of female status and respectability.

This exit from seclusion is not part of some inevitable march towards emancipation resulting from 'modernization', nor is it a result of contact with Western culture, as many would like to believe. It is rather a part of the logic of the emerging class structure. The new freedom, which women of the professional classes enjoy, is limited by the forms of male control which the class system strengthens rather than dismantles.

Yet, as the subjects of this study show from their descriptions of their own lives and struggles, women in India have also resisted these limitations. The new feminism, embodied in the various women's action groups and organizations which have developed in the past decade, is only the most recent manifestation of a totally indigenous tradition of women's consciousness and resistance. For, as the authors argue, women in India have always been able to draw upon a stock of cultural imagery which represents women not as weak and passive but as endowed with power and energy. What women in India have achieved as a result of their struggles, they owe to nobody but themselves.

1

The value of this book is that it presents the professional women neither as some exotic or dedicated deviant from the current norm of the domesticated female, nor as the representative of some future norm which all Indian women will automatically attain in some 'emancipated' future. Considered as a social phenomenon, this category of women is the product of historical forces which are amply described. They are also a group which has never ceased to contend with their own history.

The authors are eminently successful in their object of writing a book which can be read by specialist and general reader alike, having avoided jargon or an excess of technical terms without sacrificing the rigour and exactness of their argument.

Ursula M. Sharma

Preface

This book is written for two audiences. Our hope is that despite being an academic analysis, it will have a wider appeal than the academic community, especially amongst the women's movement internationally. It is meant to be accessible to general readers with no specialist theoretical background in the area, and we have deliberately given the book a style and structure that will make it more personal and readable. This is because we believe that research should be available to the people who form its subject.

As a result, certain academic conventions of style and structure have been discarded. We refer to ourselves in the active not the passive form, since the passive form depersonalises our thinking, and writes the authors *out* of the research process, lending the analysis a spurious objectivity. We have put references and technical points in footnotes at the end of each Part, rather than disturb the flow of the text. Academic readers will have to work harder as a result, but we thought it appropriate to ask a little more of them, rather than distract the general reader with textual references. And we have organised the chapters so that the general reader can omit the theoretical parts without losing the sense of the women's stories.

The first two Parts are historical discussions, Parts 3 to 6 are empirical chapters looking at the women's lives, and the final Part forms a conclusion. Chapter 2 is the most complex conceptually, and can be omitted by the general reader. The empirical Parts follow a form whereby the more analytical chapters appear near the beginning and at the end of each Part, and these chapters can be omitted by the general reader if s/he desires. The most powerful and dramatic part of the study is the women's descriptions of their experiences, many of which are kept intact in the empirical chapters.

There are many stories hidden in our research data. We have tried to remain true to the data, but inevitably we have been selective. We have chosen to tell one story — of women struggling to change their conditions — because we wanted to keep trust with the women who *had* struggled. Here is part of a letter written to us by one such woman.

The draft of the portion which you have written about me, I have gone through. I totally agree with the incorporation of the material we had discussed about. The only thing I will request is not to mention my name because the truth is always bitter and nobody will like it. My husband will not be an exception. What I told you is not only my reaction but a true statement of any professional woman desiring to have a happy family life. You are free to use the material with the exception of my name.

All the names in this book have been changed.

Our acknowledgements are due to many people. Primarily our gratitude goes to the women who agreed to be interviewed, and who gave us their time and a part of their lives. We are both grateful to the British Council, the Indian University Grants Commission and the University of Warwick, who helped to fund the visits to each other's country for the purposes of conducting the interviews (in India) and writing up the chapters (in England). We would like to thank our spouses who helped in more active ways than simply giving moral and physical support: John for helping with the interviews and commenting on literary style, Jagdish for providing valuable advice on the historical chapters. A number of people read draft chapters and gave helpful and critical suggestions: we express our gratitude to Cliff Allum, Helen Brown, Jill Hardman, Hilary Homans, Linda Pickard and Jane Rosser. And we thank Norma Bainbridge and Jeanette Whitmore for speedy and skilful work on the typewriter.

Introduction

My idea of a field study in this would be simply to look at our women . . . We have to use our eyes and ears and *see* the creative energies in us . . . Personally, I believe this energy is directly related to the Shakti cults which are still very strong in our culture. I feel it in my own body and consciousness.
Chandralekha, *The Book Review*[1]

The Problem

The women's movement has a long history in India. Much longer than the current 'second wave' movement, or even the 'first wave' of earlier this century. The Shakti cults go back centuries, and the concept of Shakti — the female power principle — was recognised thousands of years ago. In this form the women's movement represents, not merely an oppositional force fuelled by anger, a rather negative reaction to oppression, but the development of a distinctive female culture, a positive creative force inspiring men and women alike.

Women in the West have only recently rediscovered the female power principle in themselves. It finds expression in a contemporary women's movement song:

You can't kill the Spirit
She is like a mountain
Old and strong
She goes on and on.

More common is the dominant principle of male power, with which women all over the world are familiar. There is no necessity for the two principles to be opposed. The ancient religions of India celebrate the meeting, not the confrontation, of opposites. But historically the two principles were in conflict, being fought out in different forms of social organisation and religious tradition. It is the struggle between the two forces, and the effect of the conflict on women, that provide the focus for this study.

The debates in the area currently centre around two major questions. First, why are women subordinate in the sex/gender system? Amongst the approaches to this question, there is a growing body of research which suggests that women's position is intricately tied up with the development of the class to which they belong. In Britain, for example, an historian studying the rise of the middle class in an English town showed that the development of the class was associated with the increased privatisation of women, who gradually disappeared from public life and whose work became increasingly circumscribed and confined to the domestic sphere.[2]

In India a similar process linking a rise in caste status with increasing constraints on women has been noted by a number of writers. Mysore Srinivas describes the change of lifestyle required of an upwardly mobile caste as 'Sanskritisation'. This process

> alters the life-style of those who have 'arrived', and in particular, it has radical effects on the lives of women. It immures them and changes the character of the husband-wife relationship... Among the less Sanskritized 'low' castes, conjugal relations appear to be more perceptibly egalitarian than among the Sanskritized 'high' castes.[3]

If such a relationship between gender and caste exists, what is its basis, in what ways could it help us to understand the process of male supremacy and women's subordination, and what are the social processes linking the structures of caste and gender together? Srinivas goes on to draw attention to the employment of middle-class women, who have their origins in the upper castes which previously secluded them:

> High status rural women offer, however, a sharp contrast to urban, educated women, a majority of whom hail from the higher castes. They are found employed as clerks, typists, receptionists, school teachers, nurses, doctors ... this occurs generally among the urban middle classes drawn from the higher castes.[4]

This raises the second major issue of the debate. If the constraints on women arise from the caste system, what are the main influences in freeing them from the constraints? Srinivas in his earlier work connected the decrease in controls over women to a process parallel to Sanskritisation, which he termed Westernisation. This is a process stemming originally from Britain's colonisation of India, whereby the upper caste elite moved away from Sanskritised values to adopt Western cultural norms. In many ways the lower castes and the British rulers had more in common with each other than either did with the upper castes.

> The upper castes ... were further removed from the British than the lower castes. The latter ate meat, some of them ate even pork and beef, and drank alcoholic liquor; women enjoyed greater freedom among them; and divorce and remarriage were not prohibited. The Indian leaders were thus caught in a dilemma. They found that certain customs and habits which until then they had looked down upon obtained also among their masters ... The Westernized upper castes began acquiring customs and habits which were not dissimilar from those they had looked down upon.[5]

So while relating controls over women to an increase in high-caste culture,

Srinivas associated greater freedom for women with the adoption of Western culture.

Many people agreed with this position. The British rulers themselves certainly did. To the extent that they concerned themselves with women, they saw themselves as a force for enlightenment, and this was reinforced by the Christian missionaries. The British took credit for abolishing female infanticide, child marriage and sati (widow-burning). Many orthodox Indians also associated women's freedom with the influence of the West, although from a rather different standpoint. When the Indian women's movement began to introduce legal reforms in the early part of this century, they were opposed by orthodox men who argued that women's rights were a Western concept and that allowing wives to divorce and daughters to inherit would destroy the structure of Hindu society.[6] The same view was held in many of the colonised Muslim countries, where aspects of female emancipation such as shedding the veil were associated with Western imperialism, and regarded as an attack on the identity and integrity of Muslim culture.[7]

In his later discussion of women's position, Srinivas dropped this line of argument,[8] but the association of women's emancipation with the influence of Western culture is still widely held in the West. The approach is now being questioned by women writers in the former colonies such as Veena Das[9] and Vina Mazumdar.[10] The important questions on this issue seem to be: what are the main influences in freeing women from the constraints to which the caste system subjected them, how far is the impact of the West a major force in this process, and what are the social processes linking gender with the particular system of class which began to develop as a result of British intervention?

The Fieldwork

India's combined systems of caste and class provide a fascinating opportunity to examine the relationship between gender divisions and the social hierarchy. We use the term social hierarchy to refer both to caste and class systems of social stratification. We chose to look at women in professional employment because they are the people who Srinivas suggests have been subjected to the dual processes of Sanskritisation and Westernisation. That is, they are likely to have come from the upper strata of society, where the strictest constraints on women were the norm; and they have succeeded in breaking out of these constraints, emerging from seclusion to take up a profession. The empirical study of professional women will be placed in an historical context, examining the impact on upper-caste women of the British Raj and of the earlier periods which witnessed the struggle between the male and the female power principles.

Many books have been written about professional women in India. We make no claim that this group represents the 'vanguard' of progressive womanhood,[11] or that any of our 'findings' can be generalised to other groups. We have chosen this group as the best means of addressing the analytical questions posed about the relationship between gender and the social structures of caste and class.

Studying women's emergence during the process of change from high-caste seclusion to professional employment allows us to examine both the link between caste and gender subordination, and how that link is broken, adapted or sustained in the transition to a class society.

The Women

The women in this study are all educated to college level, and are employed in jobs where their education is a necessary qualification. In this respect they can be classed as professional workers. We talked to 120 women, equally divided between four professions. Two of the professions, medicine and education, are traditional occupations for women, and have been so for at least three generations. They were opened to women partially in order to maintain sex segregation — so that women and girls could receive education and health care from members of their own sex. Sex segregation also made them respectable occupations for women. The other two — the civil service and the broad category of management — are new occupations for women. Women were not allowed to enter the higher levels of the civil service until Independence in 1947, and they have only recently entered management in manufacturing and service industries.

Working in a professional job is the only feature which unites the women, and which determined their choice. In other respects they are extremely varied. They come from nearly every state in India, as well as the areas which are now Pakistan and Bangladesh. Their ages range from 22 to 59. They are single, married, divorced, widowed and separated. They include Hindus, Muslims, Christians, Jains, Sikhs and Jews. Some are from strictly orthodox families living in highly traditional areas which they themselves describe as 'backward'. Others are from fiercely liberal or radical families living in the most industrialised cities. Some have had to fight for an education at the expense of any claim they might have to family support, emotional and financial. Others have had education and employment thrust upon them out of parental belief in the need for women to be financially independent. At work, many of the women feel severely handicapped, others suggest that being a woman can be an enormous advantage in a male world.

The lecturers were chosen from one of the two universities in Delhi and three of its related colleges. Under the Indian education system, only postgraduate degrees are taken from the university campus. Undergraduate degrees are taken at colleges affiliated to the university. All the institutions were coeducational. No women's colleges were included, because the women needed to be able to compare themselves with men in similar positions in their organisation. A random sample of the women lecturers was taken within each institution.[12] The sample included lecturers, senior lecturers, readers and professors, from 20 different subject areas. Unsurprisingly, women were most strongly represented in the arts and social sciences.

The doctors were chosen from three state-owned hospitals and three private hospitals in Delhi. The sampling was done in the same way as for the lecturers, and the sample ranged from young house surgeons to professors in teaching hospitals.[13] Women were most strongly represented in gynaecology and obstetrics (in fact there were no men in these departments), paediatrics, and in the non-clinical subjects such as pathology and radiology. They were less well represented in the areas of general medicine and anaesthesia, and poorly represented in areas such as surgery, neurology and cardiology.

Civil servants are far fewer in number amongst women than are doctors or lecturers. The total number of women in the Indian Administrative Service (the highest class of civil service employees) is approximately 350, of whom less than half are resident in Delhi at any one time. IAS officers have to divide their time between central government work in Delhi and work in a state of their choice, therefore some of the officers listed in Delhi are working for Delhi state, although most are working for the central government and will be posted back to their own state in a number of years. There are also a number of specialists in government posts in research and advisory positions, including medical, educational, scientific and technical specialists, and these are included in the sample. A random sample of all the women officers listed as working in Delhi was taken.[14] The positions ranged from under-secretary to joint secretary, in 15 different ministries, and women were most strongly represented in Health and Family Planning, Education and Social Welfare, and the Ministry of Labour.

It was impossible to make any kind of systematic selection of women managers, mainly because there were so few of them. There were not enough women managers in any single organisation to take a random sample. The most helpful source of information on women in management was the University of Delhi's Management Department, who gave us the names of women who had passed through their MBA course. It was by following up these women, and the contacts they gave us, that we were able to complete the sample. We defined management widely so as to include not only general managers in the traditional areas such as marketing, finance, personnel and production etc., but also specialists in significant research and advisory positions. The specialists were found in the three areas of statistics, engineering and operations research. The women worked in five private companies, and eight state-owned companies, ranging in size from a small private firm with 30 employees, to a large, state-owned, all-India company with 55,000 employees, to a multinational organisation employing millions of people all over the world. Women were found mainly in the public sector, and predominantly in general management rather than specialist advisory positions.[15]

The managers could not be selected randomly, but we did sample women from the other three professions systematically. The refusal rate was low, at about 5 per cent. The main purpose of sampling was not to make statements about statistical significance, but to achieve a wide coverage of women in different branches of the four professions.

The Method

India is vast and complex. There are more than 20 states, some the size of the British Isles, and a few Union Territories. Even under the British, India was never 'united', since approximately a third of the territory consisted of 'independent' states controlled by Indian princes who were propped up by the British. At Independence, the predominantly Muslim areas in the north-west and the north-east became the separate state of Pakistan, from which the north-eastern part seceded in 1971 to become Bangladesh.

Because of its size, its more than a dozen major languages, its history of immigrations and invasions, its half dozen major religions, and its great variation in climatic and geographical features, India is really a country of many cultures rather than one, all of which, however, have interacted. This study is limited to the women of the professional class working in one city, the capital Delhi, in the conservative north of the country. The women themselves are cosmopolitan, only 25 per cent coming originally from Delhi.

The data in this book derive from many disciplines. We have used information from history, anthropology, sociology, psychology, law, religion, politics, statistics. Women's studies is by its nature an integrated subject. It explores the multidimensional aspects of women's lives in an attempt to understand the totality of their experiences, in contrast to the more limited perspectives of the single discipline often imposed by male researchers, particularly in a segregated society. Both authors work in multidisciplinary departments of Industrial Studies where this kind of approach is being developed. Integrating such data, however, sometimes presents difficulties in that a sharp contrast may be experienced by the reader in the *forms* of data in, for instance, a presentation of government statistics followed by a discussion of religious mythology.

Both authors are originally psychologists, the discipline which taught us the scientific method. In moving to a multidisciplinary approach, however, we have found certain limitations with the scientific method. It cannot be used in some of the other disciplines, and where it is used it often renders a spurious objectivity to complex social phenomena which cannot readily be fragmented for scientific analysis, as sociologists have argued at some length.[16] In developing the area of women's studies, our intention is to ask, not is this perspective true or untrue, but what does this perspective reveal? Although we have sampled the women to be interviewed as systematically as possible, the aim is not simply to be statistically representative, but to represent the variety of views and experiences expressed by this particular group of women. We intend to locate the experiences in the context of the social structures within which they occur, to show that the experiences are not merely personal and individual but part of a wider pattern of social relations.

The fieldwork was conducted in 1977 and the data collected by three methods.

One. A structured questionnaire containing questions on factual background information on family, education, friends and peers, and employment, as well as relevant personal data, was posted prior to the interview whenever possible. The women were asked to complete the questionnaire before the interview took place so that points in the questionnaire could be raised at the interview.

Two. A semi-structured interview containing specific questions on actual experiences and the attitudes of others, under the same four headings. These areas could be opened up for wider discussion if appropriate.

Three. An unstructured interview, with six topic areas and suggested questions under each topic, designed to explore the woman's general approach to the position of women, rather than specific experiences of discrimination, etc. The aim of this part was to explore how a woman saw the social world and her place in it, following her leads rather than asking a series of pre-set and limiting questions which could produce merely stereotyped responses.

The unstructured method was not always successful with people who had a low level of interest in the issues involved, and a more structured approach had to be used with them. The interview lasted a minimum of one hour but frequently continued longer and, with women who had the most interesting experiences and who were most interested in the study, they sometimes took half a day.

The Researchers

The interviews were conducted by three people: Joanna Liddle, Rama Joshi and John Banks. We made notes on the response we felt we received to each interview. Examining the notes and the content of the interviews, we could not discern any pattern of inhibition or openness on the basis of either sex or nationality of the interviewer. It is clear that each of us talked to women who did not speak freely in the interview, but the male interviewer was entrusted with some of the most candid information, and the foreign interviewers received both candid and reserved responses just as did the Indian interviewer. In specific cases we recognised that the sex and nationality of the interviewers did have a negative impact, but no predictable pattern could be ascertained.

The Objectives

The study has three major objectives.

One. It examines the relationship between women's subordination and their position in the social hierarchy by looking at women's conditions in the higher strata of the caste and class hierarchies, historically and empirically. We explore the basis for the relationship, and examine what an understanding of the relationship might reveal about the process of male dominance and female subordination.

Two. If the constraints on women arise from the organisation of the social hierarchy, and given that the British colonisation of India created major changes in the society, the study examines the main influences in freeing women from the constraints, and how far the impact of the West is a major force in this process, both historically and today. We look at this by examining the history of women's struggles and by an empirical analysis of high-caste women's emergence from domestic seclusion to professional employment.

Three. The study attempts to analyse some of the social processes linking the sex/gender system with the structures of caste and class. By studying women who are in a privileged position in terms of the social hierarchy, but disadvantaged in terms of the gender hierarchy, it is possible to distinguish the impact of the two systems on the position of professional women and to examine some of the ways in which they interrelate.

Notes

1. Manjulika Dubey (1983) Interview with Chandralekha, *The Book Review* VII, 6, May-June, p.272.

2. Catherine Hall (1981) 'Gender Divisions and Class Formation in the Birmingham Middle Class, 1780-1850'. In R. Samuel (ed), *People's History and Socialist Theory*. London: Routledge & Kegan Paul.

3. M.N. Srinivas (1977) 'The Changing Position of Indian Women', *Man* 12, pp.229, 231.

4. Ibid., pp.231, 233.

5. M.N. Srinivas (1962) *Caste in Modern India*. London: Asia Publishing House, p.50.

6. Jana Matson Everett (1981) *Women and Social Change in India*. New Delhi: Heritage.

7. Fatima Mernissi (1975) *Beyond the Veil*. New York: Wiley, p.vii.

8. Srinivas, 'Changing Position of Indian Women', does not mention the impact of the West in freeing women from traditional constraints.

9. Veena Das (1976) 'Indian Women: Work, Power, and Status'. In B.R. Nanda (ed), *Indian Women from Purdah to Modernity*. New Delhi: Vikas, pp.129-33, 144-5.

10. Vina Mazumdar (1976) 'The Social Reform Movement in India — from Ranade to Nehru'. In B.R. Nanda, *Indian Women*, pp.47-9.

11. Andrea Menefee Singh (1980) 'The Study of Women in South Asia: Some Current Methodological and Research Issues'. In Alfred de Souza (ed), *Women in Contemporary India and South Asia*. New Delhi: Manohar, pp.65-6.

12. The lecturers were listed alphabetically within each institution and every ninth person selected.

13. The doctors were listed in the same way as the lecturers, as above (Note 12). The positions included: House Surgeon, Assistant Research Officer, Medical Officer, Senior Medical Officer, Resident, Senior Resident, Professor.

14. The positions in the civil service included: Under-Secretary, Deputy Secretary, Secretary, Additional Secretary, Joint Secretary, Deputy Commissioner, Commissioner, Assistant Director, Deputy Director, Director, Additional Director, Joint Director, Deputy Director-General.

15. The managers constituted an incidental sample. They included 23 from the public and 7 from the private sector. They were employed in 13 companies, of which 5 had 100 employees or less, 3 had from 100 to 1,000 employees, 2 had from 1,000 to 10,000 employees, and 3 had more than 10,000 employees. Their positions included: Junior Executive, Trainee Manager, Assistant Manager, Deputy Manager, General Manager, Marketing Manager, Deputy Marketing Manager, Chief Marketing Manager, Personnel Officer, Senior Personnel Officer, Director, Managing Director, Consultant, Assistant Consultant, Export Executive, Assistant Finance Officer, Public Relations Officer.

16. The classic is C. Wright Mills (1959) *The Sociological Imagination*. New York: Oxford University Press. In Psychology the debate was taken up in Britain in the 1970s: see R.B. Joynson (1970) 'The Breakdown of Modern Psychology'. *Bulletin of the British Psychological Society*, 23, pp.261-9. For the debate in Women's Studies, see: Ann Oakley (1981) 'Interviewing Women: a Contradiction in Terms', in Helen Roberts (ed) *Doing Feminist Research*. London: Routledge & Kegan Paul; Joan Acker, Kate Barry and Joke Esseveld (1983) 'Objectivity and Truth: Problems in Doing Feminist Research', *Women's Studies International Forum*, 6, 4, pp.423-35.

Part I: Women's Organisation

1. The women rise . . .

In 1979 a new women's magazine called *Manushi* was published in Delhi. The Editorial Collective was unsure of the welcome it would receive. In the second issue they wrote:

> We were really encouraged by your response to Manushi.[1] The way it was received, the fact that we ran terribly short of copies, assures us that Manushi has come as an answer to the felt need of women in this country . . .
>
> Many women wrote us beautiful long letters, narrating personal experiences which have made them feel the urgency of the women's question. Some expressed the hope that Manushi would become a means for them to come out of their isolation, learn to communicate and work with other women. This hope is a sign of things to come.
>
> In fact, the reports and articles we received for this issue testify to a greater ferment and restlessness among women.

And they concluded: 'We hope Manushi will play a role in developing links between localized groups, and forging their struggles into a united women's movement in this country.'[2]

The magazine was the first public sign that women in India had begun to reorganise around the women's question, for which they had mobilised almost a century earlier. The magazine is still going strong several years on. The matters discussed in its pages concern all aspects of women's subordination, including sexual oppression through rape and sexual harassment, known in India as 'eve-teasing', and economic oppression through the family and in employment, with a particular focus on dowry deaths which link both economic and sexual aspects.[3]

Already the climate of opinion has begun to change. In a recent High Court judgement the clause on the Restitution of Conjugal Rights in the Hindu Marriage Act was declared unconstitutional. The clause allowed a man to demand through the courts the return of a deserting wife. Although only symbolic, since there is no longer a penalty for non-compliance, the judgement marks a significant change in judicial views of marriage. This change of perspective cannot be credited entirely to the liberality of the judge, but has to be understood as a response to the increasing articulation of women's demands.[4]

Yet as recently as 1975, a researcher who set out to look for the women's movement concluded that there was none, even though there were isolated examples of women organising against starvation wages and sexual abuse.[5] What she saw were the preliminary stirrings of a dormant movement. When we did our study in 1977, the movement had still not fully reawakened, but women had been continuing their struggles individually throughout the period of dormancy. The second rising of the movement in 1979 confirmed that, despite the achievements of the 'first wave'[6] of women's organisation, significant inequality between the sexes remained. The achievements were considerable, but inevitably they were not enough. One of the 'first wave' organisation's major problems was the limitations imposed on their achievements through having to fight the women's question on the platforms of other political issues. This problem is still relevant to the women's movement today.

2. . . . and not for the first time

> As members of the pre-Independence generation, we have always been firm believers in equal rights for women. For us the recognition of this principle in the Constitution heralded the beginning of a new era for the women of this country.
> Lotika Sarkar and Vina Mazumdar, *Towards Equality*[7]

The particular historical circumstances surrounding the development of the 'first wave' women's organisations meant that from the beginning, the women's question was closely associated with the issue of India's subordination as a British colony, and with the problem of how Indians could regain control of their own country. This and the fact that the move for reform initially came from men, affected the analysis of the women's question. The issue was further complicated because the women's organisations consisted predominantly of women from the higher strata of society. The result was that the influence of caste and class on women's subordination was neglected, whilst the emphasis on colonialism[8] as the major cause of their depressed position tended to obscure the impact of gender domination. None of this is to underestimate the achievements of the women's organisations, which did indeed herald 'a new era' for women's legal position.

Men's Organisation

In the nineteenth century the women's question was initially raised by men through a number of organisations concerned with general political reform. The issues included sati (wives 'attaining virtue' by burning alive on the husband's funeral pyre), the stigma attached to widowhood, polygamy, child marriage and female education. Many of these applied exclusively or predominantly to women of the higher castes. Ram Mohan Roy was the first to challenge accepted ideas on women. He came from an orthodox Bengali family and was given an English education, made available by the British to recruit clerks for the colonial administration.[9] He believed in the principles of reason and individual rights, which he said were common to both Hindu and Western thought, and supported his claims with references to Hindu literature. On this basis he denounced the caste system and abuses on women, and demanded civil and political rights for all oppressed groups.[10] Roy's campaign against sati arose from applying to women the 'Western' idea of individual freedom (which few people in the West had done), and was fired by the personal shock he experienced when his sister-in-law became sati.[11] The influence of the West on the social reform movement, however, has been questioned by Vina Mazumdar, since many of the reformers were not subject to the influence of Western education or Christianity.[12]

In 1828 Roy founded the Brahmo Samaj to spread his ideas, and although it remained a small elite society, its influence was considerable.[13] There followed the Arya Samaj, set up by Saraswati, which differed from the Brahmo Samaj in that it wished to revive Hinduism rather than reform it.[14] A number of other reform organisations emerged during the century, including the Muslim Reform Movement.[15] The caste system and the position of women were two aspects which received particular attention in this process. The two Hindu societies, the Brahmo and the Arya Samaj, set the pattern for the later women's organisations, which developed a revivalist branch with the aim of raising the value of women's existing lifestyle, and a reformist branch whose aim was to change women's position on the basis of equal individual rights.[16]

In 1887 the National Social Conference was set up by the reformer Ranade, one of the major aims of which was to fight on a nationwide basis for women's emancipation.[17] This was two years after he had encouraged the founding of the Indian National Congress, which was to become the main vehicle for achieving independence from the British.[18] He also believed that the social issues with which the National Social Conference was concerned, and the political issues which were the concern of the Indian National Congress, were different aspects of the same problem.[19] From this point the women's question was seen as intricately tied up with the national question.

Whilst Ram Mohan Roy had initiated the successful campaign for the abolition of sati, Ranade worked against the ban on widow remarriage, and was associated with the campaign to discourage child marriage. The campaign was not successful, but it did result in the 1891 Age of Consent Act which raised the legal age of the wife for the consummation of marriage from 10 to 12 years.[20] The reform organisations also took up the question of education for women and set up a small number of girls' schools. Education provided by the British government was restricted to males of the middle class, for whom it was a preparation for government service.[21] Christian mission schools existed, but no self-respecting Hindu or Muslim would send their daughters to them. Education for girls started towards the end of the nineteenth century,[22] and the first women's university was set up by Karve in 1916.[23]

Women's Organisation

During this time the number of men's organisations working for an improvement in women's position expanded, and some of the men encouraged their female relatives to set up corresponding women's organisations. In 1904 the National Social Conference organised a separate section, the Indian Women's Conference, which held its own annual conference and organised women's educational programmes. In 1905 the Swadeshi movement began (the boycott of foreign goods) in protest at the British decision to partition Bengal, in which women were encouraged to participate, especially through the efforts of some of the women leaders. This was the first active involvement of women in the embryonic women's movement, and outside it in nationalist political campaigning. The explicit connection which the women made between women's politics and nationalist politics against the British was one of the major factors in reducing male opposition to the women's movement at this early stage.[24]

The close links between the two movements have caused people to question how far the women's organisations constituted a 'women's movement', as opposed to a movement for general and national political reform. If we define the women's movement as autonomous women's organisations with an analysis of women's subordination and a programme for changing it, then the 'first wave' women's organisations in India must be seen as such a movement. As Geraldine Forbes points out, 'Indian women wrote and spoke about women's condition, formed organisations to secure desired changes, and eventually had an impact on the institutions of their society'.[25] They also formed organisations for women only from the early part of the twentieth century, much to the annoyance of some of their male relatives and well-wishers.[26] Geraldine Forbes dates the movement from the 1880s to the 1940s,[27] but we prefer to date it from the start of the autonomous women's organisations in the first decade of the 20th Century to the culmination of the campaign giving women legal and political rights in the mid 1950s.

The three women's organisations which were to become the largest and the most influential in the women's movement all started within the space of 10 years. The Women's Indian Association was started in 1917 by Margaret Cousins, Dorothy Jinarjadasa and Annie Besant, and was linked with the British movement for women's suffrage. The National Council of Women in India was founded by Lady Tata and Lady Aberdeen in 1925, and was the Indian branch of the International Council of Women. And the All India Women's Conference began in 1927, initiated by Margaret Cousins. The All India Women's Conference became the most influential of the organisations, incorporating the Women's Indian Association in the 1930s.[28] It originally met to discuss women's education, without any intention of forming a permanent organisation, but the women found that they could not discuss education without also addressing the social problems of purdah, dowry, child marriage and widow remarriage, and that these could not be separated from the political issue of India's subordination to Britain.[29]

The leadership of the women's movement, like that of the nationalist movement, emerged from the urban, English-educated middle class. They were not the orthodox groups, with whom the British allied themselves, but the new middle class consisting of government servants and professional people, whose jobs the British had created, and the Indian industrialists, who had developed independently of British capitalism. This class had at first been supportive of British rule, but as it developed it began to have aspirations. Its members wanted to reach higher posts in government and to make more money in industry, but they were blocked by the British at every turn, for both industry and government were controlled by the British for their own gain.[30] It was this group who founded the Indian National Congress, initially a rather conservative body, and who gradually took control of the mass movement which developed against British rule.[31] Part of Gandhi's success as the leader of the movement was his ability to mobilise the discontents of the mass of the Indian people, including those of women and the lower castes, and to direct and contain them in the interests of this group of middle-class men.[32] The organised women's movement, arising as it did from the family connection with these men, remained a largely urban, middle-class group.

The class and caste bias of the women's movement was reflected in many of the issues which the movement chose to take up. Vina Mazumdar shows that widow remarriage, dowry, polygamy and property rights were predominantly the concerns of women in the higher castes and the middle class. The Hindu Women's Right to Property Act even succeeded in depriving some lower-caste women of their customary right to the first husband's property on remarriage.[33] The reforms hardly touched the masses of Indian women, and the criticism of the reformer Vivekananda to the general reform movements also applied to the women's movement: 'Every one of these reforms only touches the first two castes'. He recommended: 'Put the fire there [at the level of the masses] and let it burn upwards'.[34] But Mazumdar also suggests that although the women's movement was elitist in class and caste terms, it had a broader perspective than its Western counterpart because of its link with the struggle against British colonialism.[35]

Of course, the women's movement was not a group of identical people with the same views. Kamaladevi Chattopadhyaya, for instance, developed a socialist analysis in the 1930s and questioned some of the priorities of the movement on this basis.[36] Vilasinidevi Shenai in the 1940s emphasised male dominance when she proclaimed: 'Today our men are clamouring for political rights at the hands of an alien government. Have they conceded their wives, their own sisters, their daughters . . . social equality and economic justice?'[37] But the dominant view in the movement defined custom, not men, as the enemy, which they saw as deriving from India's history of wars, invasions and imperialism. The movement did not adopt the term 'feminist', because it suggested that the women's question had priority over the nationalist question, whereas in fact they saw the two as inextricably linked: India was not in control of her own government, so she could hardly institute legal reforms on women's position.[38]

So we can see that the development of the women's movement was always strongly linked with the nationalist movement, first by Ranade when he set up the National Social Conference, then by the autonomous women's organisations, and later encouraged by Gandhi's leadership. This link maintained and extended the involvement of sympathetic men in the women's question, from its beginnings with Ram Mohan Roy, through the other male reformers such as Saraswati and Vivekananda, down to the nationalist leaders like Nehru and

Gandhi. The movement reflected predominantly the concerns of the middle class and the upper castes, but its elitism was tempered by the link with the nationalist movement, which influenced the women's movement to emphasise imperialism as the major cause of women's subordination. This analysis tended to neglect the influence of caste, class and gender dominance on women's position, but it had its roots in the reality into which the women's movement emerged, a reality dominated by the British colonial government.

Whilst colonialism was an obstacle to social change in many ways, its impact was often contradictory. The issue was clouded in the case of women's position because the women's cause was used by both the British colonialists and the Indian nationalists to support arguments on other political questions. In the following chapter we examine the contradictory approach of the British government to the women's question, we look at how the British used the issue to argue for the maintenance of colonial rule in India, and we show the effect of this on the women's movement.

3. The Main Enemy: Imperialism

> I am afraid that the British choose to advertise our unfortunate conditions, not with the object of removing them, but only because such a course serves well as an excuse for retarding the political progress of India.
>
> Dr B.R. Ambedkar, *Presidential Address* to the All-India Depressed Classes Congress[39]

Inevitably the British approach to the women's issue set the stage for the women's movement. The question of what the British approach to the women's issue was, recurs throughout the entire period of the 'first wave' movement, precisely because it was ambiguous. The question is important because it affected whom the women defined as the main enemy, which in turn affected the analysis of how liberation could be achieved and at what point the major goal had been reached.

The British claimed they were a force for liberation in India, especially for women, and pointed to reforms such as the law banning sati to support this. But the evidence even on sati was ambiguous, and their action on other questions contradicted their claim. The issue was confused because of the way the women's articulation of their discontents (and also that of the lower castes) was used by the British to suggest that India was not fit for self-rule, in order to preserve the financial interests tied up in Britain's continued occupation of India. It is only in the light of these interests that the British approach to the women's position can be understood.

Britain's Financial Interests in India

The important difference between British colonialism and previous foreign rule was that the British remained aliens, whereas every former ruling group had become indianised and had integrated itself into India's existing social and economic structure. The result was that the economic benefits accruing to the ruling group were no longer kept within Indian boundaries but were exported, the wealth draining from the soil of India into British coffers.[40] An indication of India's value to Britain can be seen in the fact that in 1857, the year of the Anglo-Indian War (known by the British as the Indian Mutiny), the British East India Company collected £15.7 million in land revenue alone, and taxes and customs duties brought in half as much again. In 1930-1, the land revenue provided the British crown with £27 million.[41]

The British systematically destroyed both Indian agricultural self-sufficiency and its indigenous industry. The rural wealth drained out of India through the land revenue. The British concept of private property changed the structure of rural land ownership by allowing the zamindars (revenue collectors) to evict the cultivators where previously they had only held revenue collection rights, creating large numbers of landless peasants.[42] Many of the smaller landowning peasants were forced to grow cash crops to meet their increasing debts from the land revenue. The British not only raised the percentage but also broke the traditional link with the size of the harvest.[43] The result was less food grown for the village, and more raw material grown for Britain's manufacturing industry, especially cotton, jute and indigo.[44] In 1769, 12 years after the East India Company had secured control of Bengal, an Englishman, Richard Becher, wrote: 'since the accession of the Company to the Diwani [revenue rights] the condition of the people of this country has been worse than it was before . . . this fine country, which flourished under the most despotic and arbitrary Government, is verging towards its Ruin'.[45] The prophesy proved correct: the monsoon failed later the same year and Bengal, stripped of its surplus wealth and grain, experienced the worst famine ever to have struck India, killing 10 million people or a third of Bengal's peasantry in 1770 alone.[46]

Soon after the removal of agricultural self-sufficiency came the destruction of Indian industry, with equally devastating effect. The most severe was the collapse of the Indian textile industry. In 1813 Britain imposed a duty of 78 per cent on Indian muslins imported into England, whereas they had fixed the duty on English cottons imported into India at only 3½ per cent. Between 1824 and 1837 there was a tenfold increase in the export of British muslins to India, which ruined the Indian textile towns and forced vast numbers of weavers and artisans back to the land. The population of Dacca fell from 150,000 to 30,000.[47] The balance between agriculture and industry was lost, the land could not support all the displaced craft workers, resulting in massive unemployment and poverty from which many died.[48] William Bentinck, governor-general of India reported in 1834: 'The misery hardly finds a parallel in the history of commerce. The bones of the cotton weavers are bleaching the plains of India.'[49] The figures tell the story even more clearly. The proportion of the population dependent on agriculture in the middle of the 19th Century was about 55 per cent.[50] In 1891 it rose to 61 per cent, in 1901 to 66 per cent, in 1911 to 72 per cent and in 1921 to 73 per cent.[51] These figures show the active process of underdevelopment under British rule, as India became an agricultural producer for British manufacturing industry.

The Impact of Colonial Rule on Women

We have to distinguish between the official approach of the British government and that of individuals and groups within British society. In the first place, the three major women's organisations set up between 1917 and 1927 were started mainly by British women: Margaret Cousins, Dorothy Jinarjadasa, Annie Besant and Lady Aberdeen. Lady Tata was the exception. Not all of these, however, were pillars of the British establishment. The first three supported women's suffrage, for which cause they opposed the British government at home as well as in India. Annie Besant, a supporter of Indian nationalism, was also an Irish nationalist, which alienated her still further from the British government.[52] It was Margaret Cousins who originally thought of raising the question of women's suffrage with the British government, through the women's organisations.[53] So a small number of active British women were instrumental in initiating the organised women's movement itself.

Official British policy was not to interfere in personal law, a policy which was attacked for inhibiting social change, yet in 1772 Warren Hastings, the governor of Bengal, had decreed the religious texts of the brahmins (the highest caste) as the sole authority on Hindu law. He did this to make the Hindu concept of law, based on the flexible interpretation of custom, fit in with the Britsh concept of law, which was based on the binding force of parliamentary acts interpreted according to precedent. Personal law comprised those areas which particularly affected women such as marriage and inheritance, and each religious community had its own law, usually a body of local custom. Only the brahmins used the religious texts, but these were not always consistent and were interpreted flexibly in line with present custom. The most restrictive texts prohibited women from owning family property apart from personal marriage gifts, and prescribed monogamous and indissoluble marriage, although men could be polygamous, but custom provided exceptions to the constraints, particularly in South India. Amongst the lower castes, marriage was rarely considered indissoluble, and lack of property inhibited the development of detailed inheritance rules, so lower-caste women had fewer customary constraints.[54] When the British crown took over the government of India from the East India Company in 1858, Victoria's Proclamation as Empress of India reaffirmed the policy of non-interference in personal religious matters,[55] yet from 1864 Hindu pundits were no longer consulted for interpretation; instead, Western-educated judges decided personal law on the basis of developing precedent. The result was to rigidify legal interpretation by tying it to past precedent, and to impose the moral constraints of upper-caste women on women of all castes in the form of binding legal statute.[56]

Between 1772 and 1947, the British introduced nine major laws liberalising women's legal position in British India, including those forbidding female infanticide, sati and child marriage, and those raising the age of consent, allowing widow remarriage and improving women's inheritance rights.[57] In all of these they were supported by the Indian reformers. British support for these issues, however, was often ambiguous, and their actions in other areas revealed the contradictory nature of their approach to the women's question. To show this we will look at sati, where the British appeared to be progressive, and the matrilineal family, where their influence was quite the opposite.

Sati

Sati was widespread amongst some of the upper castes when the British established themselves in India in the second half of the 18th Century, but particularly amongst kshatriyas (the second highest caste). Amongst princes, the number of women burned on the funeral pyre was often considered an index of success. Raja Budh Singh of Bundi took 84 satis with him, and Ajit Singh of Jodhpur took 64, but 20 was 'normal'. The Raja of Idar took seven queens, two concubines, four female slaves and a personal manservant to the pyre.[58] At the turn of the century, Wellesley, governor-general of India, expressed his concern over sati to the British Parliament, but they chose to ignore him and continually refused to make a decision.[59] In 1807, 300 satis were recorded within a 10-mile radius of Calcutta. In 1812, 1815 and 1817 the British government passed laws which prohibited forcing a woman to the pyre or intoxicating her for that purpose, but it still did not outlaw sati itself.[60] In 1818 the liberal provincial governor of Bengal, Bentinck, prohibited sati in his province only.[61]

On a visit to England, Ram Mohan Roy complained to the Privy Council about their refusal to make sati illegal.[62] In 1829 Bentinck, now governor-general of India, finally prohibited sati in British India. There was some opposition from the orthodox, a petition of protest was handed to the governor-general and an appeal made to the authorities in England, who upheld the ban.[63] The protest was muted compared with what the British government had feared and the expected social instability did not materialise, despite the fact that the law marked the first government intervention in the Hindu religion.[64] Of course, the law had limited effect and did not apply to the independent states in any case. But some Residents (the British representative in the 'independent' states) did endeavour to ban sati in their areas as well. Dalhousie wrote that no opportunity was lost to secure a clause on sati when any state required a favour. Some Residents took out soldiers to prevent sati forcibly, risking 'stirring up riots, and losing life [and] incurring rebuke for exceeding authority'.[65]

The British took a lot of credit for suppressing sati, which some individuals deserved. The British government was not an entirely homogeneous set of people, and Bentinck was a liberal, who served his first two years as governor-general under a Tory government. One writer suggests that Bentinck only survived Tory hostility because of a struggle in England over Indian policy, which the liberals won.[66] Previously, 20 years of inaction on sati had gone by despite the activities of reformers both Indian and British. Amongst the liberals too, British motives were not always straightforward. Two of the liberal groups challenging Tory ideas were the Radicals and the Evangelicals. The former saw India as backward, whilst the latter saw her as heathen, her people waiting to be saved from cruel and superstitious practices through the enlightenment of Christianity.[67] There was a certain irony in this group's criticism of Hindu widow-burning, since the Christian church in Europe was still burning women as witches late in the 18th Century, not so many years before Wellesley first raised the issue of sati in Parliament.[68]

The British proclaimed the suppression of sati as the first progressive action assisting in the liberation of women, although there were ambiguities in the motives behind it. In the case of the matrilineal family, however, the legal changes undertaken by the British had the effect of removing women's freedoms and imposing new constraints.

Matriliny

The Nayars of Malabar in Kerala maintained a matrilineal form of family organisation until the British imposed legal restrictions in the 19th Century.[69] A Nayar family, known as a 'taravad', consisted of a woman, her sisters and brothers and the women's children.[70] At puberty a woman undertook the tali-tying marriage ceremony with a man of a different lineage. They cohabited for three days, then the woman tore the ceremonial loincloth as a symbol of separation. Neither partner received any rights over or duties towards the other, but the woman received the right to sexual activity. She could have sambandhan relationships with visiting husbands, which could be begun and ended without formality. The husbands lived in their mother's house and could only visit their wives in the evening. There were no fathers or in-laws in the taravad, a man had no rights or duties towards 'his' children, and so there was no father-child relationship. Iravati Karve's story of taking blood samples from a Nayar family illustrates this: when she asked to take a sample from an elderly man standing at the back, a younger man said, 'You can if you want, but he does not belong to us, he is only our Nambudri father.'[71] The family land was held in common by all the members of the taravad, and could only be divided when the taravad became too big, by the consent of all. The eldest brother (the karanavan) held authority and administered the property but could not dispose of it; the taravad could remove him if they thought he was failing in his duty.[72]

In the 19th Century the brahmins succeeded in influencing the Nayars to the extent that a woman could no longer dismiss her husband without the karanavan's permission.[73] The British then took upon themselves a number of legal changes on marriage and inheritance which seriously undermined the Nayar family structure. In 1868 the British passed a law that a man had to provide for his wife and children, an idea which had no meaning in the taravad.[74] Karanavans then started trying to give taravad property to their own children, and 4,365 cases were brought against them in the Travancore courts between 1887 and 1906.[75] In 1896 the Madras Marriage Act made the sambandhan relationship a monogamous marriage. The wife and children were given the right to maintenance by the husband, and the marriage could only be dissolved through the process of law. This law, however, had little effect since sambandhan relationships were not registered.[76]

There followed various Nayar Regulation Laws, which did not require a marriage to be registered, but declared the giving of a gift to the woman (as was expected at the start of a relationship) a legal act of marriage. Polygamy was prohibited and the marriage could only be dissolved through a legal divorce. The non-Nayar father also gained the right to inherit the property of his wife's family. These laws resulted in the tali-tying marriage rite being abandoned.[77] A further influence was the opportunity for English education, which enabled men (but not women) to obtain an administrative post in the British colonial service, and thereby become independent of the taravad. This personal income was recognised in the Malabar Wills Act of 1898, which gave a man the right to dispose of his private property through a testament, so that he could pass it on to his children, which was not possible in the taravad since all property was owned in common. In 1912 the Travancore Nayar Regulations said that taravad land could be divided, and the 1933 Madras Marriage Act said that a man's heirs were no longer his sister's children, that is, the taravad, but his wife's children.[78]

The Nayars represent a form of family organisation in opposition to the patriarchal structure of the North Indian brahmin family, where property is owned in common by the men and inherited through the male line, and the men have control over the women's sexuality. In the Nayar family, property is owned in common by the men and the women, and women and men are in control of their own sexuality within certain broad limits. The separation of sexuality from subsistence is one of the most important features of the family structure for women: the people with whom the Nayars engage in sexual relationships are not the people on whom they depend for economic survival. As a result there is no basis for economic exploitation within the sexual relationship, nor does economic dependency provide a basis for sexual exploitation. There is no sati, purdah or female infanticide. It is also significant that in this region females outnumber males, in contrast to other regions of India, where lack of care if not positive neglect of females is common.[79]

The patriarchal brahmins who lived near to the Nayars in Malabar achieved an accommodation with them, but other patriarchal groups of the upper castes and the British ruling group saw the sexual freedom of the women (though not of the men) as promiscuity rather than simply a different form of family organisation, and they viewed the collective ownership of property through the female line as the dispossession of the males. After the British and orthodox indigenous onslaught against the Nayars' organisation of sexuality and inheritance, the Indian government after Independence finally destroyed the matrilineal system through land reform and the reform of personal law, supported by all the political parties in Kerala.[80] This affected not only the structure of the family but also the way men viewed it. After Independence, Iravati Karve reported that some of the younger educated men were ashamed of their parents' relationship and saw their fathers as male concubines to their mothers.[81] Today the man is the breadwinner, the woman is expected to have only one man, to look after his needs and to listen to him.[82] As Maria Mies points out, the change in family structure was not the inevitable result of urbanisation and industrialisation, but the product of concerted legal and economic actions undertaken by the British, with the support of the patriarchal groups, to eradicate a form of family living which was deeply at odds with their own.[83]

Britain's Approach to the Women's Question

The two examples of sati and matriliny show that the British approach to women was by no means unambiguously in favour of women's greater freedom. The official policy was non-interference in personal law, yet Britain also claimed to be a liberating influence. Some of that liberating influence came not from official sources at all, but from British women who were politically at odds with the British government. At an official level, the British liberalised the law for some groups, by outlawing sati for example, but imposed constraints on others by removing their sexual and economic rights. In fact, the British were highly selective both in their non-interference and in their liberalising.

On the question of non-interference, Hastings unknowingly imposed high-caste restrictions onto lower-caste women with binding legal rather than flexible moral authority. British parliaments and governors-general of India showed reluctance to intervene against sati, a practice with terminal consequences for women, but they did not hesitate to wreak havoc on the matrilineal family, which harmed no one and gave the women certain freedoms. It is significant that sati was a practice of the higher castes, with whom the British had made alliances, whereas matriliny was a form of family structure which both the British and the patriarchal higher castes found immoral. The degree of interference entailed in the Nayar legislation can best be illustrated by imagining the British imposing laws on orthodox brahmins or Muslims which enforced women's equal share in the inheritance, forbad the husband from living with his wife and children and insisted that women must be polygamous.

Where British non-interference was actually adhered to, the policy often impeded social change, since any changes desired by the Indian population could not be instituted directly but had to be fought for and the British convinced that the orthodox groups would not rise in opposition.[84] The British were always careful not to upset these groups, who maintained control in the rural areas and collected a large part of the revenue for them. The fear of social instability, either from these groups directly or from them stirring up the masses, was the paramount consideration in deciding on any reforms.

There were, of course, differences of opinion and interest within the British government. The dominance of the conservatives was successfully challenged in 1830, when policy towards India underwent some liberalisation, but control tightened again after 1857 when the Anglo-Indian War broke out. Many people thought that the Act of 1856, permitting Hindu widows to remarry, had contributed to the Indian revolt.[85] A further consideration in understanding British policy is that, as Romila Thapar suggests, women's freedoms were no more an issue for British men than they were for Indians, since J. S. Mill's election address on women's suffrage in 1865 was considered revolutionary.[86] Even Liberal governments were hostile to the idea of equal suffrage rights in Britain until 1928.[87]

Apart from allowing some liberalising of the laws on women, the split between the liberals and the conservatives in the British ranks had some unfortunate consequences. Having initially hindered reform, the conservatives were forced to accept it at the hands of the liberals. They subsequently adopted an attitude of moral superiority towards the object of the reforms. In 1828 the Tory President of the Board of Control wrote to Bentinck, 'We have a great moral duty to perform in India'.[88] This approach was reinforced by both the groups that constituted the liberals. The Evangelicals believed in Christianity as the only true religion, the Radicals believed that the principle of reason gave the Western world its superiority.[89] All three groups shared a hypocritical stance towards Indian religion and culture, interpreting them as backward, pagan or irrational compared with their own.

This stance had a self-interested side to it, for it provided the moral justification for continued British rule in India in the interests of the British economy, despite Indian opposition and demands for self-rule. The women's issue provided the British with one of their favourite justifications for foreign rule. This can be clearly seen in the storm over Katherine Mayo's book, *Mother India*, written in 1927.[90] Mayo documented in detail the effect of abuses on women arising from male dominance, such as child marriage. Her thesis was that it was this, not British colonialism, which caused India's 'poverty, sickness, ignorance . . . melancholy, ineffectiveness . . . inferiority'.[91]

The Indian socialist R. Palme Dutt commented bitterly on Mayo's charges in 1940:

It is a pity that Miss Katherine Mayo (whose book 'Mother India', follows the familiar theme of the upper class woman's lecture to poor people about their insanitary habits) could not be compelled to live under these conditions . . . and she would soon change her tune and learn to direct her anger elsewhere than against the victims of these unfortunate conditions.[92]

In contrast, Mary Daly, an American feminist writing in 1978, praises the book: 'Katherine Mayo, in an excellent work entitled with appropriate irony, "Mother India", shows an understanding of the situation which more famous scholars entirely lack. Her work is, in the precise sense of the word, exceptional.'[93] And Daly attacks Mayo's critics as apologists for male abuses on women, who rely 'upon fears of criticising "another culture" so that the feminist is open to accusations of imperialism'.[94]

Both Dutt and Daly assess Mayo's analysis from the standpoint of the single issue which is their first concern: for Dutt, British colonialism, for Daly, male dominance. Both issues affected women's lives. But Dutt and Daly both neglect the *conflating* of the two issues in Mayo's book. Whatever Mayo's motivation — and the fact that her earlier book, *Isles of Fear*, made the case against granting independence to the Philippines[95] cannot be ignored — the British seized on the book's attack on male dominance to argue against Indian self-rule. London's *New Statesman and Nation* wrote in 1927 that the book revealed: 'the filthy personal habits of even the most highly educated classes in India — which, like the degradation of Hindu women, are unequalled even among the most primitive African or Australian savages'.[96] And it ended: 'Katherine Mayo makes the claims for Swaraj [self-rule] seem nonsense and the will to grant it almost a crime.'[97]

Had the book been written outside the context of foreign rule, or had it acknowledged the part played by imperialism in the continuation of the abuses, the reactions it provoked amongst Indians could have been taken at face value as a defence of the institution of male dominance, but the influence of colonialism confounded this understanding. For Mayo's book was used by the British, not to argue for the removal of male dominance, but to maintain the oppression of imperialism.[98]

So in view of the contradictions in Britain's position over the women's question, the difficulties in implementing reforms through the British government, and the use to which both British reforms on women's issues and Indian criticisms of male dominance were put by British colonialists, it is not surprising that the Indian women's movement was reluctant to define Indian men as the main enemy and judged that the primary target should be the removal of the foreign power. This meant, however, that they relied on the alliance with nationalist men to implement reforms by legal statute, and neglected the mobilisation of support amongst the mass of women. In the next chapter we look at the nationalist movement's contradictory approach to women, and its impact on the women's movement.

4. The Freedom Alliance

The event which did more than any other single factor to speed the process [of women's rights] was the Civil Disobedience movement of 1930-31. Feeling was then so strong that those [women] already in public life joined Congress committees and took to organising pickets for liquor and cloth shops, processions and demonstrations in addition to the usual Congress activities while many thousands came out of conditions of privacy and semi-seclusion to support the cause. Some of these were so ardent that at times, as in Delhi, they directed the whole Congress movement in an area until arrested.
Percival Spear, *A History of India*[99]

The activity of women in the nationalist movement not only radicalised the women into articulating their own grievances, but also encouraged the nationalist movement to take their grievances seriously. The women won support for their cause by linking freedom for women with freedom for India, and formed an alliance with the nationalist movement for the removal of colonialism. This helped to defuse male opposition to the principle of sexual equality, which was accepted by the Indian National Congress and subsequently enshrined in the new Constitution of India.

Support for the women's cause in practice, however, was ambiguous within the nationalist movement. The alliance was united on issues where the women's demands also furthered the nationalist cause, but split over issues which posed a direct challenge to male privilege.

Women and the Nationalist Movement

The turning point in India's co-operation with British rule came after the First World War when, instead of the expected reward for supporting the war, the Indians were offered a continuation of the martial law that had been brought in as an emergency measure for the duration of the war. The massacre of hundreds of men, women and children at Jallianwala Bagh in 1919 convinced even the moderates that Britain was not going to give up India without a fight, upon which Gandhi launched the Congress's first satyagraha (non-co-operation) movement.[100]

Not until 1927 did any positive response to Indian non-co-operation come from the British government, and this was the appointment of the Simon Commission to investigate the possibility of responsible government being established in India. But the Commission was also British, which infuriated Congress. They decided to boycott the hearings, declaring for the first time that their aim was complete independence.[101] Congress insisted on immediate dominion status for India, and when it was refused, Gandhi launched the civil disobedience campaign in 1930. The British responded by declaring Congress an illegal organisation, arresting most of its leaders. At this point the women came into their own, for they took over the organisation of the campaign when the men were in jail. That they did this on their own initiative can be seen by Nehru's surprise at what happened.

> Most of us menfolk were in prison. And then a remarkable thing happened. Our women came to the front and took charge of the struggle. Women had always been there, of course, but now there was an avalanche of them, which took not only the British government but their own menfolk by surprise. Here were these women, women of the upper or middle classes, leading sheltered lives in their homes, peasant women, working class women, rich women, poor women, pouring out in their tens of thousands in defiance of government order and police lathi . . . My father had joined us later in Naini prison . . . He had been functioning outside as the leader of the civil disobedience movement, and he had encouraged in no way these aggressive activities of the women all over the country. He disliked, in his paternal and somewhat old-fashioned way, young women and old messing about in the streets under the hot sun of summer and coming into conflict with the police. But he realised the temper of the people and did not discourage anyone, not even his wife and daughters and daughters-in-law.[102]

There were, of course, differences in opinion amongst the men in the nationalist movement over the women's involvement and over their demands. Many of the Congress leaders, such as Prasad, were against any reform of women's legal position. Nehru, influenced by socialism, supported the principle of equal rights for women. Gandhi's approach was ambivalent. He was certainly the catalyst in bringing women into the nationalist movement on a mass scale. His approach appealed both to the women, whose long experience in passive resistance and silent suffering he acknowledged, and to the men, who were willing to entrust the women into his guardianship.[103] Gandhi needed the women to make the campaign into a mass movement, but he liked to be in control of the women's actions and was angry when they stepped out of line. Although he encouraged their participation in picketing cloth and liquor shops, he opposed their presence on the Salt March, a tactic he adopted to show his contempt for the onerous salt tax, by marching to the sea and making illegal salt from sea water.[104] The women protested at Gandhi's opposition, and although they failed to join the first march to Dandi, they later made salt in Bombay,[105] and after Gandhi's arrest, Sarojini Naidu directed the salt protest until she herself was arrested.[106]

A further consideration in understanding the nationalist approach is Gandhi's skill in holding the women's discontents within the overall nationalist cause. He effectively mediated these discontents so that they remained targeted exclusively at imperialism. He did this not only with the mass of women who came onto the streets to campaign, but also with the mass of peasant and working-class men who were mostly of the lower castes, but whose caste and class grievances he kept in check. Ambedkar documented how this had happened with the untouchables, when their cause was co-opted onto the nationalist platform.[107] Gandhi recognised the power of the women and the lower castes and contained it for the cause of Independence, uniting the nation behind the freedom struggle at the expense of injustices within caste, class and gender relations.[108]

To show the contradictory approach of the nationalist movement to the women's question, we want to compare two issues which the women's movement saw as central to women's position in an independent India, women's suffrage and the reform of Hindu personal law.[109] Votes for women was an issue which united the nationalist movement with the women's movement, but the nationalists were bitterly divided over personal law reform, which included issues like marriage and inheritance which were of special concern to women.

Women's Suffrage

Women's suffrage was first raised by the Women's Indian Association in 1917 when Montagu, Secretary of State for India, came to discuss Indian demands for political representation. It was not mentioned in his report, and it was rejected by the subsequent franchise report on the grounds that orthodox opinion would oppose it and it would be premature when so many men still required education to vote 'responsibly'.[110] The ensuing 1919 Government of India Act enfranchised a mere 3 per cent of Indian adults for the Provincial Assembly and 0.06 per cent for the Central Assembly.[111] It excluded women from the vote, but allowed the Provincial Assemblies to drop the exclusion clause if they wished. The British gave this concession because all the major political groupings had testified in support of women's suffrage.[112]

Most of the Provincial Assemblies did drop the exclusion clause, although this action was only a gesture, for the property qualification *dis*qualified most women, who normally had no independent share in family property. This illustrates the importance of looking beyond the formal history of legal changes for women, since the actual effect was quite different from the apparent one. But the principle was important in itself, for it demonstrated that Indians were eager to give women the vote, in contrast to the British, who resisted fully enfranchising their own women until 1928. Dumasia, a member of the Provincial Assembly said: 'It is gratifying to find that in a country where men are accused of treating women as chattels the political progress of women has been more rapid than in England.'[113] And Sivaswami Aiyer said that the political elite gave their support so readily because it allowed them to show that they were more socially advanced than the British and to counter claims that they were too backward for self-rule.[114] Significantly, women's suffrage also helped the nationalist cause: any increase in Indian political representation was likely to be unfavourable to the British.

Congress considered the political reform to be wholly inadequate and continued to agitate for greater Indian representation until the British appointed the all-British Simon Commission. Congress boycotted the hearings, declared the goal as complete independence, and published its own report in 1928 on self-government for India. Thanks to the activities of the women's movement, this report advocated the principle of sexual equality and universal adult franchise. In 1931 the Karachi session of Congress adopted the principles for a new Constitution and, thanking the women for their part in the civil disobedience campaign, pledged itself to sexual as well as caste and religious equality before the law, no discrimination in employment or offices, and universal adult suffrage when independence had been achieved.[115]

The 1935 Government of India Act initially increased the franchise to 10 per cent of men and 0.06 per cent of women,[116] intending to maintain British rule in India by placating the moderates without upsetting the orthodox.[117] Congress[118] and the women's organisations[119] united in bitterly condemning the Act. At Independence, Congress instituted universal adult suffrage and a constitutional guarantee of sex, caste and religious equality.

The nationalists gave their full support to the issue of women's suffrage, partly because of the women's movement's campaign around the issue, partly because of their gratitude at the women's part in the civil disobedience campaign, and partly to show themselves as more progressive than the British and to increase Indian voting power. The notion of equal citizens in both sex and caste terms was a revolutionary idea in Indian politics, although the impact of the change on the majority of illiterate, rural women was rather less than revolutionary, since the women's movement failed to mobilise the mass female vote.[120] But as became clear on the matter of personal law reform, many men did not accept the principle of sexual equality in practice.[121]

Personal Law

The demand for a Hindu Code reforming areas of personal law such as marriage, divorce and inheritance was initiated by the All India Women's Conference in 1934.[122] The changes to women's position embodied in the Hindu Code provoked a storm of opposition which highlighted the contradiction amongst nationalist men. They supported the principle of sexual equality and its implementation through women's suffrage, which undermined Britain's position of power. But they opposed the implementation of the principle in marriage and inheritance, which threatened their own privileges as men in the family.

In 1943 the issue came before the Legislative Assembly, who commissioned a draft Hindu Code. The draft Code gave a widow the same share as a son in the husband's property and gave a daughter half a son's share; polygamy was banned, inter-caste marriage legalised and some divorce made possible. The women's movement supported the Code whilst suggesting that it could be more egalitarian, but the Code's opponents mobilised demonstrations against it in five cities. In 1945 the Code divided the Indian political elite, for the Assembly agreed with the principle of sexual equality but found itself in conflict over how to implement it. Agreement was reached on political and economic issues (such as suffrage and employment) but not on domestic issues (such as marriage and inheritance), with the result that the clause forbidding discriminatory marriage and inheritance laws was excluded from the Constitution, and the statement that: 'The State shall endeavour to secure that marriage shall be based only on the mutual consent of both sexes and shall be maintained through mutual cooperation, with the equal rights of husband and wife as a basis' was removed from the Code and did not reappear.[123]

After Independence the Hindu Code Bill was discussed in the Assembly but there was still opposition, so Law Minister Ambedkar worked out a compromise which was debated in 1951. But the disagreements continued, whereupon Nehru withdrew the Bill and Ambedkar resigned in protest. The controversy was such that President Rajendra Prasad threatened to provoke a constitutional crisis by refusing to sign the Bill should it be passed before the general election.[124] The arguments used against the Bill by its opponents were many, but included the suggestion that the majority of women were against it, that the women assembly members were unrepresentative of women's opinion, that the reformers were influenced by Western education and law instead of Hinduism and were unpatriotic, and that women's inheritance rights would lead to women refusing to marry. In reply, the Bill's supporters argued that the constitutional principle of sexual equality had been agreed by a large majority in the Assembly, that individual equal rights was not a foreign concept but the heritage of the nationalist movement, and that political equality was meaningless without social equality.[125] The Hindu Code was finally enacted after the first general election. It was split into five parts with the least controversial parts first, and passed over a two-year period, thanks mainly to Nehru's sponsorship and his established supremacy in the nationalist government.[126]

The Code brought out the divisions over the women's question in the nationalist movement. Opposition to changes in personal law was strenuous amongst the more conservative quarters within Congress and the Assembly.[127] When it came to implementing the principle of sexual equality in the domestic arena,[128] many nationalist men were forced to admit that whilst they were determined to resist national subordination they did not want to forgo their domination of women.

The Approach of the Nationalist Movement to the Women's Question

The examples of women's suffrage and the Hindu Code suggest that the nationalists were not unambiguously in favour of greater freedom for women any more than the British were. They supported the principle of sexual equality, but they were divided over how to implement it. Women's suffrage was supported partly because it also fulfilled nationalist purposes, but opinion on the Hindu Code was split since the Code represented a challenge to male dominance rather than to British colonialism. It was no accident that the resistance encountered by the women's movement came in the *personal* areas of marriage and inheritance in the Hindu Code and the guarantee of domestic equality in the Constitution. Equality in the areas of politics and employment was granted, but it was in precisely the area which characterises women's subordination, the very feature which distinguishes gender oppression from other forms, namely in personal, domestic, sexual and family relations, that the men resisted conceding their privilege.

This resistance demonstrates just how political the personal arena is in gender relations, for it is the place where women have to negotiate the conditions of their lives on an individual basis within the male-dominated family organisation. Legal reforms do not work well in this area: they are difficult to enforce precisely because they concern private, or privatised, matters. This again shows the difficulties of legislating for women's equality, a problem which is multiplied in the case of the majority of uneducated rural women who neither know their legal rights nor have the means to pursue their grievances through the courts. In fact, the legal changes had little impact outside the urban, educated middle class.[129] This was partly because of the nature of the reforms, as discussed above, partly because the urban middle-class composition of the women's movement inhibited the mobilisation of mass female support for the reforms, and partly because the strong historical connection with the nationalist movement encouraged reliance on the male political elite for the implementation of the changes. The Code's opponents could argue that the women's movement was unrepresentative of the mass of Indian women, which was true, but the educated and propertied members of the political elite were equally unrepresentative of the mass of the Indian population. The Assemblies even after Independence consisted mainly of professional men from the higher castes, whose motivation in freeing themselves from British rule was to share in the rulers' spoils, rather than to give up their own privileges.

So the freedom alliance between the nationalist movement and the women's movement broke down on the personal issue, both before and after the goal of political independence was attained. Both organisations wanted freedom from British rule, but the women also wanted freedom from male domination, which not all the nationalists were willing to concede. The women obtained a great deal of support for their cause, and achieved revolutionary legal changes, through fighting the women's issue on the nationalist platform. But the breakdown in the alliance demonstrated that although the two issues were related, they were not identical. The women gained from the alliance in that nationalist political activities radicalised them into expressing their own grievances and defused male opposition to the cause, but the nationalists also limited the women's movement in as much as they kept control over the women's activities and could not be relied upon to support the women's demands when male privilege was under threat.

5. Freedom for India, and Women?

> The inseparable links between the liberation of women and national liberation are constantly being reaffirmed by women activists from the Third World. At the same time, the limitations imposed on women's organisations by political parties, together with the international development of the women's movement, have opened up a growing debate on the question of autonomy.
> Miranda Davies, 'Women in Struggle'[130]

The women's movement, having achieved a radical change in the concept of gender relations, from the orthodox religious view of women as lifetime dependants, to the adoption by the secular state of sex equality based on individual rights, went into decline as a force for political change, even though the All India Women's Conference and the National Council of Women in India continued to exist without their political drive.[131] The movement had fulfilled its major purpose, the goal was achieved: national independence, universal adult suffrage, a constitutional guarantee of sex equality in political and economic life and a comprehensive reform of Hindu personal law.

The effect of these changes, however, on the majority of women was limited by the fact that many of the reforms, such as divorce and inheritance, were problems only for the upper castes, and changes in the area of personal law were in any case difficult to enforce without the awareness and co-operation of the broad mass of people. The social composition of the women's movement meant that they could not articulate the particular oppressions of women of the lower castes and class, nor could they recognise that some aspects of their own oppression were not universal. On the question of divorce, for instance, the opposition's arguments could have been undermined had the women opened the discussion to a wider audience, since large numbers of the lower castes had neither religious objection nor customary prohibition against divorce.[132] In addition, there was repression even in the reforms. The Hindu Code, which liberalised the law for women in the high-caste patriarchal groups, consolidated the deterioration of women's position in some matrilineal groups, by imposing upon them economic dependence within the marital rather than the natal family, and removing their inheritance and marital rights.

The other major limitation on the effectiveness of the women's movement was that the political agendas were set by the British colonialists and the Indian nationalists, with the result that the women's question was fought on the political platforms of foreign imperialism and national liberation. Both the

British and the nationalists supported the women on issues where their interests coincided, and obstructed the women where their interests conflicted. This inhibited the women's analysis and their actions, since not only had they to fit their understanding of women's oppression into the conceptual framework of the nationalist movement, but they were also limited in how far they could confront male dominance as a major cause of women's subordination because of the way this would be used by the foreign rulers against the whole nation. British rule was obstructive to the women's cause in many ways, and women needed to free themselves of this constraint as much as the men did, but the women's cause was not identical with the nationalist one, and the political liberation of the state did not automatically lead to the liberation of women from male domination.

The women in the movement recognised this and attempted to free women from male control through the personal law reform. Valuable lessons can be learned today from those experiences. One, that to make changes in the personal area effective, women have to *negotiate* changes in personal relationships on an individual basis with other members of the family. Two, that when organisations with their own specific aims of liberation form alliances to achieve common ends, the *specific* interests that differentiate them must be confronted, not conflated or submerged. In fact, the liberation of women and of India after Independence was strictly limited, for India continued to be constrained by economic pressures imposed by the West despite political independence from Britain. Had the leaders of the Indian nationalist movement seriously addressed the discontents of the women, the lower classes and the untouchables, and been willing to forgo their caste, class and gender privileges, it is possible that they could all have achieved a more effective victory over Western imperialism. Finally, women too must recognise the specific interests that distinguish different groups within their movements, if they are to be an effective force for the liberation of all women.

Notes

1. All non-English words will be found in the glossary.
2. *Manushi* (1979) 2, March-April. Editorial, p.3.
3. *Manushi* has run a regular feature reporting the specific circumstances of dowry deaths, and participated in a campaign to prevent such deaths. See issues no. 3, 4, 6, 8, 9, 12, 13.
4. Andhra Pradesh High Court Judgement delivered 1 July 1983 and reported in *Hindustan Times*, 2 July 1983. The clause was introduced by the British, and allowed a person to take punitive action against a spouse who withdrew from a marriage. The wife thereby lost an opportunity to exercise choice within the arranged marriage system: Dagmar Engels (1983) 'The Age of Consent Act of 1891: Colonial Ideology in Bengal', *South Asia Research*, 3, 2, Nov., pp.108–9. *Manushi* claims that the judgement cannot be regarded as progressive since the clause was used as a means of divorcing an unwilling spouse (*Manushi* (1983) 3, 5,

p.27). Whether this was beneficial for women, however, depends on the proportions of men and women taking advantage of the remedy. Given the economic inequality between the sexes it is likely to have favoured men.

5. Gail Omvedt (1980) *We will Smash this Prison!* London: Zed Press, pp.155-68.

6. As has been pointed out by Elizabeth Sarah (1982) *Women's Studies International Forum* 5, 6, pp.519-20, the terms 'first wave' and 'second wave' require parentheses, because they suggest that feminism disappeared when there was no visible movement. This suggestion has been undermined by Dale Spender (1983) *There's Always Been a Women's Movement This Century*. London: Routledge & Kegan Paul. We address the issue in Part II, Chapter 6.

7. Lotika Sarkar and Vina Mazumdar (1974) 'Note of Dissent', in Dept. of Social Welfare, *Towards Equality: Report of the Committee on the Status of Women in India*. New Delhi: Government of India, p.355.

8. We use 'imperialism' as a general concept to signify any relationship of dominance and subordination between nations, including the modern form using economic control, and 'colonialism' to indicate the specific historical form of imperialism which uses direct military and political control. See Harry Magdoff (1978) *Imperialism*. New York: Monthly Review Press, pp.117, 139.

9. Jawaharlal Nehru (1939) *Glimpses of World History*. London: Lindsay Drummond, p.436.

10. Percival Spear (1970) *A History of India*, vol.2. Harmondsworth: Penguin, pp.161-2, 164. See also S.N. Mukherjee (1974) 'The Social Implications of the Political Thought of Raja Ram Mohun Roy', in R.S. Sharma (ed), *Indian Society: Historical Probings*. New Delhi: People's Publishing House.

11. Romila Thapar (1963), 'The History of Female Emancipation in Southern Asia', in Barbara Ward (ed), *Women in the New Asia*. Paris: UNESCO, p.495. To 'become' sati is the correct expression, since sati means 'virtuous woman'.

12. Vina Mazumdar (1976) 'The Social Reform Movement in India', in B.R. Nanda (ed), *Indian Women from Purdah to Modernity*. New Delhi: Vikas, pp.47-8.

13. Thapar, 'History of Female Emancipation', p.495.

14. Nehru, *Glimpses of World History*, pp.436-7.

15. Dept. of Social Welfare, *Towards Equality*, pp.52-4.

16. Thapar, 'History of Female Emancipation', p.481.

17. Ibid., p.483.

18. Stanley Wolpert (1977) *A New History of India*. New York: Oxford University Press, p.252.

19. Thapar, 'History of Female Emancipation', p.485.

20. Jana Matson Everett (1981) *Women and Social Change in India*. New Delhi: Heritage, p.60.

21. C.E. Trevelyan (1838) *On the Education of the People of India*. London: Publisher not given, p.48. Quoted in B.B. Misra (1961), *The Indian Middle Classes*. London: Oxford University Press, pp.151-2.

22. Thapar, 'History of Female Emancipation', p.482-3.

23. Dept. of Social Welfare, *Towards Equality*, p.52.

24. Everett, *Women and Social Change*, pp.50-1, 54-5, 61, 68.

25. Geraldine Forbes (1982) 'Caged Tigers: "First Wave" Feminism in India', *Women's Studies International Forum* 5, 2, p.525.

26. Ibid., pp.527-8.

27. Ibid., p.525.

28. Everett, *Women and Social Change*, pp. 68-69, 126.

29. Forbes, 'Caged Tigers', p.529.

30. Nehru, *Glimpses of World History*, pp.435-9.

31. Bipan Chandra (1974) 'The Indian Capitalist Class and British Imperialism', in Sharma (ed), *Indian Society*, pp.390-3.

32. Gail Omvedt (1975) 'Caste, Class and Women's Liberation in India', *Bulletin of Concerned Asian Scholars* 7, 1, pp.43-8, Jan-March. See also: B.R. Ambedkar (1945) *What Congress and Gandhi have done to the Untouchables*. Bombay: Thacker & Co.

33. Mazumdar, 'Social Reform Movement', pp.51-3.

34. *Selections from Swami Vivekananda* (1957), Almora: Publisher not given, pp.129-30. Quoted in ibid., pp.64-5.

35. Ibid., pp.62-3.

36. Kamaladevi Chattopadhyaya (1939) *The Awakening of Indian Women*. Calcutta: Publisher not given, pp.1-7. Quoted in Everett, *Women and Social Change*, p.139.

37. Forbes, 'Caged Tigers', p.532.

38. Ibid., p.529.

39. B.R. Ambedkar (1930) Presidential Address to the All-India Depressed Classes Congress, August. Quoted in R. Palme Dutt (1940) *India Today*. London: Victor Gollancz, p.262.

40. Jawaharlal Nehru (1946) *The Discovery of India*. New York: John Day, p.302.

41. Joan Beauchamp (1934) *British Imperialism in India*. London: Martin Lawrence, pp.25, 86.

42. Wolpert, *New History of India*, pp.196-7.

43. Anupam Sen (1982) *The State, Industrialisation and Class Formations in India*. London: Routledge & Kegan Paul, p.65.

44. Ibid., p.72.

45. Letter from Bengal written by Richard Becher, 24 May 1769 and laid before the Secret Committee of the East India Company. Reprinted in *Secret Comm. Cons., India Office Records*, Range A9 pp.92-5. Quoted in Wolpert, *New History of India*, p.188.

46. Ibid., p.188. See also Beauchamp, *British Imperialism*, pp.22-3. Extracts from India Office Records.

47. Henry Noel Brailsford (1943) *Subject India*. London: Victor Gollancz, p.134.

48. Nehru, *Discovery of India*, p.302.

49. William Bentinck (1834). Quoted in Karl Marx (1976) *Capital*, vol.1. Harmondsworth: Penguin, Ch.15, Section 5, p.558.

50. Nehru, *Discovery of India*, p.298.

51. Census figures, quoted in Beauchamp, *British Imperialism*, p.84.

52. Thapar, 'History of Female Emancipation', p.496.

53. Margaret E. Cousins (1941) *Indian Womanhood Today*. Allahabad: Kitabistan, pp.32-3. Quoted in Everett, *Women and Social Change*, pp.102-3.

54. Everett, ibid., pp.141-3.

55. Wolpert, *New History of India*, pp.240-1.

56. Everett, *Women and Social Change*, p.144.

57. Sati was prohibited in 1829, widow remarriage allowed in 1856. The age

of consent was fixed at 10 in 1860 and raised to 12 in 1891. Female infanticide was prohibited in 1870, child marriage forbidden in 1929, and various laws improving women's inheritance rights were passed in 1874, 1929 and 1937. A number of other laws were enacted within particular provinces. See Everett, ibid., pp.144-5; Thapar, 'History of Female Emancipation', pp.482, 487; G.G. Mirchandani (1970) 'Status of Women in India', *India Today*. Delhi: United News of India Research Bureau, Ch.14, p.253.

58. Edward Thompson (1911) Quoted in Tara Ali Baig (1976) *India's Woman Power*. New Delhi: S. Chand, p.20.

59. Spear, *History of India*, p.123.

60. Mirchandani, 'Status of Women in India', p.253.

61. Baig, *India's Woman Power*, p.21.

62. Thapar, 'History of Female Emancipation', p.495.

63. Mirchandani, 'Status of Women in India', p.253.

64. Spear, *History of India*, p.125.

65. Edward Thompson (1911) Quoted in Baig, *India's Woman Power*, pp.20-1.

66. Spear, *History of India*, pp.123-4.

67. Ibid., pp.121-2.

68. Mary Daly (1978) *Gyn/Ecology*. London: The Women's Press, pp.183-4. Daly quotes Matilda Gage (1972) *Woman, Church and State*. New York: Arno Press, who estimates that 9 million persons were burned as witches in Europe in the 300 years from 1484 to 1784. The great majority of these persons were women.

69. The information in this section is taken from Maria Mies (1980) *Indian Women and Patriarchy*. New Delhi: Concept, pp.84-90.

70. Joan Mencher (1965), 'The Nayars of South Malabar', in M.F. Nimkoff (ed), *Comparative Family Systems*. Boston: Houghton Mifflin, p.169.

71. Iravati Karve (1965) *Kinship Organisation in India*. Bombay: Publisher not given, p.298. Quoted in Mies, *Indian Women*, p.86.

72. Mies, *Indian Women*, pp.84-5.

73. M.S.A. Rao (1957) *Social Change in Malabar*. Bombay: Popular Book Depot, pp.78-80.

74. Ibid., p.133.

75. K.M. Kapadia (1968) *Marriage and Family in India*. Calcutta: Oxford University Press, p.344.

76. Mies, *Indian Women*, p.87.

77. Rao, *Social Change*, pp.98-100.

78. Ibid., pp.139-44.

79. Mencher, 'Nayars', p.165.

80. Joan Mencher (1962) 'Changing Familial Roles among South Malabar Nayars', *South Western Journal of Anthropology* 18, p.241.

81. Karve, *Kinship Organisation*, pp.297, 299.

82. Mencher, 'Changing Familial Roles', p.241.

83. Mies, *Indian Women*, p.89.

84. 'An alien government can seldom introduce social reform, because every change it seeks to introduce is resented by the people.' Nehru, *Glimpses of World History*, p.431.

85. Thapar, 'History of Female Emancipation', pp.484-5.

86. Ibid., p.485.

87. See Midge Mackenzie (1975) *Shoulder to Shoulder*. Harmondsworth: Penguin, p.x.

88. Spear, *History of India*, p.124.

89. Ibid., pp.121-3.

90. Katherine Mayo (1927) *Mother India*. New York: Harcourt Brace.

91. Ibid., p.22.

92. Dutt, *India Today*, p.57.

93. Daly, *Gyn/Ecology*, p.119.

94. Ibid., p.129.

95. Robert Hardy Andrews (1967) *A Lamp for India: The Story of Madame Pandit*. London: Arthur Barker, p.114.

96. Quoted in ibid., p.110.

97. Quoted in ibid., pp.110-11.

98. Joanna Liddle and Rama Joshi (1985) 'Gender and Colonialism: Women's Organisation under the Raj', *Women's Studies International Forum*, 8, 5.

99. Spear, *History of India*, pp.213-14.

100. Wolpert, *New History of India*, pp.297-301.

101. Everett, *Women and Social Change*, pp.113-14.

102. Nehru, *Discovery of India*, pp.29-30.

103. Aparna Basu (1976) 'The Role of Women in the Indian Struggle for Freedom', in B.R. Nanda (ed), *Indian Women*, p.37. See also Manmohan Kaur (1968) *Role of Women in the Freedom Movement (1857-1947)*. Delhi: Sterling.

104. Everett, *Women and Social Change*, pp.75-8.

105. Basu, 'Role of Women', p.24.

106. Everett, *Women and Social Change*, p.114.

107. Ambedkar, *Congress and Gandhi*.

108. Omvedt, 'Caste, Class', p.47. See also Gail Omvedt (1973) 'Gandhi and the Pacification of the Indian Nationalist Movement', *Bulletin of Concerned Asian Scholars* 5, July.

109. A useful historical study of these two issues has been conducted by Jana Matson Everett. Most of the following information on the two issues comes from her study: Everett, *Women and Social Change*, especially chapters 6, 7.

110. Ibid., pp.102-6.

111. Dilip Hiro (1976) *Inside India Today*. London: Routledge & Kegan Paul, p.53.

112. Everett, *Women and Social Change*, p.106.

113. Legislative Assembly Debates File No.28, Public of 1926. Quoted in Geraldine Forbes (1979) 'Votes for Women', in Vina Mazumdar (ed), *Symbols of Power*. New Delhi: Allied Publishers, p.6.

114. P.S. Sivaswami Aiyer (1928) *Indian Constitutional Problems*, Bombay: Publisher not given. Quoted in Everett, *Women and Social Change*, p.108.

115. Everett, ibid., pp.113-15.

116. Brailsford, *Subject India*, p.42.

117. See the comment of Sir Samuel Hoare (author of the 1935 Act) to the Commons in this respect: 'It will be impossible, short of a landslide, for the extremists to get control of the federal centre'. Quoted in ibid., p.42.

118. Wolpert, *New History of India*, p.322.

119. Everett, *Women and Social Change*, p.133.

120. Ibid., pp.134-8.

121. Ibid., pp.94-5.

122. Ibid., p.148.

123. Ibid., pp.155-62.

124. Ibid., p.186 and Lotika Sarkar (1976) 'Jawaharlal Nehru and the Hindu Code Bill', in Nanda (ed), *Indian Women*, p.87.

125. Everett, *Women and Social Change*, pp.175-82.

126. The Acts are: the Special Marriage Act 1954, the Hindu Marriage Act 1955, the Hindu Succession Act 1955, the Hindu Minority and Guardianship Act 1956 and the Hindu Adoptions and Maintenance Act 1956.

127. 'Only a few Congress members came out strongly in support of the Bill.' Sarkar, 'Jawaharlal Nehru', p.93.

128. The suggestion that housework should be included in the National accounting process was rejected by the Assembly. See Mazumdar, *Symbols of Power*, p.xvi.

129. Ibid., pp.xi-xii.

130. Miranda Davies (1983) 'Women in Struggle', *Third World Quarterly* 5, 4, October, pp.878-9.

131. The British women's movement, too, went into decline for 30 or more years after winning the vote. See Sarah, 'Towards a Reassessment', p.520.

132. Mazumdar, *Symbols of Power*, p.xi.

Part II: Gender and Hierarchy

6. Roots of Women's Resistance

The other dimensions of thought which have gone into the Indian family structure . . . have brought out more clearly than perhaps in any culture that women have relevance even when under-privileged; are strong, not weak; and that they continue to be the acknowledged repository of unknown, unseen yet tangible elements of human power.
Tara Ali Baig, *India's Woman Power*[1]

The specific interests which distinguish the Indian women's movement from those of the Western countries arise from India's distinct cultural traditions and social structure. Having established that the influence of British colonialism was not unambiguously progressive in terms of women's liberation, it is nevertheless tempting to think that women's resistance to male domination in India was initiated by the British women who started the women's organisations and helped to define their aims. But just as the impact of colonial domination on women was complex and contradictory, so too the influence of the British women's movement was not a simple importation of the Western organisation, but represented a single intervention within the totality of Indian history. Women's resistance to oppression in India neither began nor ended with the British women's intervention, but had its roots in the Indian social structure and cultural heritage.

This heritage both preceded and followed on from the British women's initiatives, which meant that the two movements had very different starting points and developed in distinctive directions. The common strand was that in both countries the institutions of male supremacy supported male privilege, but the forms of male supremacy were different in each case, with different implications for the formation of gender relations and the development of women's resistance. The specific form of male supremacy in India affected men's views and treatment of women, as well as how women saw themselves and constructed their demands.

We have made the comparison between India and the West, not to examine the historical roots of Western women's subordination,[2] but to draw attention to the distinct character of the movement for women's liberation in India, so that we can understand the women who are the subject of this study, and so that today's women's movements in the West might learn from and be inspired by the history and heritage of women in India.

In Part II we will examine the roots of women's inequality and of their resistance in India, by looking at what we see as the major influences on the formation of gender relations, that is, the development of the patriarchal form of family organisation, the formation of the caste hierarchy, and the impact of foreign domination. We will argue that:

One, the patriarchal form of family organisation and its associated ideology did not emerge as a universally accepted or natural way of living, but was the scene of a struggle, in which the patriarchal form gained dominance without a final victory. This struggle reveals the historical roots of women's resistance to male domination, and provides the basis for a distinct view of women as strong and powerful;

Two, the subordination of women was crucial to the development of caste hierarchy, the women being subject to increasing constraints the higher the caste in the hierarchy. Caste, too, was the subject of struggle, and the anti-caste movements were always associated with the removal of constraints on women. The upper castes maintained their supremacy by incorporating some of the opposing cultural traditions into their own, while increasing the social distinction between themselves and the lower castes. These efforts illuminate the historical connection between women's subordination and social hierarchy, and provide the basis for strong physical controls over powerful women in a patriarchal society;

Three, the impact of foreign domination on the formation of the social classes had a contradictory effect on the position of women in the middle class. The class structure appeared to build on the existing gender divisions within the caste system, reinforcing women's subordination though changing its form. But it also allowed a small number of women from the urban, educated middle class to survive independently of the patriarchal caste system in the higher levels of waged work.

As a result of these influences, we suggest that women's desire for emancipation in India did not stem primarily from the initiative of the British women who started the movement, but from the way this intervention combined with Indian women's unique cultural heritage which provides a tradition of women as strong and powerful beings, and with their position in the social structure which offered them the possibility of an independent existence.

7. Patriarchy and the Matriarchal Heritage

> The Brahmins would have liked to annihilate the Shakti [female power principle] cults altogether and replace the female with the male as the dominant and superior principle. The roots of these cults . . . are so powerful that they have persisted even to this day . . . We need to . . . understand Shakti . . . as an energy within ourselves which generates the power to act.
> Chandralekha, *The Book Review*[3]

Women in India have a unique cultural heritage. It is not always easy, however, to trace its history, since the best preserved stories are normally those of the groups who achieved dominance. India's earliest written history is recorded in the Vedas, the religious books written by the priestly groups of the Aryan-speaking race, known as the brahmins. It was the males of these groups who eventually achieved social and religious supremacy, although not without opposition.

If we only look at the dominant groups' history, we see only one side of the story. To find the other stories we have to look at alternative sources such as later written history, oral history, archaeological evidence, and surviving religious practices and social organisation. This is particularly necessary in the case of women's history, since most written history is recorded by men and represents predominantly male concerns. Piecing the picture together from other sources indicates that male supremacy was not a natural or an inevitable development in the history of gender relations, but was the result of a struggle between the female power principle and the idea of the male as the dominant source of power.

What is distinctive about this heritage compared with that of women in the West is that although the male principle attained supremacy in both areas of the world, in India the idea of women as powerful was accommodated into the patriarchal culture and retained its visibility. It also remained strong amongst certain sections of the population who opposed the patriarchal ideas of the brahmins. The visibility of women's power was maintained in Muslim cultures too, as indicated by Fatima Mernissi[4] and Azizah Al-Hibri.[5] We want to examine the struggle over the male and female principles by identifying two areas where it can be seen to have taken place. One of these is in the different forms of family structure, the other is in the different forms of religious culture.

We use the term patriarchy to refer to the particular system of family organisation which includes patrilineal inheritance, the sons and daughters-in-law staying in the father's house, and the authority of the father over the women and the younger men, supported by a cultural tradition which emphasises the supremacy of the male power principle.[6] We do not use it to refer to male dominance, since we wish to distinguish betwen patriarchy as a specific family system, and male dominance as a general system of sexual hierarchy.

The definition of matriarchy is as much in dispute as is the definition of patriarchy.[7] When we refer to the matriarchal heritage, we do not mean the obverse of patriarchy, that is, a system of family organisation where mothers have authority over men and the younger women. There is no evidence for a matriarchy having existed anywhere in the world, in the sense of women's rule over men being embodied in the family or social structure.[8] What we do mean by the matriarchal heritage is a history of struggle where the idea of female power was constantly reasserted through the religion and where family forms giving women greater freedom existed despite the opposition of the dominant patriarchal groups. The evidence for the struggle is found in the conflicts and accommodations between different modes of religious thought, and between the matrilineal and patrilineal family systems.

Matrilineal Family Organisation

The matrilineal systems of descent, although by no means constituting a matriarchy, did provide the basis for a greater degree of freedom for women compared with the patrilineal system. This freedom differed in its form and extent in different matrilineal communities; we have already seen one example amongst the Nayars of Kerala.[9] The important factor is that matrilineal groups depend on retaining a similar degree of control over both male and female members, whereas control over women is much more severe than control over men in patrilineal descent.[10] Kerala today has the highest female literacy rate,[11] the highest ratio of females to males,[12] and the second highest age of marriage for women in India.[13] These indices of women's relatively better position in the state of Kerala are normally attributed to the continued existence of the matrilineal family and the associated cultural worth attached to women.[14]

When the Aryans migrated to India around 1500 B.C., they brought with them the patrilineal form of family organisation, where the line of descent is from father to son, and the women leave their father's house on marriage to live with the husband and father-in-law. The Aryans are believed to have destroyed the superior civilisation which they encountered in the Indus Valley, in the north-west of the subcontinent, and gradually to have established dominance over the Dravidians who were the indigenous inhabitants of the main peninsula.[15]

Many historians believe that the Aryans encountered matrilineal family organisation amongst the indigenous people.[16] This they deduce from communities in outlying areas of India where matriliny has persisted. In the South of the country, Kerala and Tamil Nadu certainly seem to have been matrilineal.[17] We have already discussed the Nayars of Malabar, whose matriliny survived to British times, but similar family forms continued amongst almost all the communities in this region of Kerala, assisted no doubt by the isolation created by the sea to the West and the mountains to the East.[18] The hills and forests of Travancore and Cochin and other parts of South India have a number of tribes, of which many are matrilineal, some are patrilineal and others use both systems, passing half the property to the sons and half to the sister's sons.[19]

In the Himalayas, the Khasis to the north and the Garos to the east are both matrilineal.[20] and there are matrilineal traces in the Brahui who live in Baluchistan in the west of the subcontinent.[21] The brahmin scriptures refer to the Arattas in the Punjab, whose heirs are their sisters' children, not their own, and to a matrilineal system in Mahishmati in central India, where women could choose a plurality of husbands.[22] This was, of course, anathema to the brahmins, where only men could have several spouses at once.

The struggle between the two family systems can best be seen in the division of castes into two factions, the Right Hand and the Left Hand. Hutton concludes that the division reflects the two descent systems, since the division occurs throughout Dravidian South India except for Malabar, where the patrilineal system barely penetrated. He suggests that the division signifies the refusal of some matrilineal groups to accept the new patrilineal system:

> The inference that the factions of the Right and Left Hand arose as a result of the introduction of the [patrilineal] principle, which some castes were unwilling to accept, is inescapable. The fact that the women of one or two castes belong to one faction while the men belong to another does nothing to weaken this inference, since there is nothing more likely than that the women of a caste might be opposed to it while the men were wishful to adopt it.[23]

Hutton's 'inescapable' inference illustrates not only the struggle between the two family forms, but also the political divisions and the conflict of interest between men and women associated with the two systems of descent. The struggle in the structure of the family is paralleled by the struggle in the religious culture between the male and the female deities as the dominant power principle.

Matriarchal Religious Tradition

Many countries, including India, have matriarchal myths. Several writers have warned that the myths, on examination, may confirm male superiority rather than provide a history of female power, since they tell of how the women were vanquished because they ruled irresponsibly.[24] Consequently, it is important to distinguish myth from reality,[25] and to make clear the level at which myths are significant. Although the myths read like a story, they are not to be taken as a history of what happened, but as a conceptual framework within which people viewed the world. The religious myths and beliefs represent a cultural history, embodying a struggle over ideas, meanings and interpretations. The persistence of the female power principle symbolises the continued visibility of the power of women as part of the cultural heritage.

Before the arrival of the Aryans, the population of India is believed to have consisted of agricultural communities who lived according to the seasons. God was female, representing life in the form of the Earth Mother.[26] The religion of the Indus Valley was based on fertility, and the people worshipped the mother goddess together with other fertility symbols, all of which are found in Hinduism today.[27] Terracotta figurines of the mother goddess, like those excavated at Mohenjo-Daro in the Indus Valley, were also found at Buxar in Bihar, which suggests the extension of the Indus Valley culture, with its goddess religion, into the Ganges valley in the North-east.[28] Kali the destructive goddess was also known in the Indus Valley, and the Shakti cult (female power) may be traced back to this time.[29] There may also be an early form of the god Shiva.[30] Kali and Shiva are pre-Aryan deities which became more important than Indra, the major god of the early Aryan scriptures,[31] indicating that the cultural struggle for supremacy was by no means always resolved in favour of the immigrants.

Apart from numerous goddesses, a snake cult associated with the mother goddess is found in many regions of the South, and in the Himalayas to the North. Devi, the goddess in the hills, is explicitly known as Devi Mata, the mother goddess.[32] Devi is important in local ceremonies all over India, but she is also involved in the national Hindu festivals of Holi and Dasserah.[33] The Holi spring festival is associated with fertility rites and sexuality, and some of its features are thought to go back to a prehistoric 'matriarchal' stage.[34] At a local level, one study showed that half of the 90 deities worshipped in the village belonged to the 'non-brahmin tradition', and most of these were mother goddesses.[35] The 'brahmin tradition' consists of the specialist scriptures written by the brahmins and requiring a guru for interpretation,[36] although the rigid division of the religion into two parts is not really tenable, since both 'traditions' are a result of conflicts and compromises between the orthodox brahmins and the common people.

Nevertheless, significant differences occur in the 'brahmin' and the 'non-brahmin' traditions, which symbolise the opposition between the male and female principles. The concept of marriage, involving male control of female sexuality, is important for understanding how the mother goddess was incorporated into the patriarchal brahmin religion.[37] In the villages, the old matriarchal religion was brahminised by providing orthodox male deities as husbands for the mother goddesses. In Madura, the goddess is married every year to the god, but the goddess is still recognised by the people as the real deity, not the brahmin god.[38] In Bengal, the scriptures report that Adya, the mother of the gods, was married to Shiva.[39] Durga, also known as Parvati, was married to Shiva and Lakshmi was married to Vishnu.[40] Krishna married several thousand mother goddesses, and one in particular at an annual ceremony, indicating that prior to Krishna, the human representative of the goddess's consort was sacrificed every year.[41]

The features of the goddess in the 'non-brahmin' religion symbolise popular resistance to the control of women's power in the 'brahmin' religious tradition. An excellent illustration of this is found in a study of goddess worship in the region of Chattisgarh by Lawrence Babb.[42] He shows that in the 'brahminical' version, the goddess has a dual, changing nature. As Kali, she is a malevolent destroyer, the manifestation of a terrible sinister force, black anger, implacable and bloodthirsty. The story of Kali — India's matriarchal myth — is that she was created to save the gods from their more powerful enemies, but having done so, she continued on a rampage of uncontrollable killing, which could only be stopped by her husband Shiva lying down in front of her. In her malevolent aspect she receives blood sacrifice. As Lakshmi she is benevolent, bestower of wealth, progeny and happiness, and passively devoted to her husband. In this aspect she never receives blood sacrifice. The goddess is Lakshmi when she is under the control of the male god. In this aspect she is seen standing meekly beside her husband Vishnu. When she is in her terrible aspect, she stands alone, and if Shiva is there he is not her husband but her servant, also in terrible form but subordinate to the goddess. As Susan Wadley suggests, it is marriage and the dominance of the male that transforms the goddess's dangerous power into benevolence.[43]

Significantly, in the 'brahminical' form, the goddess has both aspects, but is more commonly subordinate. In the 'non-brahminical' form, however, the goddess is never represented as married, and is always dominant. In this form, the local goddess is known by many different names, one of which is Shitala, the smallpox goddess. A case of smallpox is treated as possession by the goddess, and certain things are likely to enrage her, particularly the sight of a pregnant woman, who must never approach the patient, and a married couple, who may only approach the patient singly. Remembering that the 'non-brahminical' religion belongs to the people, requires no specialists and is passed on and contributed to by the people themselves, it appears that Shitala's hatred of marriage and pregnancy symbolises the local people's rejection of the patriarchal brahmin attempts to control women's sexuality. The religious myths of the brahmins may tell the story of women's destructive power and how it was constrained by men through control of the women's sexuality, but the religion of the common people tells the story of women's continuing power and their resistance to male control.

Women's Heritage

The worship of the mother goddess does not constitute a matriarchy, but it does constitute a matriarchal *culture*, in the sense that it preserves the value of women as life-givers and sources of activating energy, and it represents the acknowledgement of women's power by women and men in the culture. Nor does the matrilineal family constitute a matriarchy: there is no guarantee that women will be as free as men in such societies, but the evidence from Kerala suggests that matrilineal organisation has had beneficial effects on women's current position compared with women in patrilineal communities.

Both of these aspects form part of the heritage of women in India. From this heritage arises a view of women as powerful and strong. Women in India have managed to maintain the visibility of their power, despite its incorporation into the patriarchal culture, and unlike in the West, the concept of women's power is built into the common cultural assumptions. Consequently, the dominant image of woman is different in India from that of the West, and has different implications for women's liberation in India.

The implications for women are that they see themselves as powerful and strong, an image upon which they can act. The heritage also demonstrates that the roots of women's struggle and resistance go back a very long way, and provide the Indian women's movement with a history of its own, in which the intervention of the British feminists represented only one strand amongst many. The heritage informs both the desire for emancipation amongst women, and the nature of their demands.

The heritage has implications for men too, in terms of how they see women, and the systems they devise for controlling women. In male-dominated societies, women's power must be contained: there are different methods of doing this. Western women are defined as weak and in need of protection. In India, amongst both Hindu and Muslim cultures, women are seen by men as dangerously powerful. Men have to constrain women since women are incapable of controlling themselves; not because they are too weak to do so, but because their power is too great. Such a view legitimates a system of strong physical controls to restrain women's power, which makes no sense within the Western concept of women as the weaker sex. The male-dominated cultures of both India and the West control women's power but in different ways, depending on the specific historical development of gender relations in the two regions. In the following chapter, we discuss the nature of the controls over women in India in the context of the historical development of the caste system.

8. Women and Caste

The most radical of the nineteenth century reformers had seen the subjugation of women as an instrument for perpetuating brahminical domination in society.
Vina Mazumdar, *Symbols of Power*[44]

The connection between gender and caste has been recognised for some time, and it is this we want to explore. The women's question in the 19th and 20th Centuries revolved around issues such as sati, child marriage, purdah, divorce and widow remarriage. It is significant that these issues concerned the control of women's sexuality, and that most of them affected only the two highest castes. We will argue that control over women's sexuality was essential to the development of the patriarchal caste hierarchy, both for the maintenance of the caste and for the legitimation and control of inheritance, and we will show how the constraints on women developed historically with the formation of the caste system.

In relating gender to social hierarchy, we are suggesting that women's subordination needs to be understood not in terms of their powerful sexuality alone, but also in terms of the material and ideological dangers that it posed for the caste structure. Our argument is that the development of the gender division, based on the control of female sexuality, was integral to the formation of the social structure, based on the control of economic resources, revealing the crucial link between women's sexuality and the economic position of the community.

If women are viewed as 'too powerful', it is relevant to ask what exactly was their power going to destroy? Was the threat a purely abstract notion, or was there something concrete and material that their power endangered? The key to this question lies in the system of caste. There are two systems for understanding caste: 'varna', the national system, and 'jati', the local system. We will concentrate on the national system, since although it is too crude to clarify the detailed operation of caste at local level, it does have sufficient generality to be useful for discussing caste nationally.[45]

Features of the Caste System

Caste divides the population into four major groups: the brahmin (priestly caste) at the top, followed by the kshatriya (warrior caste), then the vaishya (commoners, usually known as trading and artisan castes), and at the bottom the sudra (agricultural labourers) some of whom are beyond the pale of caste and are known as untouchables. The sudra is not allowed to take the caste initiation ceremony, at which male members of the other three castes receive the sacred thread and are 'reborn' into the caste (and therefore known as 'twice-born' castes). Within the four major groups there are thousands of sub-castes, which vary regionally.

Caste is both a structural system and a cultural one. The structure consists of a hierarchy of in-marrying groups, organised into hereditary occupations.[46] 'In-marrying' means that they will in general not marry outside their own caste or sub-caste. There are exceptions, notably of women marrying 'up' to men of a higher caste. The hereditary division of labour is also not rigid: a person from a weaving caste does not have to be a weaver, but a weaver could not be a brahmin priest, nor is a brahmin agricultural labourer likely.

The cultural system comprises belief in karma (that the circumstances of birth depend on previous actions), commitment to caste occupation and lifestyle, belief in the hereditary transmission of psychological traits associated with occupation, tolerance of distinct lifestyles for other castes, and belief in a hierarchy of values along a scale of purity and pollution.[47] In the scale of purity and pollution, brahmins are generally, but not always, the purest and sudras the most polluted. Brahmins are not 'naturally' pure; they can become polluted and in extreme cases lose caste, if they behave in impure ways or fail to perform important rituals. This ritual purity is in the nature of a religious status, but it usually coincides with economic wealth and social esteem.[48] Three of the major signs of purity are vegetarianism, teetotalism and tight constraints on women,[49] indicating that a significant degree of ritual purity comes through domestic activities.

The caste system has survived for 2,000 years, though not without modification.[50] As we shall see, the caste system was subject to many challenges over the years both to the position of the dominant castes and to the structure itself, but although the challengers established oppositional movements and changes in relative ranks, they did not succeed in eradicating the hierarchy as a whole. The system's resistance to revolt is thought to lie traditionally in the unity of manufacture and agriculture. The craft workers in the village manufactured all the tools needed by the peasants in exchange for a share in the peasants' produce, so that the community was entirely self-sufficient, but the individual never became independent of the community.[51] The cultural autonomy of the system meant that the upper castes never tried to impose their strict rules of conduct on the lower castes; in fact they forbade the lower castes from following the upper caste lifestyle, and used the differences to distinguish the lower orders from themselves.[52] This cultural autonomy was important because it enabled alternative cultures to flourish, including, as we saw earlier, a distinctive matriarchal culture in the face of a predominantly patriarchal structure.

The Impact of Caste on Women

Increased control over women is one of the factors that a caste must observe along with vegetarianism and teetotalism before it can claim to be ritually pure. Specifically, this control involves two major aspects. One is women's disinheritance from immovable property in the form of land, and their exclusion from the productive economy, involving removal from public life to the domestic sphere of the home in the form of seclusion or purdah. The second is the far greater control exercised by men over women's sexuality, through arranged marriage, child marriage, the prohibition of divorce, and strict monogamy for women, leading to sati and a ban on widow remarriage, including infant or child widows. These strictures were enforced most severely by the higher castes, particularly the brahmins, but some of the lower castes also adopted them. A lower caste that had improved its economic position could attempt to move up the hierarchy over a number of generations, but economic power alone was not sufficient. The caste had also to adopt the cultural attributes of ritual purity, which meant constraining women's freedom.[53] This pattern of social mobility accompanied by increased control over women is not restricted to Hindus. Amongst Muslims, the Ashrafs are the former ruling groups, whilst the non-Ashrafs are the lower-caste converts from Hinduism. The control over Ashraf women is severe, and similar controls are imposed by non-Ashraf men when they improve their economic position.[54]

We want to show that the increased constraints on women are an essential part of a rise in caste hierarchy, by looking at the ideological and material basis for it. Several writers on caste have observed the relationship, but being normally more concerned with caste than with the position of women, they have failed to note the significance of the relationship for an analysis of women's subordination. For example, Hutton states:

> There are also drawbacks to the caste system in India which arise not so much because of the nature of the system as *incidentally* to its development. One of these is the hardship entailed to generations of women in all those castes that aim at raising their position in the social scale. Any caste or sub-caste that wishes to rise . . . finds it *essential* to conform to . . . the marriage of girls before they reach the age of puberty, and [to] the forbidding their remarriage even if widowed in infancy.[55]

The two words 'incidental' and 'essential' reveal a remarkable inconsistency in this passage. Hutton suggests that the hardship to women entailed in raising the caste's position is nothing to do with the nature of the system. And yet he is forced to admit that the hardship is essential to higher status. How can it be 'essential', and at the same time not 'in the nature' of the caste hierarchy? What

Hutton glosses over is the essential gender division which allows the men to benefit from higher caste status at the expense of the women, for the hardship is not experienced by all the members of the caste. The women alone are subject to it, whilst the men gain privileges both in relation to the men of the lower castes and the women of their own caste.

Amongst writers who have noted the relationship between caste and gender division is Srinivas, but he treats it descriptively rather than analytically. Whilst documenting the increasing constraints imposed on women as castes attempt to raise their position, he discusses it only as an index of 'Sanskritization', a term describing cultural social mobility. For instance:

> the institutions of the 'low' castes are more liberal in the spheres of marriage and sex than those of the Brahmins. Post-puberty marriages do occur among them, widows do not have to shave their heads, and divorce and widow marriage are both permitted and practised . . . But as a caste rises in the hierarchy and its ways become more sanskritized, it adopts the sex and marriage code of the Brahmins. Sanskritization results in harshness towards women.[56]

Srinivas does not use this relationship to reach an understanding of women's subordination, nor does he provide any analytical framework which could help to explain why caste and gender might be related in this way. It appears in his accounts to be a cultural accident.

More significantly, Nur Yalman has drawn attention to the essential nature of the relationship between gender and caste, although his discussion is specifically concerned with rituals to ensure women's purity rather than the actual constraints which limit their freedom. He links the sexual purity of women with the purity of the caste, suggesting that female sexuality presents a threat because of the danger of her introducing impure or low caste blood into the lineage.

> It is through women (and not men) that the 'purity' of the caste-community is ensured and preserved . . . [The] danger of low quality blood entering their caste . . . only exists with women. The male seed they receive should be the best available . . . The 'dangers' here are . . . the low-caste men.[57]

But his analysis does not help us to understand (nor was it his intention) why some women's lives were so much more restricted than others, regardless of the religious rituals around their sexuality, for amongst the matrilineal Nayars the rituals were purely symbolic,[58] limiting their sexuality relatively little in practice.

Veena Das takes Yalman's analysis a stage further, adding to the notion of purity the question of access:

> Women were literally seen as points of entrance, as 'gateways' to the caste system. If men of ritually low status were to get sexual access to women of higher status, then not only the purity of the women but that of the entire group would be endangered. Since the main threat to the purity of the group came from female sexuality, it becomes vital to guard it.[59]

Her suggestion is that women are so strenuously guarded by the higher castes because sexual contact with lower caste men would not only pollute the purity of the caste, but also allow the lower castes access to it, undermining its social exclusiveness as well as its biological purity. This is important, but we need to go further, to see whether this cultural explanation has any material basis. The notion of the gateways to the higher castes being guarded against the dangers posed by female sexuality is much the same as the idea we encountered earlier about women's sexual power being potentially destructive to men. We need to know what it is that could be destroyed by lower-caste access if female sexuality were insufficiently guarded. We want to look at this by tracing the impact of the early patriarchal immigrants, as expressed in brahmin writings, on the existing culture of the common people, as depicted in Chapter 7, and examining how this process of struggle and accommodation affected women.

The Aryan Impact on Women

Our knowledge of this period comes from the Vedas, the Aryan religious books which constitute the earliest written history of the region. They were written mostly by brahmin males, so it is not clear how far their ideal view of women was actually practised, and there are contradictions even within the theory. Nevertheless, this was regarded by some of the 19th Century reformers and the revivalists of the 20th Century women's movement as the 'Golden Age', to which they looked back with nostalgia as a time of liberality for women. Yet compared with the value accorded to women in the matriarchal culture, it was far from ideal.

The Aryans held a radically different view of women from that prevailing within the indigenous culture. They brought with them a pantheon of predominantly male gods, the patriarchal joint family, and a three-class social structure, divided into kshatriyas (warriors and aristocracy), brahmins (priests) and vaishyas (commoners).[60] At first there was no caste consciousness, no hereditary occupations and no rules about marriage within the class. The development of this form of social organisation into a caste structure was a slow process which only began when the Aryans, having established dominance over the native population around 1500 B.C., began to class the indigenous people and those of mixed descent as outsiders, relegating them to a fourth category of sudras (servants) and excluding them from the Vedic religion.[61]

At this time the king was the supreme political force and the kshatriyas held the highest rank, but the brahmins began to stake their claim as the primary caste by claiming that only they could bestow divinity on the king. Slowly the brahmins established an alliance with the kings to maintain the position of both groups at the top of the hierarchy. Caste became hereditary, rules of in-marriage were established, and it became impossible for individuals to rise in the hierarchy except as members of entire sub-castes. These new strictures were laid down by the brahmin law-givers, and although they were portrayed as rigid rules, there was in fact a great deal of flexibility within the system.[62]

Within the patriarchal joint family, women were considered as part of the males' property in the same way as a field belonged to the men of the family. The analogy of the field and the seed was used to describe the right of the men to the use of women and to the women's issue.[63] Only sons inherited immovable property, the daughters taking with them a dowry in the form of goods to their marital family. These economic facts of patrilineal inheritance ensured that sons were valued and daughters were not, amongst propertied families in particular. Women could not sacrifice to the gods, because their presence was considered polluting, so a man had to have male children to perform the sacrifices which would allow his soul to rest after death.[64] However, women in propertied families had access to learning and could become scholars, poets and teachers. Women in commercial circles took an active part in business transactions, and in the lower strata they worked in agriculture, military manufacturing, weaving, dyeing, embroidery and basket-making, amongst other occupations.[65] Women also took part in the administration of the country, for the marriage hymn expresses the hope that the bride will be able to speak with composure and success in the democratic assemblies until her old age.[66]

Marriage was not compulsory for women, and young men and women could mix together socially.[67] Later, when caste rules on marriage became more important for the higher castes, the woman could choose her husband from a group of suitable men.[68] Widows could remarry and monogamy seems to have been the norm, but polygyny and polyandry were not unknown.[69] However, women were also classed with dwarfs, humpbacks, lean, lame and blind men, idiots and eunuchs, as unfit to attend the king's court.[70] That women's position was better than in later periods was true, but compared with the value given to women by the matriarchal culture, it represented a sharp decline, from woman as life-giver and equal sharer in property and produce, to woman as impure and herself the property of men.

Challenge and Response

Caste supremacy, however, with its emphasis on a social elite and the superiority of the male, did not go unchallenged either by women or the lower castes. The resistance arose at various times over the centuries, usually corresponding with some change in the economic order. The Muslim invasions later posed a further challenge to the caste hierarchy from outside the society. The high-caste response was to tighten up on caste divisions by distinguishing themselves more clearly from other castes, and to compromise by incorporating some aspects of the opponents' culture into their own.

The first major change occurred around the last few centuries B.C., when trade with other countries began to expand, currency was introduced, and large urban centres developed. The expansion in trade opened up opportunities to all the castes, and some members of the lower castes were able to raise their economic position. A large number of atheistical sects developed at this time, including Buddhism and Jainism, which appealed to the lower-caste members of this rising class, and Ghurye has suggested that the two religions represented the assertion of kshatriya superiority over the religious authority of the brahmins.[71] For vaishyas, whose economic position did not now accord with their religious position, and for sudras, whose ritual status did not permit them caste initiation or religious knowledge, the new atheistic religions represented a humanitarian, anti-caste, anti-brahmin protest. Another radical difference was that women were allowed to join, to participate in learning and devotions, and to become nuns.[72]

The response of the brahmins to kshatriya supremacy, to vaishya and sudra protest, and to the atheistic challenge to the Vedic religion, was to defend their position by tightening up the rules on social relationships. This affected both women and the lower castes. The relationships between the four castes and their legitimate social activities were rigidly defined and strict controls over the lives of women were laid down. The brahmins at this time began to emphasise their superiority over every other group in society.[73]

The increasingly strict sex and caste orthodoxy for brahmins was imparted through the new law books known as the Smritis. These advocated for the first time a strict monogamy for women, reflected in brahmin opposition to polyandry and widow remarriage. They also advocated marriage before puberty for girls, and backed it up with the social sanction that a brahmin man who married a girl over 10 years old would be treated as the husband of a sudra woman, and not allowed to eat with other brahmins.[74] Significantly, these strictures were not adopted by the kshatriyas, the lower castes or the matrilineal groups.[75] At this time too, brahmin men increased the exclusiveness of education, by limiting it mainly to themselves. Kshatriya and vaishya men were allowed only restricted access, and sudras and women virtually none.[76] Women were no longer allowed to attend the democratic assemblies, and high-caste women were withdrawn from their previous occupations in education and the arts.[77]

The new orthodoxy finds many expressions in the Smritis. Although from the earliest Aryan times a woman's purpose had been defined only as producing sons for her husband, the Smritis introduced an additional element of total dependence, as in the famous statement from the Code of Manu: 'A woman should never be independent. Her father has authority over her in childhood, her husband in youth, and her son in old age.'[78] The reason for this was her evil nature: 'Manu (the creator) allotted to women a love of bed, seat and ornament, impure desires, wrath, dishonesty, malice and bad conduct.'[79] More specifically: 'Women remain chaste only as long as they are not in a deserted place and do not get the chance to be acquainted with any man. That is why it is necessary that respectable women should always be guarded by friends.'[80] And: 'Women, even when they are of good family, beautiful and married, do not hesitate to transgress morals . . . At the first opportunity they leave wealthy and good-looking husbands to share an adulterous bed with other men.'[81]

When caste distinction became more pronounced, women's unbridled lust for men had to be firmly controlled. According to Manu, a man could only achieve merit by protecting the purity of his wife and, through her, of his sons.[82]

Since she could not be expected to control herself, he had to do it for her. The importance of sexual control over women to the maintenance of caste distinction can be seen in the low status classifications given to the children of various mixed caste unions, of which the Chandala was the lowest, born of a sudra man and a brahmin woman.[83]

The brahminical ideal of the pativrata woman (husband worshipper) was emphasised at this time: a brahmin woman's first duty was to worship her husband as god, no matter how cruel, unfaithful or immoral he might be. The most famous example of the ideal is Sita of the Ramayana Epic, who is abducted by a demon king but, even though she has resisted seduction, has to prove her innocence through ordeal by fire after her rescue and subsequent rejection by her husband Rama. In the Mahabharata Epic, Gandhari blindfolded herself for life when she discovered at her wedding that her husband was blind.[84]

The next major decline in women's position came in the 'classical age' around 500 A.D. The word 'classical' in fact refers to the prosperity of upper-caste men in the Northern regions only. Amongst the upper castes, *women's* position deteriorated during this period. Child marriage was compulsory and widows were regarded as contemptible, and forbidden to remarry. The earliest evidence of widow-burning was in 510 A.D., and was demanded more and more by upper-caste men, especially kshatriyas, during the next few centuries. It was claimed that the act brought the woman the highest religious merit, hence the meaning of the word sati, 'a virtuous woman'. The only way a high-caste woman could be sure of avoiding such a fate was by becoming a Buddhist nun, a theatrical entertainer or a prostitute.[85]

The decline in women's position was directly connected with the brahmins finally establishing economic and social supremacy in Northern society,[86] for it was in this period that they consolidated their land holdings. The brahmins eventually won the contest for primacy over the kshatriyas and vaishyas of the mercantile communities by becoming landowners, thus providing the material basis for their caste supremacy and their power over women. The maintenance of land and other property within the joint family was the material basis of the patriarchal family structure and the in-marrying nature of the caste system, which was regulated by the religious laws.[87] The family structure was patrilineal, property passing down the male line, and patrilocal, the sons staying with the father. The daughters went to live with the husband's family on marriage. The property laws forbade the daughters from inheriting immovable property, since such property would have passed to their husbands' family at marriage. Instead, women were given a portion of movable property to take with them, known as dowry.

The transmission of property to the daughters through dowry had important implications for women, as is suggested by Jack Goody[88] more generally, and Prabhati Mukherjee more specifically in relation to India.[89] It meant that within the patriarchal family, significant portions of the property were removed from the patrilineal line of inheritance, and distributed to the daughters' marital families. This provided a substantial material reason for anxiety over the birth of daughters. And if the daughters were allowed to marry freely, the accumulated property could not be retained within the group, but could soon be redistributed amongst families without property. To retain differentials in economic position required daughters to marry as closely as possible within the group, and this entailed both strict general rules of in-marriage for the upper castes, and control over the particular man that the woman married. The consequence was tight constraints on female sexuality and on any movements or activities which might interfere with such constraints. The more property a woman had, the more important it was to control her sexuality, since the distribution of her property coincided with her sexual attachment. So the rule of in-marriage and the control of female sexuality not only maintained the purity of caste, but also ensured that the property remained within the caste.

That women were regarded as men's property amongst the upper castes, and that control over women was important for the retention of property is suggested by the numerous references in the religious texts at this time to women and property together. For instance, it was said that 'A virtuous man never interferes with the wives or properties of others, the source of all trouble.'[90] The institutions of private property and the patriarchal family were regarded as the main reason for the origin of state authority: 'In a kingless state, private property cannot be retained and a wife is not under control.'[91]

In this time too, women and sudras were regarded as equally contemptible. The Code of Manu distinguished between the twice-born castes on the one hand, and women and sudras on the other.[92] Women and sudras were regarded as life-long slaves from birth to death, with slavery inborn in them;[93] the same value was attached to the life of a woman and a sudra, for anyone who killed an artisan, a mechanic, a sudra or a woman had to perform two penances and give 11 bulls to atone for it.[94]

Here we can see two links between gender and caste. Women's position deteriorated with the economic supremacy of the caste. And this deterioration had a material basis in the maintenance of property within the caste.

The next major challenge to brahmin supremacy came with the Muslim invasions, of which the most significant were the arrival of the Arabs and the Turks in the 11th and 12th Centuries, and the Mughals in the 16th Century. The Muslims did not destroy the caste structure, but used it to establish an administrative system designed to collect revenue and maintain law and order.[95] The invasions led to another tightening up by the brahmins on women's position. Around 1000 A.D. the rule of no remarriage for widows amongst the top castes was extended even to child widows, of whom there were large numbers because of the low age of marriage.[96] The incidence of sati increased, particularly amongst the warring regions of the North, the women often being forced onto the pyre by their husband's relatives and sometimes by their own sons.[97] And the seclusion of women, purdah, became more common amongst the higher castes.[98] Baig suggests that conquest made the people defensive, inducing particularly the upper castes to retreat into more rigid orthodoxy and providing a solid reason for protecting women from the foreign invader.[99]

The coming of the Mughals in the 16th Century consolidated Islamic power in India. They established an empire which lasted until the arrival of the Europeans in the 18th Century. During this time women's lowly position amongst the upper castes of both Muslim and Hindu communities was reinforced. Purdah, child marriage, widow discrimination and the pativrata (husband worshipping) ideal were the norm amongst high-caste Hindu women, and were regarded as symbols of prestige. Purdah in particular spread under Mughal rule, especially in areas where Muslim-Hindu conflict was strongest, based on the fear of abduction and rape from the opposing side.[100]

Muslim women, however, had a better legal status than Hindu women, even though their rights often did not work to their advantage. For example, Muslim women were allowed to study the religious books, divorce and remarriage were possible (although divorce was at the discretion of the husband) and they had rights of inheritance. Polygyny was allowed in both religions, but Islam restricted the number of wives to four, whereas Hindu law specified no limits.[101] Clearly these could be considered improvements only within a patriarchal context, but the original egalitarianism of Islam did bring a small measure of protection to Muslim women. For example, the Sharia defines suicide as illegal, and becoming sati comprised suicide, but even though the matter was discussed, no restraint on its practice by Hindus was attempted.[102] The Islamic law against suicide did, however, prevent sati being adopted by Muslims.

Resistance and Integration

So far we have looked only at the way the upper castes tightened the caste and gender divisions in response to challenges to their supremacy from below and outside. But the upper castes also responded to the challenge by loosening some of the cultural divisions and accepting certain 'non-brahmin' traditions into the orthodox religion, including aspects of the matriarchal culture. This was not as contradictory as it appears, because the notion of woman as powerful was incorporated to legitimise strong controls. The particular constraints imposed on upper-caste women had rarely applied to women of the lower castes, although they experienced their own hardships. But lower-caste women were not secluded, since their labour was needed in the fields for survival. There was no sati and widows could remarry. Many lower-caste communities allowed divorce, and polygyny, though permitted, could not be practised by those who could not afford to support a large family.[103] Amongst these communities, women's involvement in wider areas than those specified by the brahmins was a fact of life, and the demand for women's inclusion in religious and social activities became a feature of all the socio-religious reform movements in India.[104]

At the same time as brahminism was tightening its hold on its own women and the lower castes, two new movements began which embodied matriarchal and populist resistance to patriarchal brahmin elitism. One was a resurgence of mother goddess cults and fertility worship, of which the most famous was Tantra in the 5th Century A.D. and which had its centre in the non-Aryan regions of the North-east. Tantra was open to all castes and to women. It was explicitly against both the orthodox ritual of the Hindu religion and the patriarchal caste structure of the brahmins. It worshipped the mother goddess, since life was created in the womb, and had its roots in the pre-Aryan culture. The cult influenced Buddhism to form a new school, adding female saviours, Taras, to the existing male ones. The worship of Taras still exists in Nepal and Tibet. And it influenced Hinduism, which developed the Shakti cult, representing the female power principle. Shakti believes that the female is the source of all energy and action, and only she can activate the male god.[105] Shakti is the active, practical, violent goddess, compared with the passive, contemplative, non-violent god.[106] The cults also influenced artistic expression in the form of erotic poetry, such as the story of Krishna and Radha,[107] and in the form of erotic temple sculpture such as that found at Khajuraho.[108]

The other movement was the Bhakti cult in the 6th and 7th Centuries A.D., which was strongest in the non-Aryan South, but later spread all over India. Bhakti means devotion, and was based on the belief that a direct personal relationship with god was possible, without the mediation of a brahmin expert or the performance of esoteric ritual.[109] This cult too opened religion to ordinary people, and was anti-caste and anti-establishment, representing a resistance to brahmin culture with its emphasis on caste and gender superiority. Their saints and followers included women and men, and were predominantly of the lower castes.[110] But significantly their number included women from the higher castes, particularly widows, otherwise condemned to a life of penance.[111]

So despite brahmin supremacy, the matriarchal and populist cultures continued to make their opposition felt. They found a common interest in their exclusion from the brahmin religion and the ownership of land and in the restrictions on their activities, which formed the basis for an alliance of women and the lower castes against patriarchal caste elitism. Here we can see another link between gender and caste, for the partnership against caste supremacy and male dominance was to be repeated many times over the centuries.

We have already seen that the brahmin religion, under the pressure of economic change and the threat of opposition movements, maintained supremacy by becoming more orthodox, tightening the divisions between castes and increasing the sexual controls over women of their own caste. But they also adopted a more liberal approach to other cultural groups and incorporated their different interests into the brahmin religion. They became at the same time more orthodox themselves and more tolerant of others. This was possible for two reasons. First, the high degree of integration between the religious ideology and the rural economy prevented the revolts from destroying the economic basis of the caste system in the villages.[112] And second, the tradition of cultural autonomy not only allowed other cultures to flourish, but also enabled the brahmins to use the cultural differences to accentuate caste divisions.

The brahmin priests made two important concessions. They conceded that women and the lower castes could have a direct relationship with god based on personal devotion, without the intervention of a priest, even though women, vaishyas and sudras were still classed together as lower forms of life. This can be seen in the Bhagavad-Gita:

> For whosoever makes me his haven,
> Base-born though he may be,
> Yes, women too, and artisans, even serfs,
> Theirs it is to tread the highest Way.[113]

In making this concession the brahmins maintained control by modifying some of the popular secular writings to give them religious authority, propounding the doctrines of karma (that the circumstances of birth were determined by previous actions) and dharma (the sacred law which regulated the morality of the actions). And second, they dropped some of their own gods, incorporating the matriarchal fertility cults into the worship of Shiva and providing 'brahminical' husbands for the 'non-brahminical' mother goddesses.[114] Since the mother goddess could not be suppressed, she was finally incorporated into brahmin ritual,[115] but this integration could not occur without contradiction. It is intriguing to consider the brahmin priests, holding Manu's opinion of women, yet allowing the introduction of matriarchal goddesses into the pantheon. The mother goddess was associated with magic, sexual orgies and blood sacrifice, representing the miracle of birth, the creation of life through sexuality, and menstruation as a symbol of fertility. To the brahmin, childbirth, sexuality and menstruation were all sources of pollution, yet this polluting matriarchal culture was absorbed into the pure patriarchal religious ritual in the form of mother worship.[116] The success of such an integration was a tribute both to the persistence of the matriarchal culture and to the adaptability of the brahmin patriarchy.

Having acknowledged women's power, the contradiction was resolved culturally, as we have seen, by defining it as dangerous unless controlled by men. But the underlying material basis of this ideological resolution, as we have also seen, was the preservation of wealth within the caste, for which purpose the women had to be sexually controlled by men.

We can now answer the question of what precisely women's power endangered. Lakshmi is benevolent because her controlled sexuality bestows legitimate heirs for the maintenance of caste wealth and retains family property within the caste. Kali is malevolent because her uncontrolled passion is liable to introduce impure blood into the caste and to dissipate caste wealth, making a mockery of patrilineal inheritance and the accumulation of property, and thereby destroying the caste system itself. Unconstrained, mortal women are as much to be feared as potential destroyers and robbers of the patriarchal heritage — cultural and material — as are members of the lower orders. As the scriptures say:

> Women constantly suck the blood of men like leeches . . . That very woman whom man considers his beloved robs him of his manhood through sexual indulgence, and of his mind, his wealth and all his possessions. Hence is there any greater robber than woman?[117]

The ideas about women's ritual impurity which arose, along with the physical constraints on their activities, stressed that women's menstrual, reproductive and sexual functions made them inherently impure. These ideas justified her low ritual status within the caste and her inability to control her own sexuality in the interests of the caste. Her sexual insatiability was at the root of all problems, and the lower castes' failure to control their women's sexuality was partly what made them impure. This idea reinforced the caste divisions, for if the lower castes behaved like the brahmins, the distinctions would dissolve. So the gender division reinforced the caste division, and the gender ideology legitimated not only the structure of patriarchy but also the organisation of caste.

9. The New Middle Class

The attempt on the part of some women to cast off their shy temperament and adopt certain useful professions like nursing, teaching and other public services, ushered in an era of socio-economic freedom for the womenfolk . . . The changing pattern of socio-economic life ultimately led to a remarkable awakening in women in general.
Pratima Asthana, *Women's Movement in India*[117]

Caste is defined primarily by social honour, attained through personal lifestyle, in which the domestic arena is crucial. The ownership of property is usually a precondition for social honour, in that a certain economic minimum is needed to maintain the lifestyle.[118] For example, the caste has to be able to afford to maintain the women if they are withdrawn from labouring in the fields. Social mobility in the caste structure is closed for individuals both in principle and practice, but in practice whole communities can change in rank over a long period of time.[119]

Class, however, is defined primarily by the ownership of property (land under feudalism, capital under capitalism), although social honour is usually associated with property ownership. Class within a capitalist structure is defined by the wage relation, that is, whether a person earns wages or pays them, for which the occupational arena is crucial. Social mobility in the class structure is open to individuals in principle but limited in practice.[120]

Traditionally, social, economic and political power largely coincided in the caste structure, but the development of the class system introduced certain changes. The formation of social classes in India was largely the effect of the new capitalist economic structure, resulting from the British conquest and the integration of India into the British and world economy.[121] The British entered India at a time when the power of the state was weakened because of the decline of the Mughal empire. Some Indian merchants had accumulated capital from trade and begun to invest it in urban industrial enterprises, but the strength of the caste system in the villages made it difficult for the merchants to develop into a social class which could successfully challenge the power of the state, as had happened in England.[122]

The British stepped into the vacuum, and took over the administrative system designed by the Mughals for the control of the population and the collection of revenue. They destroyed Indian industry and undermined the rising merchant class. They commercialised Indian agriculture so that it produced less food for immediate consumption and more raw materials for British industry. And they changed the nature of property from collective to individual ownership.[123]

As we saw in Part I, the changes forced large numbers of people back to the land which was unable to support them. Many of the peasants found themselves in debt because the British had also changed the tax into a rent so that the size of the payment no longer varied with the harvest, but was a fixed sum which increased periodically. But the methods of agriculture did not improve since production was still precapitalist and without the benefit of machinery, so the peasants had to pay more and more rent on the basis of the same amount of production. This development created a class of money-lenders from amongst the zamindars (landlords) and the better-off peasants. The change in land ownership meant that the zamindars were able to turn the peasants off the land for non-payment of rent, creating a class of landless labourers.[124] In England the landless labourers provided the wage labour for the new urban-based capitalist industries, but in India the British inhibition of indigenous capitalism created a large surplus of pauperised 'free' labour. This was the origin of India's chronic poverty, which persists and increases to this day.

Creation of the Middle Class

The middle class arose from the British need for English-educated Indians to administer the country under British superiors. The British set up education in India for this purpose, and explicitly encouraged the men of the upper castes to avail themselves of the new opportunities. The British created the new middle class out of the existing public officials from the Mughal times, out of the money-lenders, and out of the literary class of educated brahmins.[125] The literary groups were almost exclusively brahmins, the money-lenders were predominantly brahmins and kshatriyas, and the industrialists were mainly vaishyas, since they were traders by caste occupation, although some also came from sudra, kshatriya and brahmin castes.

As a result the people who took over the adminstration of the state under the British came predominantly from those groups who had been powerful in the rural areas. The administration also needed lawyers, teachers and accountants, and soon these groups wanted their own professional services such as doctors. So the middle class in India came to consist primarily of the educated professional groups, with the merchants and the industrialists in the minority.[126] The position of the professionals in the class structure is ambiguous because, although they are wage-earners not employers, the discrepancy between their income and that of the manual labourers is sufficient to place them economically and socially closer to the larger-scale employers. The professional groups therefore constitute part of the middle class, and in India their position is particularly important since they outnumber the industrialist groups.[127]

The discontent that resulted in the formation of the Indian National Congress by the middle class (which led but did not initiate the mass movement against British imperialism)[128] grew from the discrepancy between the supply of and demand for government jobs, and from the barriers to further progress placed by the British on the professionals and the industrialists. More people had acquired an English education than the British needed, and the pressure on agriculture and the obstruction of industry left this newly-educated middle class with few opportunities apart from the British administrative posts, over which there was increasing competition, and increasing dissatisfaction for those who were unsuccessful. Public servants could not rise to the top because the British held all the senior posts, professionals who had arisen around the administration were similarly blocked at the top levels,[129] and industrialists were inhibited in their accumulation of capital by British domination of the market and control over private investment and public finance.[130]

It was the new middle class who rose to power and took over the political and administrative machinery of the state after Independence. The circumstances of its development meant that although there was some breakdown of the caste structure, the new power elite still consisted of the higher castes.[131] A sample survey conducted in one of the states 20 years after Independence found that the professions were still dominated by the upper castes. Amongst Hindus in the Indian Administrative Service, 65 per cent were brahmins, 30 per cent were kshatriyas, and 4 per cent were vaishyas. There were no sudras.[132] There is evidence from Jamshedpur that caste is no barrier to factory employment,[133] but this is qualified by evidence from five factories in Poona which showed that although sudras are not excluded, they are given low-level jobs whilst brahmins are given high-level ones.[134] These findings on the relationship between caste and class in industrial and professional occupations suggest that the capitalist class structure is building upon the existing divisions in society, and is breaking them down to only a limited extent.

The Impact on Women

The rise of the middle class had a contradictory effect on the position of women. Similar strictures on women's activities to those prevailing amongst the rural upper castes are also imposed on women of the urban middle class, and similar discrepancies between the strictures imposed on upper- and lower-caste women in the villages seem to occur between middle- and working-class women in the towns. For example, Kamla Bhasin argues that in the middle class: 'There has been some improvement because of various social and economic factors, but even today the majority of women live in perpetual subservience, self-denial and self-sacrifice.'[135]

In the city of Chandigarh, despite the fact that the number of women taking outside employment increases towards the top of the occupational and educational hierarchy, the vast majority of educated middle-class women are still confined to domestic activities. By far the largest proportion of employed women occurs in the lowest occupational class.[136] Studies such as these suggest that the class structure, rather than destroying the gender divisons within the caste system, may be building upon them, whilst changing their form.

The other effect was that new economic opportunities became available for some women of the middle class. The British had not allowed women to enter the new administrative occupations, but women did begin to move into other professions serving the Indian community, especially in medicine and teaching. This happened partly in response to demands for education and health care amongst female relatives of middle-class men, and partly because the maintenance of sex segregation and female seclusion demanded that these services be provided by other women.[137] Independence widened opportunities for middle-class women still further, especially in government service and public sector industry, thanks to the constitutional guarantee against discrimination in employment and offices, and expanded opportunities in the existing women's areas of education and health. So the rise of the middle class, combined with the continued segregation of the sexes, provided opportunities for women from the more liberal families of the class to enter professional occupations.

The result was that women from the middle class began to see new possibilities for change in women's position, since some of them now had access to an independent source of income and could survive outside the patriarchal caste structure. This posed problems for the traditional organisation of society, for women who were economically independent could less easily be controlled. Because of their crucial position in the organisation and maintenance of the social hierarchy, women had the potential to undermine the entire social structure. It was no accident that the women's organisations developed out of the middle class, nor was it surprising that the changes they demanded met with resistance, since many of the demands fundamentally challenged the organisation of the social hierarchy, particularly those concerning personal law.

We can now see that the resistance of women in India did not arise primarily from the liberalising influence of British imperialism (since the effect of imperialism was contradictory), nor from the direct influence of the British women's movement (although that was one intervention amongst many), but from the powerful influence of the women's own cultural heritage, and from their particular position in the social class structure which provided economic opportunities and potential independence from the existing relations of gender and social hierarchy.

10. The Problems Remain, So Does the Struggle

Do we really believe that when all the movements subsided, all the feminists who were involved with them vanished? . . . Maybe the difficulty lies with our definition of what constitutes participation . . . The example of India raises a lot of questions about . . . our categories and definitions.
Elizabeth Sarah, *Towards a Reassessment of Feminist History*[138]

At Independence in 1947 the women's movement succeeded in bringing women's legal position to a level in advance of many of the rich countries of the West.[139] The Constitution conferred equal rights and status on all citizens, forbidding any discrimination on grounds of caste, creed, religion or sex. The state was required to secure to all citizens — men and women — equality, the right to education and to adequate means of livelihood.[140] Women acquired full political rights including the right to vote, to contest elections and to enter the administrative services.[141] Labour legislation to protect the interests of women workers was included in the Factories Act, the Plantation Labour Act and the Mines Act, passed between 1948 and 1952, which regulate working conditions where 50 or more women are employed, providing for equal pay for equal work, maternity benefits, creches and nursing time, and specifying a maximum load and maximum hours for women. It is illegal to employ women on night work and on underground and dangerous operations, to restrict the recruitment of women, and to terminate employment on the grounds of pregnancy.[142] Under the Hindu Code, many of the disabilities suffered by Hindu women were removed by the five Acts on personal law. Monogamy was established as a rule for both men and women, divorce became permissible under certain conditions, the minimum age of marriage was fixed at 18 for women and 21 for men, and women were given the right to inherit and adopt.[143] Later laws included the Prohibition of Dowry, the Suppression of Immoral Traffic,[144] and a liberal abortion law providing social reasons as grounds for abortion.[145]

Sushila Mehta describes these laws as 'paper tigers'. They are enforced neither by the machinery of the state nor by women themselves, and equality remains a distant dream for most women even after 30 years of Independence.[146] For example, in spite of the law on equal pay, women in lower paid jobs generally receive between 10 per cent and 60 per cent of men's wages, depending on the industry.[147] The protective legislation has been used to restrict recruitment, which is itself illegal. For example, the National Commission on Labour concluded that the ban on night work, underground and dangerous operations had adversely affected women's employment.[148] Employers often pay women daily wages in order to avoid insurance benefits, and may restrict the number of women workers to below 50, to avoid the obligation to provide equal pay, maternity leave or a creche.[149] Dowry, far from being eradicated, has grown to greater proportions — a doctor can now demand 3 lakh rupees or £20,000 in dowry — and dowry deaths have replaced sati as the married woman's fear in the urban middle class.[150]

The contradiction for women today is that despite the liberality of the laws, the inequalities remain. The implementation of the laws to secure equality continues to be hindered by patriarchal family structures and by barriers of caste and class. The position is made worse by the West's continued drain on the Indian economy, which is now preventing all but the most economically privileged middle-class women from earning an independent living.[151] Mehta draws attention to these persistent problems when she suggests that although male-dominated society has paid lip service to the new laws, most men have not accepted their practical implications. The laws also require honest implementation by the male-dominated administrative machinery. And a majority of women are both illiterate and poor, unaware of their legal rights, and without the resources to fight for them through the courts.[152]

What makes male supremacy particularly resistant to legislative change is the fact that women's subordination remains embodied in the personal relations of the patriarchal family, and patriarchal relations are part and parcel of the social structure. The former makes legal changes difficult to enforce, the latter means that many of the laws which are not directed at changing the social structure itself are attacking the symptoms rather than the causes of women's inequality.

The Movement Disappears, the Ideas Remain

The struggle for women's equality goes on. In 1977, when we did our study, the women's movement had no clear organisational focus such as the Independence movement had provided. But there were women whose ideas had their history in that movement. The women who speak in the following pages are from that privileged group of the educated middle class who work in professional occupations. They are from two of the traditional professions for women, education and medicine, and from two of the more recent areas, government service and public and private sector industry. They have similar social origins to the activists in the earlier women's movement, and they are the bearers and beneficiaries of the movement's heritage. Our study came just before the rise of the 'second wave' movement in Delhi, and 30 years after the demise of the 'first wave'. Throughout that time women had retained both the ideas of the movement and its struggles on an individual or collective basis.

Some writers have begun to question the assumption that when a movement is no longer active, the ideas on which it was built fall into disuse, and the people who acted collectively disappear.[153] In India the ideas of sexual equality and the challenge to male domination which were raised by the women's movement continued to inspire women activists. For example, Renuka Ray of the All India Women's Conference and Romola Sinha, both in their seventies, are still at work organising women into consumer action groups, and providing refuge for battered wives, prostitutes, women refugees and runaways.[154] Nor did the ideas evaporate as the women actively involved in the movement grew older, for they passed on their inspiration to the next generation. Reeta Rao, one of the women we talked to, was 19 at Independence. Her orthodox father had kept her at home, but she took comfort and inspiration from her aunt:

> My mother's elder sister was a great influence. I thought of her as my real mother . . . She stood by me through all my problems. My aunt had studied in purdah, married out of caste, worked with Gandhi, gone to jail, lived in an ashram. I wanted education desperately. My aunt had fought to learn herself. I took on my aunt's values, I knew I had to have education.

Promilla Khanna was only three in 1947, but the experience of Independence and Partition (when India and Pakistan were separated) changed her parents' lives, and their outlook. This they passed on to their children by bringing them up to continue the struggle against sexual inequality.

> My mother and father believed in equality but the social institutions gave pre-eminence to male children. My parents were trying to bring us up equally and I resented unequal treatment. I was always taught to question the social institutions, and I always rebelled against male-dominated institutions.

A significant number of women who spoke to us in 1977 expressed, without prompting, ideas which derived directly from the women's movement.[155] These women were evenly divided across age groups, and included women from all four areas of work (education, medicine, government service and industry). They were no more dormant or passive in recognising male domination and fighting for their rights in 1977, than they were in 1947. They know they are not treated as individual people but as sexual stereotypes. They experience their subordination at work and in the home. They are angry about it, and this anger is expressed in different ways. But none of these women accepts the inequality, and many of them are determined to change it.

In Part III we will examine how the gender division relates to the divisions of social hierarchy in terms of caste and class, by focusing on the change that occurs when women struggle to emerge from domestic seclusion to professional employment. In looking at the change, we will analyse the social processes by which the women's personal experiences can be seen to be not purely individual, but crucially related to the social structure.

Notes

1. Tara Ali Baig (1976) *India's Woman Power*. New Delhi: S. Chand, p.xiv.

2. See for example Merlin Stone (1976) *The Paradise Papers*. London: Virago.

3. Manjulika Dubey (1983), 'Interview with Chandralekha', *The Book Review* VII, 6, May-June, p.272. Chandralekha is a woman activitist, Bharata Natyam dancer, graphic artist and writer, who works in villages teaching low-cost communication and media techniques.

4. Fatima Mernissi (1975) *Beyond the Veil*. New York: Wiley.

5. Azizah Al-Hibri (1981) 'Capitalism is an Advanced Stage of Patriarchy: but Marxism is not Feminism', in Lydia Sargent (ed), *Women and Revolution: the Unhappy Marriage of Marxism and Feminism*. London: Pluto.

6. The definition of patriarchy is problematic. See Veronica Beechey (1979) 'On Patriarchy', *Feminist Review*, 3.

7. See Michelle Zimbalist Rosaldo and Louise Lamphere (1974) *Woman, Culture and Society*. Stanford, Calif.: Stanford University Press, Introduction.

8. Paula Webster (1975) 'Matriarchy: A Vision of Power', in Rayna Reiter (ed), *Towards an Anthropology of Women*. London: Monthly Review Press. We use 'matriarchal' as a cultural concept, and confine its use to an adjective describing a culture rather than a noun implying a structure.

9. See Part I, Chapter 3.

10. David Schneider (1962) 'The Distinctive Features of Matrilineal Descent Groups', in D. Schneider and K. Gough (eds), *Matrilineal Kinship*. Berkeley: University of California Press, pp.5-6.

11. Female literacy is 54.3 per cent in Kerala compared with 18.7 per cent in the whole of India. Tamil Nadu is the next highest state with female literacy of 26.9 per cent. Source: Ashish Bose (1975) 'A Demographic Profile of Indian Women', in Devaki Jain (ed), *Indian Women*. New Delhi: Government of India, p.163.

12. The sex ratio in Kerala is 1,016 females per 1,000 males, compared with 930 females per 1,000 males in all India. In all other states and union territories except Dadra and Nagar Haveli, males outnumber females, although females normally outnumber males in other countries. Source: Department of Social Welfare (1978) *Women in India: a Statistical Profile*. New Delhi: Government of India, p.6. For a discussion of the implications of the declining sex ratio, see: Kumudini Dandekar (1975) 'Why has the Proportion of Women in India's Population been Declining?', *Economic and Political Weekly* 18 Oct, pp.1663-7, and Asok Mitra (1979) *Implications of Declining Sex Ratio in India's Population*. Indian Council for Social Sciences Research: Programme of Women's Studies I. For sex ratio in selected countries, see Bose, 'Demographic Profile', p.145.

13. Mean age at marriage of women in Kerala is 20.88 years, compared with 17.23 in all India. Source: Department of Social Welfare, *Women in India*, p.59.

14. Department of Social Welfare (1974) *Towards Equality. Report of the Committee on the Status of Women in India*. New Delhi: Government of India, pp.54-6.

15. Stanley Wolpert (1977) *A New History of India*. New York: Oxford University Press, pp.14, 24, 27.

16. For example ibid., p.77, and Romila Thapar (1966) *A History of India*, vol.1. Harmondsworth: Penguin, p.103.

17. Wolpert, *New History of India*, p.77.

18. Kathleen Gough (1962) 'Nayar'; 'Tiyyar'; 'Mapilla', in Schneider and Gough, *Matrilineal Kinship*, chs.6-9. For ecology of Kerala, see pp.299-302.

19. J.H. Hutton (1963) *Caste in India*. Bombay: Oxford University Press, p.9.

20. Ibid., p.29.

21. Ibid., p.151.

22. Ibid., p.154.

23. Ibid., p.167.

24. Joan Bamberger (1974) 'The Myth of Matriarchy: Why Men Rule in Primitive Society', in Rosaldo and Lamphere, *Woman, Culture and Society*. Mandy Merck (1978), 'The City's Achievements: the Patriotic Amazonomachy and Ancient Athens', in Susan Lipshitz (ed), *Tearing the Veil*. London: Routledge & Kegan Paul.

25. Margaret Stacey and Marion Price (1980), 'Women and Power', *Feminist Review* 5, pp.35-6.

26. Baig, *India's Woman Power*, pp.4-5.

27. Thapar, *History of India*, p.43.

28. Hutton, *Caste in India*, p.152.

29. B.G. Gokhale (1959) *Ancient India*. Bombay: Asia Publishing House, p.18.

30. Ibid., p.18 and Hutton, *Caste in India*, p.224.

31. Ibid., p.225.

32. Ibid., p.152.

33. Maria Mies (1980) *Indian Women and Patriarchy*. New Delhi: Concept, p.40.

34. D.D. Kosambi (1965) *The Culture and Civilization of Ancient India in Historical Outline*. London: Routledge & Kegan Paul, p.47. Kosambi uses the word 'matriarchal' without indicating whether he means a structural or a cultural concept.

35. McKim Marriott (1955) 'Little Communities in an Indigenous Civilization', in McKim Marriott 'Village India: Studies in the Little Community', *The American Anthropologist* 57, pp.171-2. Quoted in Mies, *Indian Women and Patriarchy*, p.40. The 'Little Community' is equivalent to the 'non-brahmin tradition'.

36. Mies, *Indian Women and Patriarchy*, pp.39-41.

37. Lawrence Babb (1970) 'Marriage and Malevolence: the Uses of Sexual Opposition in a Hindu Pantheon', *Ethnology* IX, pp.137-49.

38. Hutton, *Caste in India*, pp.153-4.

39. B.K. Sarkar (1917) *Folk Element in Hindu Culture*, quoted in Hutton, ibid., p.154.

40. Kosambi, *Culture and Civilization*, p.170.

41. Ibid., p.116.

42. Babb, 'Marriage and Malevolence'.

43. Susan Wadley (1977) 'Women and the Hindu Tradition', in Doranne Jacobson and Susan Wadley, *Women in India: Two Perspectives*. New Delhi: Manohar.

44. Vina Mazumdar (1979) (ed) *Symbols of Power*. New Delhi: Allied Publishers, p.xvii.

45. See M.N. Srinivas (1962) *Caste in Modern India*. London: Asia Publishing House, ch.3.

46. Surajit Sinha (1967) 'Caste in India', in Anthony de Reuck and Julie Knight (eds), *Caste and Race*. London: Ciba Foundation, p.94.

47. Ibid., p.95.

48. Ibid., p.97.

49. Srinivas, *Caste in Modern India*, ch.2.

50. Thapar, *History of India*, p.48. See also Max Weber (1958) *The Religion of India*. New York: The Free Press.

51. Anupam Sen (1982) *The State, Industrialization and Class Formations in India*. London: Routledge & Kegan Paul, p.18.

52. N.K. Bose (1951) 'Caste in India', *Man in India* 31, pp.107-23. Quoted in Sinha, 'Caste in India', pp.96-7.

53. M.N. Srinivas (1977) 'The Changing Position of Indian Women', *Man* 12, pp.221-38.

54. Zarina Bhatty (1976) 'Status of Muslim Women and Social Change', in B.R. Nanda (ed), *Indian Women from Purdah to Modernity*. New Delhi: Vikas, p.110.

55. Hutton, *Caste in India*, p.129. Emphasis added.

56. Srinivas, *Caste in Modern India*, p.46.

57. Nur Yalman (1968) 'On the Purity of Women in the Castes of Ceylon and Malabar', *Journal of the Royal Anthropological Institute* 93, 1, pp.43-4.

58. Ibid., pp.45-6.

59. Veena Das (1976) 'Indian Women: Work, Power and Status', in B.R. Nanda, *Indian Women*, p.135.

60. Wolpert, *New History of India*, pp.26, 32.

61. Thapar, *History of India*, pp.37-8.

62. Ibid., pp.38-40, 54.

63. Mies, *Indian Women*, pp.55-7.

64. Wolpert, *New History of India*, p.28.

65. A.S. Altekar (1962) *The Position of Women in Hindu Civilization*. Delhi: Motilal Banarsidas, pp.179-81. Padmini Sengupta (1960) *Women Workers of India*. Bombay: Asia Publishing House, pp.1-4.

66. Rigveda X, 85, 86. Quoted in Altekar, *Position of Women*, p.190.

67. G.G. Mirchandani (1970) 'Status of Women in India', *India Today*. Delhi: United News of India Research Bureau, p.249.

68. Romila Thapar (1963) 'The History of Female Emancipation in Southern Asia', in Barbara Ward (ed), *Women in the New Asia*. Paris: UNESCO, p.476.

69. Mies, *Indian Women*, pp.47-8.

70. Mahabharata (Shanti Parva). Quoted in Ashok Rudra (1975) 'Cultural and Religious Influences', in Jain, *Indian Women*, p.43.

71. G.S. Ghurye (1932) *Caste and Race in India*. London: Routledge & Kegan Paul, p.69.

72. Thapar, *History of India*, pp.64-9.

73. Ibid., pp.109, 121-4.

74. Mies, *Indian Women*, pp.47-51.

75. Altekar, *Position of Women*, p.58.

76. Thapar, *History of India*, p.123.

77. Maitrayaniya Samhita IV, 7, 4. Quoted in Altekar, *Position of Women*, p.190.

78. Manusmriti, Dharmashastra IX, 3.

79. Ibid. V, 147.
80. Arundhati, Diva Purana. Quoted in Rudra, 'Cultural and Religious Influences', p.47.
81. Mahabbarata, Anusasana Parva. Quoted in ibid., p.47.
82. Manusmriti, Dharmashastra IX, 14.
83. Ibid., III, 13.
84. Mies, *Indian Women*, p.45.
85. Thapar, *History of India*, pp.136, 151-2.
86. Ibid., p.166.
87. Thapar, 'History of Female Emancipation', pp.252, 476-7.
88. Jack Goody (1976) *Production and Reproduction*. Cambridge: Cambridge University Press.
89. Prabhati Mukherjee (1978) *Hindu Women: Normative Models*. New Delhi: Orient Longman.
90. Krsnajanma Kanda 35, 77-86. Quoted in Ram Sharan Sharma (1966) *Light on Early Indian Society and Economy*. Bombay: Manaktalas p.24.
91. Ayodhya Kanda 67, 11. Quoted in ibid., pp.23 and 27-8.
92. Manu V, 139. Quoted in ibid., p.30.
93. Ibid., p.33.
94. Parasara VI, 16. Quoted in ibid., p.29.
95. Sen, *State, Industrialization and Class Formations*, p.132.
96. Mies, *Indian Women*, p.48.
97. Thapar, *History of India*, p.247.
98. Mies, *Indian Women*, p.60.
99. Baig, *India's Woman Power*, pp.12, 258.
100. Mies, *Indian Women*, pp.51-2, 65-8.
101. Thapar, 'History of Female Emancipation', p.478.
102. Thapar, *History of India*, p.292.
103. Mies, *Indian Women*, pp.65-8.
104. Thapar, *History of India*, p.67.
105. Ibid., pp.160, 261.
106. Mies, *Indian Women*, pp.40-1.
107. Nigel Frith (1975) *The Legend of Krishna*. London: Abacus.
108. Thapar, *History of India*, pp.258-61.
109. Ibid., pp.133-4.
110. Ibid., pp.184-8.
111. Department of Social Welfare, *Towards Equality*, p.43.
112. Sen, *State, Industrialization and Class Formations*, p.18.
113. Bhagavad-Gita IX, 32. In R.C. Zaehner (1966) *Hindu Scriptures*. London: J.M. Dent, p.289.
114. Thapar, *History of India*, pp.131-4.
115. Ibid., p.161.
116. Mies, *Indian Women*, pp.46-7.
117. Devi Bhagavat. Quoted in Rudra, 'Cultural and Religious Influences', p.47.
117. Pratima Asthana (1974) *Women's Movement in India*. Delhi: Vikas, pp.57-8.
118. André Beteille (1971) *Caste, Class and Power*. Berkeley: University of California Press, Ch.VI.
119. See Chapter 8.

120. Beteille, *Caste, Class and Power*, Ch.VI.

121. A.R. Desai (1959) *The Social Background of Indian Nationalism*. Bombay: Popular Book Depot.

122. Sen, *State, Industrialization and Class Formations*, pp.37-45.

123. Ibid., pp. 132, 48, 53, 64.

124. Ibid., pp.65-9.

125. Ibid., pp.80-6.

126. B.B. Misra (1961) *The Indian Middle Classes*. London: Oxford University Press, pp.307, 12-13.

127. Ibid., p.12.

128. Bipan Chandra (1974) 'The Indian Capitalist Class and British Imperialism', in R.S. Sharma (ed), *Indian Society: Historical Probings*. New Delhi: People's Publishing House, pp.390-1.

129. Jawaharlal Nehru (1939) *Glimpses of World History*. London: Lindsay Drummond, pp.434-9.

130. Chandra, 'Indian Capitalist Class', pp.394-7.

131. Misra, *Indian Middle Classes*, p.307.

132. Richard Taub (1969) *Bureaucrats under Stress*. Berkeley: University of California Press, pp.63-5.

133. M.D. Morris (1960) 'The Labour Market in India', in W.E. Moore and A.S. Feldman (eds), *Labour Commitment and Social Change in Developing Areas*. New York: SSRC, pp.173-200. Quoted in Sinha 'Caste in India', pp.102-3.

134. R.D. Lambert (1963) *Workers, Factories and Social Change in India*. Princeton: Princeton University Press, pp.34-6. Quoted in M.N. Srinivas (1966) *Social Change in Modern India*. Berkeley: University of California Press, p.174.

135. Kamla Bhasin (1972) 'The Predicament of Middle Class Indian Women — an Inside View', in Kamla Bhasin (ed), *The Position of Women in India*. Srinigar: Arvind Deshpande, p.40.

136. Victor S. D'Souza (1980) 'Family Status and Female Work Participation', in Alfred de Souza (ed), *Women in Contemporary India and South Asia*. New Delhi: Manohar, p.129.

137. Pratima Asthana, *Women's Movement in India*, p.23. See also E.C. Gedge and M. Choksi (eds), (1929) *Women in Modern India*. Bombay: D.B. Taraporewala, Ch.3, 4.

138. Elizabeth Sarah (1982) 'Towards a Reassessment of Feminist History', *Women's Studies International Forum* 5, 6, pp.520-1.

139. See comparisons, notes 140-3, and 145 below.

140. Sushila Mehta (1982) *Revolution and the Status of Women in India*. New Delhi: Metropolitan, p.104. In the USA, the most 'advanced' capitalist country of the world, the Equal Rights Amendment, adding a guarantee of sexual equality to the Constitution, failed to reach the statute book during the 1980s because the required number of states did not ratify it.

141. Ibid., p.104. Women in Switzerland, one of the richest countries of Europe, did not receive the vote until the 1970s. In at least one canton, women still do not have the vote on canton affairs.

142. The Factories Act was passed in 1948, the Plantation Labour Act in 1951, and the Mines Act in 1952. See Kamala Mankekar (1975) *Women in India*. New Delhi: Central Institute of Research and Training in Public Cooperation, p.19.

The Equal Pay Act and the Sex Discrimination Act came into force in Britain in 1975. There is no legal provision for creches or nursing time.

143. Five Acts were passed between 1954 and 1956:

1. Special Marriage Act (1954) provided for civil marriage for all Indians and divorce by mutual consent. Minimum age of marriage, 21 for men, 18 for women. If married under this Act a Hindu man would be automatically regarded as independent of the joint family, and inheritance would be governed by the Indian Succession Act.
2. Hindu Marriage Act (1955) stipulates monogamy and provides for divorce and inter-caste marriage.
3. Hindu Succession Act (1955) provides equal shares of property for widow, daughter, mother and son, in the case of non-testamentary death. Women have absolute right of ownership and disposal over property with the condition that male successors have a presumptive right to acquire any property of which the female successors wish to dispose.
4. Hindu Minority and Guardianship Act (1956) gives custody of a child under 3 years of age to the mother, and the natural guardian thereafter is first the father and second the mother.
5. Hindu Adoptions and Maintenance Act (1956) provides for the adoption of daughters, and allows women to adopt children as well as men. See Jana Matson Everett (1981) *Women and Social Change in India*. New Delhi: Heritage, pp.187-8, and Sushila Mehta, *Revolution*, Ch.7.
   Eire does not allow divorce even today.

144. Suppression of Prostitution and Immoral Traffic Act 1958, Prohibition of Dowry Act 1961. See Sushila Mehta, *Revolution*, pp.115, 121.

145. Department of Social Welfare, *Towards Equality*, pp.327-9. In Spain abortion is not legal under any circumstances.

146. Mehta, *Revolution*, pp.125-6.

147. Mankekar, *Women in India*, pp.30, 31.

148. Rama Joshi (1978) 'The Status of Female Labour and the Law', *Bulletin of Comparative Labour Relations* 9, pp.225-6.

149. Mankekar, *Women in India*, p.34.

150. Mehta, *Revolution*, pp.207-8, 243-4. Most issues of Manushi carry reports of dowry deaths. See Note 3, Ch.1.

151. For a discussion of the Indian economy in 1977 in the context of world capitalism, see Andre Gunder Frank (1977) 'Emergence of Permanent Emergency in India', *Economic and Political Weekly* XII, 11, March 12. Recognition of the West's role in pauperising the Third World is expressed (more ambiguously than by Frank) by Willy Brandt (1980) *North-South: a Programme for Survival. The Report of the Independent Commission on International Development Issues*. London: Pan. 'A long and assiduous learning process was necessary until it was generally accepted that higher wages for workers increased purchasing power sufficiently to move the economy as a whole. Industrialized countries now need to be interested in the expansion of markets in the developing world.' Ibid., pp.20-1. The analogy means that if the Third World is made so poor that it cannot buy Western capitalism's goods, then the West would also suffer through the collapse of its markets. So the poverty of the Third World is seen to threaten the very structure of Western capitalism's political, industrial and financial institutions. Ibid., p.239.

152. Mehta, *Revolution*, pp.125-6.

153. Elizabeth Sarah, 'Towards a Reassessment', p.520. Dale Spender

(1983) *There's Always Been a Woman's Movement this Century*. London: Routledge & Kegan Paul.

154. Geraldine Forbes (1982) 'Caged Tigers: "First Wave" Feminists in India', *Women's Studies International Forum* 5, 6, p.535.

155. 20 out of the 120 women explicitly identified themselves as feminists, without being asked.

Part III: Emergence from Seclusion

11. Experiences of Orthodoxy

You planned to tame a swallow, to hold her,
In the long summer of your love so that she would forget
Not the raw seasons alone, and the homes left behind, but
Also her nature, the urge to fly, and the endless
Pathways of the sky.
Kamla Das, 'The Old Playhouse'[1]

Vathsala Rajaram is a brahmin of 59, from the southern state of Tamil Nadu. She has taught at the university for 19 years.

My parents only expected me to marry. I was married at the age of 10 . . . I began studying for my degree shortly after Independence when I was thirty . . . My grandfather was a great educationist, and in favour of women's education, as were my parents, but they had no effect on me, it was my husband who suggested I could do it . . . My husband's family didn't agree with education for women, his father was very strongly against it, but my husband was in favour of it and only his arguments overcame my in-laws' objections. Orthodox people are still critical of women taking paid work, but not educated people.

Vathsala was one of the millions of girls married shortly before the Child Marriage Restraint Act of 1929. The Act raised the minimum age of marriage for girls to 14, but there was a six-month wait before it came into force, which was used to beat the Act. The result was a vast increase in the proportion of child marriages, and subsequently of child widows.[2] Vathsala was one of the lucky ones who didn't lose her husband till much later in life. She raised her family and only then started her degree. Her parents' views on education and paid work for women mattered little since she had been married so young. It depended entirely on her husband. Her sister, whose husband was unsympathetic, was not allowed an education. Because she has economic independence Vathsala, now a widow, has no need to follow orthodox strictures which lay down a life of penance for widowhood.

Nor did Puja Shukla when she was widowed in her twenties, although her aunt was less fortunate. Puja is 37, a brahmin, and she started her first job at the age of 30, teaching literature at the university. She comes from the far North of India, from a very conservative state.

> Where I come from, it's very difficult to be liberal. My mother and grandmother are very cautious of the family image. My father's sister has never even seen the main road outside our house. She's still living in the 17th Century. She's old now, but she was married at the age of 9. She never saw her husband because he died before they met, so she's a widow and she has never left the house since.

Puja's aunt lived her whole life in penance, widowed even before puberty. Puja's seclusion was less severe. She was allowed education, but not paid employment. We will see later how Puja was able to avoid her aunt's fate when her own husband died.

Anjana Vishwanatan is a brahmin from Delhi and a civil servant in the Ministry of Labour. Her mother, only 16 years older, was given an education, but she received it in purdah — and it would have been unthinkable for her to have remained unmarried until 30, as her daughter has.

> My mother was married young, and she had me, her first child, when she was 16. She was educated to high school level, and to get her education, she had to sit separate from the boys at school, with a curtain between her and them. That's still a problem in the rural areas.

Lastly, Parvati Sahni, 58, from a kshatriya family. She was born in Lahore, but moved to Delhi at Partition. She is now a professor of medicine.

> I married into a very conservative family. They didn't want me to study or to work as a doctor. My husband married his choice, but I had decided against the marriage because I knew I wouldn't be able to do what I wanted. My father forced me to marry — he was very traditional.

We shall see how Parvati resisted her father and husband later in the book.

The experiences of the women we talked to, together with those of their immediate relatives, give a clear picture of what is involved for women from an orthodox high-caste background. First there is early marriage, preferably before puberty, the husband being chosen by the girl's family with or without her consent. Second there is a prohibition on work outside the home. Third, there is a varying degree of seclusion, which might mean not being allowed to leave the house under any circumstances, or being allowed to go out in public whilst maintaining purdah in the form of a curtain or veil. And fourth, there is a strict life of austerity and penance for widows, who are not allowed to remarry, are regarded as inauspicious and contemptible, the cause of their husband's death even if they were infants at the time, and subjected to the most rigorous control over their behaviour.

12. The Significance of Seclusion

In her discussion of male dominance, Heidi Hartmann identifies the material basis for men's power over women as resting on their control over two major features: women's access to economic resources, and women's sexuality.[3] The four effects on women of patriarchal caste orthodoxy, noted above, coincide with Hartmann's definition. Women's sexuality is controlled by seclusion, by early arranged marriage with or without the bride's consent, and by the ban on widow remarriage. Women's access to economic resources is controlled by forbidding work of any sort outside the home. This is reinforced by law and custom permitting only males to inherit immovable property, ensuring women's economic dependence on men. Women's economic resources in the form of movable property are controlled and retained within the group through the constraints on female sexuality.

The significance of seclusion is that it provides a means for controlling both the sexual and economic aspects of women's subordination. It entails a restriction on women's mobility and a removal from the public gaze, physically enforcing their maintenance as exclusive sexual property. And it prevents women from contributing to the economic income of the group either through paid work outside the home or through unpaid but productive family labour in the fields, restricting their contribution to the domestic sphere. Seclusion in terms of the removal of women from public life cements the dual control of men over women's sexual and economic autonomy, the one reinforcing the other.

Seclusion is strongly associated with orthodox patriarchal upper-caste communities in North India. It is first mentioned in the religious books around 100 B.C., when it was adopted by some royal families, but not without resistance from women. There are examples of women resisting the infringement of their freedom in the books of three of the major Indian religions. The Hindu heroine of the Ratnaprabha proclaims: 'The strict seclusion of women is a folly produced by jealousy. It is of no use whatsoever. Women of good character are guarded by their own virtue and nothing else.'[4] In Islam, a niece of the Prophet's wife Ayesha protests: 'On me God has set the seal of beauty, and I rejoice when my beauty is seen and the mercy of God therein acknowledged. Never shall I cover my face, for no flaw or fault finds a place in God's work.'[5] And Gopa, the Buddha's bride-to-be, refused to wear a veil on her betrothal, on the grounds that 'The pure in thought require no such artificial protection.'[6]

Although the resistance failed in the North, it was successful in the South, where the heritage of women's power was sufficiently strong to reject this imposition on women's freedom.

Seclusion was generally confined to royal, aristocratic and merchant-prince families before about the 10th Century A.D., but the arrival of the Muslims consolidated its hold on upper-caste women and extended its imposition to some middle-caste women too.[7] It came to signify respectability and high breeding, since it distinguished the wealthy and better-off sections of the upper and middle castes from the poorer middle and lower castes. Its link with wealth and property can be seen in the fact that peasant and lower-caste women were never secluded. Men required women's economic contribution for survival and could not afford to protect their sexuality from other men.[8]

In rural communities today, at the bottom of the caste hierarchy, landless labourers, men and women, work for wages on other people's land. Wages are their only source of income, and waged work of this sort is considered the lowest form of labour. At the middle levels, tenant farmers, men and women, cultivate their own rented land (that is, unpaid but directly productive family work), and may also undertake waged work for landowners during busy seasons, depending on their economic position.[9] The work involved in subsistence cultivation for even a fairly well-off, socially mobile family who do not need to work for others, is both time-consuming and back-breaking.[10] The withdrawal from physical labour by both men and women of the upper-caste landowning families therefore represents a release from the degradation and exhaustion involved in subsistence agriculture, as well as symbolising the family's wealth.

The sexual division of labour is maintained throughout the caste hierarchy, but in different forms. Amongst the lower and middle castes, the women normally weed and transplant, whilst men plough. Oxen are men's responsibility, fowls women's, but either sex may rear sheep and buffaloes, the income from the sale of the products belonging to the person doing the rearing. Amongst the higher castes, the men supervise the work of servants, hired labourers and tenants, whilst the women are responsible for domestic work. Neither sex labours in the fields, but amongst all the castes, domestic work is performed exclusively by the women.[11] For upper-caste women, then, withdrawal from work outside the home (paid or unpaid) marks a release from arduous physical labour and a significant reduction in the amount of labour required of them. No hardship is involved here; in fact, it is a reduction in hardship.

So with a rise in caste status, it is not so much that the women stop working as that the kind of work they do changes, along with the economic reward attached to it. Amongst the lowest groups, the women are compelled to undertake waged work alongside the men whenever they can get it. These women (and men) live a precarious existence, combining abject poverty with grinding labour in the fields, on top of their domestic labour. Despite being paid lower wages than men, the economic contribution of women to survival is visible and necessary.

At the middle levels, the women withdraw from waged work, but perform unpaid labour in the family fields, as well as their domestic work. The work is equally hard, but is performed for themselves not for employers, and they may have their own income from dairy produce. At the highest levels, the women withdraw from outside work altogether and work only in the house. They receive no income, but the work is equally vital to the maintenance of life. These women, whose work has now been privatised, lose what little economic power they might have had and become totally dependent economically on men. They receive material benefits from their economic position in the caste hierarchy, in that their economic survival and security is ensured and they have no need to perform physical labour in the fields on top of their domestic labour, but they lose the visibility of their independent economic contribution.

The economic aspects alone, however, do not explain why it is the *women* who withdraw from outside work. It is the sexual aspect, the control of women's sexuality for the maintenance of property within the group, that explains why it is women who are secluded rather than men. Although both women and men gain economically from a rise in caste hierarchy in relation to lower castes, men gain sexually in relation to the women of their own caste. The removal of women's sexual and social autonomy, epitomised by seclusion, is the price paid by the women alone for the economic benefits accruing to both sexes. Lower-caste women, by contrast, experience far fewer controls over their physical freedom. The economic benefits and the social constraints of seclusion are unknown to them. Sati was never demanded of them, widowhood was no curse, divorce was allowed in many lower-caste communities and widows and divorced people could remarry without disgrace.[12]

So the hardship involved in seclusion derives less from the economic than from the sexual aspects, although the two are connected. The nature of the hardship is described by Dr Rukhmabai.

Open air and sunlight may not be denied to plants and animals if healthy growth is to be secured and yet, under strict Purdah conditions, they are denied to women young and old all through their lives. From the time they attain puberty, numbers of young girls, Hindu and Mahomedan, often just children in instinct and feeling, retire into seclusion. They see no men except those of their own household; they go out veiled or in closed and curtained conveyances when they do go out at all; and even this degree of liberty is denied them under the stricter Purdah conditions.[13]

Rokeya Hossain describes how, prior to marriage, a bride was secluded in a room for anything from a few days to a whole year.

It would last a year if the wedding was delayed. The girl was supposed to keep her eyes closed and someone had to feed and bathe her, even comb her hair. If the family neglected her, her eyesight would be severely impaired. When Rokeya visited her stepdaughter's two daughters who were in this maiya khana, she says: 'I could not stay in Mangu's cell for long. I felt suffocated in that close room . . . I failed to stay in Sabu's cell for even a minute. Those poor girls at that time, had already stayed in those rooms for six months. Ultimately Sabu had a spell of acute hysteria. This is how we are trained to endure seclusion.'[14]

Many of the examples given by Rokeya Hossain involve women's sickness, injury or death as a result of seclusion; in such cases, arguably it might be preferable to be a lower-caste woman on the edge of starvation, but at least free to move around in the open air. When the alternative of waged work in white-collar and professional occupations becomes available with the rise of the class system, women's acceptance of seclusion is even less firmly based. Women's desire to break out of the domestic sphere and into paid employment amongst the middle class, has to be seen in terms of what a secluded domestic life means for an upper-caste woman, and what it meant historically.

We have already seen in Part II that the material benefit to men of controlling upper-caste women's sexuality was the reproduction of legitimate heirs and the maintenance of caste purity for the retention and continuity of caste property and culture. However, the acquisition of exclusive sexual property rights over women also became for men a material benefit in its own right. This can be seen in the change from a widow being allowed to marry the husband's brother, to not being able to remarry at all.[15] In the former case, the widow's property was retained within the family without disrupting her existing lifestyle. But some other motive must have initiated the total ban on widow remarriage which developed later, for whilst men could have any number of wives from the appropriate caste group and sexual relations with women of any other caste group, eventually a high-caste woman could only have one husband, even if married and widowed before puberty with no consummation of the marriage.[16] She was kept in strictest seclusion, could not attend celebrations because she was inauspicious, and had to lead a life of austerity, shaving her head, eating only one meal a day and shedding all decorations in dress.[17] This change, depriving widows of the economic comforts of the caste, of sexual and reproductive activity, and of any self-esteem, can only be explained by the increasing importance to men of maintaining women as their exclusive sexual property even after death.

In summary, seclusion is not a specific set of constraints on behaviour, but an approach to how women should live in a patriarchal society. It ranges from the strictest purdah to the general idea that a woman's place is 'in the home'. Its essential feature is that it privatises women and confines them to the domestic sphere, which helps to control both their sexuality and their economic independence from men. Paid work is forbidden, and women's work is defined as domestic, private and unpaid. Such work is often not even considered to be real work.[18] The study of women's transition from unpaid domestic work to professional employment can clarify the processes of change in women's position occurring in a male-dominated hierarchical society.

Figures on the relationship between paid employment and the social hierarchies of caste and class confirm the significance of women's work in the connection between gender and social hierarchy. Andrea Menefee Singh shows that at the middle-class level, only a small proportion of women are employed,[19] whereas a much higher proportion of lower-caste migrant women in Delhi are employed.[20] D'Souza's figures for Chandigarh show that the lowest level of occupational class contains the largest proportion of women in paid work, the middle levels contain very few women in waged work, and increasing numbers of women are in paid jobs towards the higher levels.[21]

The rest of Part III documents our women's emergence from domestic seclusion to professional employment, examining the basis for the women's power to initiate change and the internal and external influences that stimulate it. We look at the basis for women's seclusion within the caste system, by examining the objections that women from orthodox high-caste families encounter when making the transition. And we see how the class system builds upon the gender divisions inherent in caste, whilst transforming them, by examining the differences and similarities in the experiences of women from orthodox and non-orthodox families.

Specifically, we will show that:

one, the external influences which stimulate the change arise from personal experiences of the system of male domination, and from the social movements of political opposition to caste, class and imperialism;

two, the internal influences which stimulate the change at the level of consciousness lie in the contradiction between the women's own experience and the ways in which that experience is constructed within a male-oriented gender ideology;

three, the basis for women's power to initiate the change rests not only on their determination to resist subordination and to break free of the stultifying effects of seclusion, but more significantly on their potential for economic independence, and often too, on the support given by other family members;

four, the basis for the women's seclusion in the caste system is the maintenance of men's position in the social hierarchy, the men deriving their status from the position of the women. When women from orthodox families resist seclusion and move into professional employment, the social honour and economic benefits they receive from a high position in the occupational class hierarchy can be incorporated by the men of the family so that in the class system, too, they derive social status from the women. Within the class structure, the forms of women's activities providing men with social status are different from those in the caste structure, but the underlying reasons for the restrictions remain essentially the same.

13. Forces for Change

The women in our study come from families with a wide range of views on women's work. Some women faced total opposition from their orthodox families when they tried to move out of the domestic arena, others came from families where it is regarded as natural and desirable for women to work outside the home. Not all the women made the transition from domestic seclusion to paid employment themselves; in many cases it had been made by a previous generation of women in the family, sometimes going back three generations. Female employment was often encouraged by members of the liberal Indian religions such as Jainism and Buddhism, and amongst people from the Southern states of India. But many women, particularly from the North and from the more conservative religions such as Hinduism and Islam, felt the weight of orthodoxy in some form, whether from their own experience or that of other members of the family.[22]

Women whose families regard female employment as perfectly acceptable are in marked contrast to those women who spoke at the beginning of Part III. Amrit Soni, for example, is 29 and comes from Delhi. Being of the Jain religion, she is not a part of the caste system. She is a member of the Indian Administrative Service (IAS), which selects people through a competitive examination. Amrit never had to think about whether she would get a job: it was assumed all along. Many women in her family are employed, and she grew up surrounded by professional people and employed women, particularly in the fields of medicine and education. When asked whether she had ever experienced any pressure from the family against taking a job, she was emphatic: 'Quite the opposite. They shoved me into it. They don't want me to sit at home any more than I do.'

Sumitra Kaushik spoke in similar vein. Sumitra is a 30-year-old accountant, a brahmin from Bombay, educated in England, who now works for a foreign-owned chemical company. Her aunt and mother are both practising doctors, her father was a lawyer, and she was always expected to take up a career.

My mother was upset when I gave up my job to have a child . . . She thinks women should be financially independent of their husbands, in case something happens . . . When I went back to work, she was so pleased she wrote me a congratulations letter.

This positive encouragement is repeated in many of the families, including those of women who are first-generation professional workers, and especially amongst younger women. We want to look first at some of the external influences which stimulated the change from seclusion to employment. The influences which women have identified derive from their personal experiences of the institution of male domination and from the social movements that sprang up as a response to the privileges of caste, class and imperialism. In this section we are examining the facilitators, not the inhibitors of change, which will be discussed in Part IV.

Social Movements against Caste, Class and Imperialism

Throughout India's history there have been opposition movements to the privileges of social hierarchy, many of them linked with opposition to the subordination of women. Amongst our women there are families whose political opposition to caste or class affected their approach to women's employment. Anjana Vishwanatan's father was strongly opposed to caste hierarchy and privilege, and questioned the orthodox approach to women's position. Anjana is a 30-year-old brahmin civil servant from Delhi.

> My father's an idealist, a reformer, he didn't conform to traditional social norms. He expected me to do well and have my own status and position. He didn't think I was inferior to his 2 sons. Mother says he used to brag about how good his daughter would be.

Sunanda Rao's father was radically opposed to class privilege, which affected his view of women's dependency on men. Sunanda is 54, a Bengali brahmin originally from Bangladesh but settled at Partition in the Indian part of Bengal, a state renowned for its tradition of reformist and radical politics, which has for many years had a Marxist state government.

> My father was a Marxist — he was very progressive and wanted me to lead an independent life and career. Even my grandmother was liberal and progressive . . . It was my own decision to work, but my father dreamed of our success, so he was very encouraging from the earliest stage. Everyone is independent in our family.

So the movements opposed to caste and class privilege still maintain their connection with the issue of gender privilege, and may help to facilitate women's emergence from seclusion.

One of the most radical influences of imperialism on the position of women occurred in the resistance movement which developed against it, and in the quitting of India which involved the Partition into India and Pakistan.

Vijaya Ambujam and her family were influenced by the nationalist movement. She's now 42, comes from the southern state of Karnataka and works in management.

> I wasn't aware of it at the time, but in retrospect I think it's because of the freedom movement that we were encouraged to work. Everyone went to prison and

worked for it, even though we were a backward middle class family. All the women proved themselves and I was expected to as well . . .

The freedom movement was a source of inspiration for many women. The increased awareness of national subordination which came with the freedom movement also raised people's consciousness about women's dependent position on men. The impact of Partition, however, was traumatic. Many families fled over the newly-created borders, taking with them only what they could carry. Many lost relatives, as did Leela Das, whose father was killed in what is now Pakistan. All of them were destitute unless they had relatives to go to. Kapila Ahuja was 20 when she and her family left Lahore for India. She's 50 now, a civil servant from the kshatriya caste.

My parents expected nothing from me. They didn't discourage me, but it was a closed society before Independence. There was only marriage. But from the beginning I had the desire to be more, to establish myself. My parents lost everything at Partition, and their attitudes underwent a radical change. My elder sister encouraged me to finish my education and supported me financially. The Indian Administrative Service was only available after 1947 and I applied straight after finishing my education. I was the first woman in the state to get into the IAS. My family regards me with great pride and distinction. Everyone said I couldn't do anything except be a teacher or a doctor.

Sushila Banerji was 9 when her family fled across the Bengal border. Now she is 39, a brahmin, trained as a chemical engineer, and working as a deputy manager in a state-owned engineering company.

My parents influenced me, especially my mother. They wanted me to be a doctor because there was no doctor in the family . . . My family were made refugees *twice*, first from Burma during the second world war, and then from East Pakistan in 1947. Those experiences changed the attitudes of the family very much. They were determined we should all have an education and get a good position. We were very mature children compared with our friends because of our experiences.

The abrupt loss of economic security at Partition had a radical effect on many previously orthodox families. The men could no longer keep the women in seclusion, nor could they support them financially. In the changed circumstances of independent India, economic security lay in each individual being able to earn a living, including the women.

The System of Male Domination

One of the problems with a prescriptive philosophy of women defined as men's dependants is that such a position cannot be guaranteed. The system of male supremacy 'fails' women, for example, when the male provider dies or is too ill to fulfil his duty. Awareness of this possibility affected Bharati Kapoor's father. Bharati is 31, a civil servant from the vaishya caste married to a kshatriya man of her own choice. She comes from the state of Bihar.

My father came from the village, and had to go to great pains to educate himself. He refused an arranged marriage and married a women of his own choice. It's because of him that my mother had a job, though she didn't need to financially. He always pushed her and us . . . He's different from the rest of his family, he's a self-made man and a strong nationalist [against British rule]. He knows how hard life can be for a woman if she's not independent. He expected us all to have jobs, especially the girls to be independent. My father was seriously ill when we were younger, which compounded the idea that we should be independent.

There are also circumstances under which the system of male supremacy 'fails' men, and this can cause men to reassess women's position. The patriarchal caste structure requires sons for inheritance, religious ritual and the care of parents in old age, so sons are highly valued. But some men produce no sons, or not as many sons as they would like. Lakshmi Mitra, a young non-brahmin civil servant from Bengal, is certain that she benefited from being one of three daughters.

My parents expected me to join the civil service like my father, and have a career. I was brought up like a man. That's important — I had no brothers. I was encouraged to play games, climb trees, do what boys do. Usually women are protected. My sisters are the same. Our parents attitude was always encouragement and pride.

The same consideration was important for Kalpana Kunnur. Kalpana is 43, a brahmin from Madras. Independence opened up opportunities that had previously been closed to women, but her father's desire for a boy when she was born was a significant influence for her.

For a girl, the only idea was to marry . . . going out to work wasn't done in those days. My four sisters never had jobs. I was unique because I was the youngest and my father wanted a boy. He was disappointed — I'm the sixth and last child, and only one boy amongst us. So he said I should do all the things a boy would. I'm the only girl who studied . . . Girls were just beginning to think they could branch out. The Indian Administrative Service only started after Independence, there was no chance of women getting in before. I came in at the turn of attitudes. The independence movement was a big boost to women — women fought too.

The other way in which the institution of male domination prompts change *against* itself is through the resistance it creates in women. Under certain circumstances the effects may also adversely affect men. Most commonly, it is the woman's own mother who has learnt from her experience of a purely domestic existence that it is right for women to reject their seclusion, and encourages her daughter to take the step she wishes she could have taken herself. Pushpa Saxena is a 38-year-old lecturer from Kashmir, a brahmin who married out of caste.

My parents wanted me to be well educated, not just to marry. They gave me a lot of encouragement . . . My mother never worked outside, she had too much spare time — she used to say I should grow up and work and do something creative.

And Kusum Gupta's mother was determined that her only daughter would have an education. Kusum is 55, originally from Bombay, and a civil servant of the vaishya caste.

> My mother wanted me to be a doctor because she was uneducated and she wanted her own daughter to have an education. She was the strongest influence — she never allowed me to cook.

The experience of Namita Iyengar's mother affected both her parents. Namita, whose family comes from Kashmir, is now 39, a doctor and a brahmin.

> My parents wanted me to be educated for independence. My father was keen for me to work, and very helpful. My mother was illiterate and she had been harassed and suppressed by her husband's family. That's why they wanted their daughters to be independent.

The same problem afflicted Rekha Rohtagi's father. The effects of male domination meant that he could not have the kind of relationship with his wife that he would have liked. Rekha is 50 now and originally comes from Pakistan. She is a lecturer from the kshatriya caste.

> My father was very liberal. From the beginning he inculcated the attitude that daughters should have equal education with the sons. He was unusual. Partly it was because he was educated and partly because he didn't find companionship with his wife, who was uneducated. I always felt the incompatibility between my mother and my father.
> He also thought women should have economic independence as well as an equivalent intellect and education . . . My father was responsible for initiating me.

Many of the women were encouraged to come out of seclusion by male and female members of the family. The support of another woman in the family is often a vital feature of women's emergence from seclusion. It may be the example of an older female relative who has already taken the step and serves as an inspiration for the younger woman. Or it may be the older woman's experience of seclusion which drives her to make sure her younger relative's life is different, as we have just seen. Or both factors may be influential, as with Seetha Jayalakshmi, a brahmin from Bombay working as a manager.

> My parents expected me to have a proper career and be economically independent in a prestigious job. I was different from my friends because of the expectations and encouragement of my parents, especially my mother who couldn't complete her own education. I had a lot of influence from older women in the family — my aunt and my grandmother were both doctors and several of my mother's friends worked as doctors and teachers.

The problem with sponsorship from other women is that, because of their subordinate power position in the family, their support may be less successful than the support of a man. Amongst the women to whom this applies, less than a quarter were assisted by a woman, the rest having been sponsored by men.[23]

This does not mean that men are more likely to be radical, but that they are more likely to succeed against opposition.

The problem of male sponsorship can be seen below. Indrani Vijayalakshmi is 41 now, a brahmin from Madras.

> My parents expected me to go into the civil service. We were all influenced by my father. My younger brothers have had a say in what they did, but we older ones didn't put up any resistance at all. I wanted to become an academic pyschologist, but my father wanted me to be a civil servant like him . . . My father wanted it for stability and for economic reasons. Prospects in an academic career were not good in those days.
>
> I had a teaching job for 3 years in Madras, but my father forced me to take the Indian Administration Service exam. I passed, but I miss the academic life. There's no scope to use my knowledge, it is a boring job, I don't feel fulfilled.

Sahar Srinivasan is also 41, and experienced the same problem. She is a Muslim from Uttar Pradesh. 'I never had any control over my profession . . . I didn't make the decision, my father did. I wanted to be a scientist, but my father wanted me to be a doctor. The decision was taken for me.'

The problem with male sponsorship is that, although it tends to be more successful against opposition, it is often associated with the male still wishing to control the outcome. The woman's emergence into employment is on his terms. Of course, this does not happen with all the men, but the impact of the power relationship between men and women in a male-dominated society is such that this can be one of the limitations of male sponsorship.

The experiences of these women and their families of the system of male domination laid the foundation for the development of the women's movement in the early part of this century, along with the oppositional movements to caste, class and imperialism. It is clear from the examples that the change in attitude about women's place did not arise in isolation from the external environment, but was heavily influenced by the political and economic changes occurring in the social structure. Equally important was the change in consciousness and in the material basis of women's power. In examining these, we will be able to analyse some of the social processes whereby the gender division is related to the social structure.

14. 'The Urge to Fly'

We want to discuss in some detail three women from orthodox high-caste families, and two women from non-orthodox lower-caste families, to see how they were able to challenge accepted ideas about women's place and how the families responded. The first three are Puja Shukla, Reeta Rao and Shikha Munshi, of whom Puja and Reeta come from the strictest brahmin backgrounds. Neither of them was in purdah, but they were both confined primarily to the home. They encountered two major restrictions: on the kind of man they might marry, and the kind of work they might do.

Caste and Women's Work

We have already met Puja Shukla in Chapter 11. Puja started her first job only after becoming a widow.

> My parents expected me to marry a rich, high status person — he *must* be a brahmin. I was *not* supposed to have a profession. My sisters are both good scholars with MAs in Economics and Anthropology, but they never had jobs after college. My father was a college principal, but he never encouraged me to teach, in fact quite the opposite, he opposed any idea of a profession. . . . It had to be marriage. My father's pressures on me ended only when he died. If he were alive today, he wouldn't have allowed me to come to Delhi to take this job.
>
> A personal incident in my life resulted in my decision to get a job. My first husband died in an accident — it was a terrible shock . . . I decided I must become financially independent. I had continued to study and to write at home during my marriage, and I was able to get this job. A university job is very prestigious and so my family is very proud of me now . . .

Puja subsequently married a second time, to a man of her own choice — not a brahmin. Both he and his family would prefer her to write at home rather than to serve at the university, but, unlike her father and first husband, are unable to enforce their preference because she is now economically independent of any man.

Puja was faced with the contradiction that what she saw as good — the desire to contribute to society, to serve humanity — was seen as bad by her father. To him, a respectable woman did not serve humanity in public, but her husband in private. When this was not enough for his daughter, he compromised by allowing her to write at home, as a result of which she published several books. The books formed a link with the outside world, and later helped to get her a job.

For Puja's family, education was acceptable, even publishing novels from home was respectable, but doing the same thing in an institution as a paid employee was not. The big barrier was employment: work conducted outside the home which provided a wage and therefore financial independence. In this way Puja's access to economic resources of her own was controlled by her father and later her husband. She was only able to break out of her secluded form of work on the death of the two men who controlled her life. Her father's refusal to allow her to move from domestic work to professional employment was closely connected to his insistence that she marry within the caste to a man of riches and status. These two aspects — the prohibition on employment and the insistence on a high-caste marriage — are bound up together, in that marriage and employment are mutually exclusive for women within the orthodoxy of caste. Only when one aspect of the link breaks, at the death of her husband, can Puja break the hold of the other aspect, and emerge from her secluded life.

This done, two astonishing changes occur. Her family changes from implacable opposition, to pride at her prestigious position — a mystery we will discuss later. And Puja herself, from being a brahmin widow, takes control of her own sexuality to the extent of marrying a second time, to a man who is not a brahmin, not even an Indian but a foreigner, and a man of her choice. All of them impossible for an orthodox brahmin widow. The contrast between her and her widowed aunt, who was housebound from the age of 9, is extraordinary, and was made possible not only by changing cultural values but also by the financial independence furnished by her profession.

Reeta Rao also had to break the link between compulsory marriage and prohibited employment, before she could emerge into the professional world. Her struggle was much harder than Puja's. She had to fight even for an education and then could only continue her study and work after sacrificing the security of marriage. Reeta's story began in Chapter 10, where she talked of her aunt, who had worked with Gandhi and been to jail for the cause of India's freedom. Reeta wanted her own freedom, but she came from a strictly orthodox brahmin family where her desire for learning was regarded as a whim.

My parents expected me to marry. My teachers at the convent school I went to thought the same . . . I went to an elite finishing school where again we were expected only to marry. I wanted to study even though I didn't know what it would lead to. My father was an industrialist, educated at Cambridge in England. He thought education for girls was ridiculous, but my mother said, 'Let her go till we find the right man.' I fought my father to let me have an education.

I graduated in a women's college where everybody was marking time to get married. I came first at university but no one expected me to do anything. Then I got married. My husband expected me to be a good housewife and help his career. Since he was well educated, he wouldn't marry a non-graduate — but it was for his own image not mine . . . I had a child, and left my husband a year later. He never supported me to study further or take up a job. I had no identity after marriage — I was just somebody's wife. His attitude towards me and his family's orthodoxy made me leave my husband's home after my first son was born.

My father and brother brought great pressure to bear on me. They couldn't do anything about my sister because her husband supported her. My sister had made up her mind she wouldn't copy *my* life . . . I did an MA course to save the family's face, but I was made to go back to them after the MA.

I got a scholarship to do a PhD., but my husband's family wouldn't let me go . . . I stayed with my husband for another 6 years, during which time I had my second son. When I could tolerate it no longer, I finally left and did my PhD. After I got a divorce I started work in teaching.

Getting a job had no effect on my husband's family because I only got it after the divorce. In my own family, everybody's very happy now. Their attitude towards me changed after I got my PhD. My sons are very proud of me, which made my parents re-think their attitude to me. Formerly there was only total opposition. Still, no one helped me except my mother. She did extra jobs in the house for me after I had to go out to work.

I didn't apply for my first job, I was offered it by the college I did my MA in. Apart from financial considerations, I wanted to do something where I could give the children an identity. Now they have respect for me and through me, I wanted them to be able to have esteem for me after the divorce. I'm still supporting my youngest son so I can't stop working yet, but if I had another income I wouldn't do this . . . I like the teaching, but I would much prefer a more meaningful job with a different sense of involvement. This job is doing no good. But something good came out of it. I learned to sort myself out in the process. I spent 10 years as someone else's identity, but then you have to learn to be yourself.

Reeta faced a major contradiction over her education. To begin with, her father decreed it as unnecessary for girls, and yet it was what she most desperately wanted. His Cambridge education was no source of liberal ideas about women. The contradiction between her own experience and the rule of her father was given concrete form in her mother's sister, who had struggled before her to come out of seclusion and had sacrificed her hard-won freedom for the liberation of the country. Having won an education, Reeta faced a further contradiction. She had taken up this struggle for education against her father for her own development and fulfilment, but her father used her success only to make a more prestigious match with an educated man, and her husband added *her* achievement to *his* status. So the battle she thought she had won for herself turned into a victory for her husband. Her self-development made her more discontented with the patriarchal organisation of the family. It did nothing to change the approach of the men — husband, father and brother continued to oppose her — towards her, and her subordinate position in the family. Since they would not change, she was forced to leave.

Reeta's only support came from other women; from her aunt, her sister and her mother. After marriage, it was even harder to get an education, for none of her in-laws supported her. She had to leave her husband before she could complete her education or get a job. Two factors allowed her to do this. She had the emotional and moral support of the three women of her own family, and she had sufficient ability to win a scholarship and be offered a job. So she was able to be financially independent of the family.

In one way Puja's and Reeta's stories are the same, for in both cases they could only emerge from seclusion into employment after their marriages were broken. The link between the necessity of marriage and the prohibition on employment can be clearly seen. In another way Reeta's story is quite different from Puja's, for Reeta did not wait for her marriage to be broken by chance or mischance. She did not merely take advantage of an unfortunate occurrence which released her from the constraints of an orthodox marriage; instead, she took the initiative and broke the marriage herself, sacrificing the security of marriage for the uncertainties of earning her own living. She was forced to leave her husband to complete her education, but it was her economic independence that allowed her to make the break a permanent one. Reeta emerged from seclusion by taking power into her own hands. The basis for her power lay in her own courage and determination bolstered by the support of other women in the family, the strength of her personal desire and ability to fulfil herself academically, and finally her financial independence. Reeta's struggle didn't only change her, it also radically changed her family. All the members of her own family changed from opposition to her education and employment to pride and pleasure at her success.

Shikha Munshi is also a brahmin, but her family is not so strictly orthodox, possibly because their financial circumstances did not permit it. She is now 43, and has only been lecturing for seven years. For ten years prior to her marriage she was a secretary. She did not have to struggle as hard as Reeta against the men in her family, but the same concerns about the nature of her work and its effect on the position of the men can be seen.

> My parents had high expectations of an education . . . They saw education as an improvement and higher education as an insurance. I started work in an office at 18. I became a secretary so I could contribute to the family finances . . . I had wanted a professional career earlier, but I lowered my expectations due to the family's economic circumstances. The family wasn't happy with me being a secretary because there was no future and no respect in it. I rebelled to work.
>
> I was good in Maths, my teachers hoped I would be a mathematician if I'd gone to university straight from school, but I didn't, I had to study on my own in the evenings, so Maths was too difficult. I chose Economics instead. I left school in 1948 at the age of 14, because my parents couldn't afford any more education for me. I started working at 18, studied in the evenings, and got my BA at 22. Then a friend said, 'Don't give up, do an MA', so I continued on my own and did an MA in Political Science as an external degree. They didn't do external degrees for women before the mid 1950s. I got my BA in '56, my MA in '60 then I had a break for marriage.
>
> My marriage only lasted 6 months. I had resigned my job after I got married because my husband left Delhi, so I went too. He was not happy that I had been working, particularly being a secretary. It was too low status and I was too independent. His family didn't like it either. That marriage led me to a mental breakdown, and my marriage broke up . . . It was only after that, that I could complete my education and get a lecturing job . . . Now my parents are very happy that I'm a lecturer.

The story of how Shikha came through her mental breakdown is a remarkable one, and will be told in Part VI. In the meantime she was faced with a number of contradictory experiences. In the first place, her education was terminated early because of financial problems, but her family disapproved of her secretarial job because of its low status. The job was in fact in keeping with their economic position, but not with their religious status or their desired social position. In addition, her job and her struggle for education required not a little energy and initiative, so that by the time of her marriage, she was an independent, self-confident, autonomous woman, qualities which were regarded by her husband and his family as undesirable if not unnatural in a woman. She was induced to leave her job when her husband left Delhi shortly after their marriage. Along with the job went her economic independence together with much of her self-confidence. Financially dependent and with her identity submerged under her husband's, the contrast between her autonomy as a single woman and her powerless condition as a wife was simply intolerable. Without a job there was no way out; her mind broke down under the strain. Puja and Reeta had never known anything different, although they envisaged an alternative. Shikha, however, had experienced it.

All three women had to break the bond of marriage before they could emerge or re-emerge from seclusion. Shikha's family didn't approve of her work, but their disapproval was tempered over time by her economic independence and their own need for her financial contribution. Her husband, however, wanted her to be dependent on him — and this he achieved; unlike her father, he could afford to put his disapproval into practice, because his financial position provided the material basis for greater control over Shikha's work activities.

The concern which united Shikha's father and husband was the nature of her work. Its status was too low and it gave no 'respect'. Here we can see in practice the link between women's work and the social position of the family, discussed theoretically in Part II. From an orthodox point of view, women's employment reduces the prestige of the family as a whole, including the *men* in the family. The effect is increased with a lower-level job. The concept of respectability raised by Shikha's father and husband provides the clue to the nature of the link, for its meaning is gender specific. Respectability for men signifies a high position in the social hierarchy. For women it signifies sexual purity. The two are connected in that a significant part of male respectability, in the sense of social position, is derived from female respectability, in terms of sexual purity. We can see empirically that the man's control of the woman's sexuality is essential for his position in the social hierarchy. But this control is undermined by the woman's independence, whether social or economic. Women's financial independence prevents men from controlling their access to economic resources. Women's social independence inhibits men's control of their sexuality. Employment violates both strictures, requiring physical mobility and providing an independent income.

These processes affect not only Hindus, but also Muslims of the upper strata. Mumtaz Ahmad is a lecturer of 42 and comes from an orthodox 'high-caste' Muslim family.

I was a very serious student . . . My parents just expected me to marry. They wanted to educate their children but only for show . . . After I completed my PhD I saw this job, applied for it and got it. My parents opposed me — they were very angry . . . but after some time they adapted, they accepted it after I started working.

The fears which form the basis for the families' resistance to female employment are expressed by Aruna Sharma, a civil servant of 31 who comes from an orthodox kshatriya family: 'When I wanted to work, my father thought it would be difficult to marry me, and it would bring shame on the family.' A high-caste woman is only acceptable as a bride by an equally high-caste man if she is sexually pure — 'respectable'. Anything which casts doubt on this respectability — physical mobility, work relationships with men, a show of social or financial independence — undermines her chance of marriage into a 'respectable', that is, high-caste family. A job could preclude marriage — and that would bring shame onto the entire family. More specifically, the loss of the woman's sexual respectability brings about the loss of the male relative's caste respectability. Amongst this high-caste orthodox group at least, the basis for the women's seclusion is the maintenance of the men's caste position.

Finally, one of the most surprising features of the stories is the mysterious change of heart that occurs in the families' attitudes to female employment, from opposition, to acceptance, to pride at their daughters' rebellion. How can this extraordinary change be understood?

We suggest that the turnaround reflects a shift from the evaluations of caste hierarchy to those of class hierarchy. Caste, as a system of social organisation, is collectively based, that is, all the groups involved are dependent on one another for survival, even though the higher groups in the hierarchy experience better conditions of life at the expense of the lower groups. Being collectively based, individuals cannot improve their position in the caste hierarchy. There is simply no place for an individual once s/he has left her/his own group. Social mobility within the caste system occurs not with individuals but with entire groups and an individual's attempt to rise brings dishonour.

In contrast, mobility in the class system based on wage labour is individually based. Each individual is assumed in theory to be free to sell her/his labour on the market in return for a wage. The wage may be insufficient for survival, for not all individuals enter the labour market on an equal basis. Women as a group, for instance, are at the lower end of the occupational hierarchy.[24] Nevertheless, the payment of wages to individuals means that a small number of individuals from subordinate social groupings can rise in the class system, normally through the acquisition of a professional education. When a woman achieves a high position within the class system on the basis of personal ability, her merit is acknowledged and, apart from certain sex-specific limitations to be discussed in Part IV, she shares with men the material and social benefits of that occupation. This is not to say that the class system is more egalitarian than the caste system in terms of either social hierarchy or gender hierarchy, but that the basis of inequality and mobility is different: collectivist for caste, individualist for class. Where whole groups rise in caste, individuals, including women can rise in class.

The fathers' radical change of heart can be understood with reference to these two systems of social evaluation. We are not suggesting that the fathers abandon the caste system as a frame of reference when their daughters refuse to conform to its constraints, but that they adopt a class perspective on this particular issue. The individualist mobility of the class system means that social honour can be conferred for an individual expression of personal ability which would be viewed as shameful or dishonourable for a woman under the caste system. In this way, honour can be gained from the woman's rebellion instead of lost. However, the honour can only be gained from occupations high in the class hierarchy. This is why lecturing or the civil service is acceptable for women, but not secretarial work. And the respect so hard won by the woman does not remain solely with her. The honour returns to the families who earlier had bitterly accused her of bringing them shame.

Class and Women's Work

Vimla Gupta is a widow of 53. She is now chief marketing manager in one of the biggest state-owned companies in India. She is from a wealthy vaishya caste family from Bengal. Vimla's family represents not high-caste orthodoxy, but the top end of the occupational class hierarchy.

> My family expected me to marry and have children. I graduated young and I was academically good, but everyone at school and college and in the family advised me to get married. I should have gone to Oxford University in 1942, when I was 18, but I couldn't because of the war. So I married and had children. My three sisters are all highly educated, but they never had jobs. We had no brothers — I am the boy of the family! My father was educated at Oxford and was an ambassador in the Indian Foreign Service.
>
> I *longed* for a career when I was younger, but we lived in a small town where there were no opportunities. I was married to a very senior man with a large income. My husband's family didn't want me to work in any low-level job, and there were no opportunities for anything else, so I could only do social work until my husband's death. My husband died when I was 33, and then I was determined to have a career. I only started work after I become a widow. I took the lowest paid job in line management. It was the only executive job I could get, the other jobs were service jobs or technical jobs in statistics for instance. I started very low and too late. I haven't got as far as I want because of that, but at least I'm in control of my career now . . .
>
> The inhibitions of Indian culture didn't affect me . . . we were a westernised family.

The lifestyle of Vimla's family was highly westernised, cosmopolitan, unconstrained by traditional caste considerations of controls over women. They measured their social prestige on the class hierarchy, and had no compunction about marrying out of caste, religion, even nationality, acts which would have destroyed high-caste purity. The contradiction that Vimla faced was that although none of her family insisted on seclusion in principle, the pressure to marry, to abandon education and to take only high-status employment ensured her domesticity in practice. For Vimla's in-laws, the predominant concerns were women's economic dependence, and the social prestige attached to the work. The effect on Vimla was as constraining as for any woman from the most orthodox brahmin family, since no sufficiently prestigious jobs were available. Just like Puja Shukla, Vimla could not take paid work until the link between the necessity of marriage and the prohibition on employment was broken by her husband's death. And the reason underlying the restriction was the same in this wealthy middle-class family as in the high-caste families: the woman's low occupational status would undermine the class position of the entire family, including the men.

In the caste structure, the women either have to break the link between the necessity of marriage and the prohibition on employment, or use a chance break in the link, forcing a change in power relations on the basis of their economic independence. In the class structure, a change in power relations may also be necessary, as with Vimla Gupta, but it may be accomplished by persuasion rather than force, because the criteria of respectability for women are different in the class system, and do not include a total ban on women's employment, but, as we shall see, the underlying reason for the control over women remains the same.

Kasturi Verma is 50, a civil servant from the far North of India, from a vaishya caste family. She was not encouraged to have a profession, but nor did she have to force her way out of domesticity, for her family was not orthodox in caste position or aspiration. She was able to change her family's attitude before taking the job, by convincing the family of the job's high *class* position — the same process which the more orthodox families went through only *after* their daughters were employed.

> My parents wanted me to be well educated, but not to work . . . My mother wanted an education but she was denied it because she was a woman. My father was a mathematician in government service. He was a great influence. I thought I'd be a maths teacher, and I liked teaching. My father wasn't keen for me to work, especially outside Delhi. When I did my postgraduate course, there was only one women's college in Delhi, and they didn't need a maths teacher. In the meantime someone suggested statistics training . . . I did that whilst still doing my PhD at university. Then a renowned statistician wanted someone with a background in maths and stats. I was attracted to the job, that man was so eminent. My father didn't want me to work, but he allowed me to since he was an eminent man. I persuaded him. He hoped I'd marry. But he came around completely. I worked . . . for 6 months, then the project became a regular government job, so the staff became government staff. My mother was also unhappy initially with the government job, she wouldn't have minded teaching. Most of my family didn't expect me to carry on, but now they've quite come round.

Kasturi's parents disapproved of her having any occupation only because she was a woman. But there were certain conditions under which they would have agreed to her employment. Teaching was acceptable, in a women's college, and in Delhi. The conditions of respectability, then, were: no physical mobility, not mixing with men at work and a job that was an extension of women's traditional childcare role. Her parents were willing to modify the practical details of the constraints on their daughter's activities, but the underlying basis for the constraints, sexual control, remained the same. Kasturi's family eventually changed their views when she convinced them that she would be working with 'an eminent man', already distinguished in terms of class position in the occupational hierarchy. Class honour overcame gender dishonour.

The prohibition on employment in the class system, then, is not as severe as in the caste structure, for women may work outside the home without dishonour provided the job is high enough in the occupational class hierarchy. The concern with respectability in women's employment is expressed by many of our middle-class women who are not bound by the rules of caste honour. Asha Paul is 31, a civil servant from Bombay. Although she is a kshatriya, she married out of caste and religion, to a Christian man of her choice.

> My father used to encourage me to do the exam for the Indian Administrative Service. That's the only sort of work he approved of because of its status. He regards me with great pride. My husband's family don't mind me working at all. It's not so unusual amongst the educated classes, provided it's this profession and status.

Lakshmi Mitra talked in the last chapter about how she was brought up 'like a man.'

> In India women are not bread-winners, they're not supposed to work. Some have to for economic necessity, but in the middle and upper-middle classes, you have to have a job which gives standing since we're not bound to work.

So middle-class women may work outside the home, but there are still criteria of respectability to be upheld. The concern with respectability amongst the middle class is confirmed in a study of women school teachers by Malavika Karlekar, where almost half the respondents attributed their choice of occupation to this consideration.[25] One in five of our women raised this as an important influence, without prompting. The evidence from our women suggests that respectability can be retained by minimising the woman's sexual freedom in the job, and through emphasising the economic and status benefits attaching to her occupation. At the highest levels of the occupational class hierarchy, any dishonour associated with the sexual freedom inherent in the job (mixing with men, physical mobility) can be outweighed by the honour associated with the job's high material and social rewards. The class division can precede the gender division, and the family, specifically the men, can again derive social status from the women.

15. The Basis of Women's Subordination

In Part III we have examined the relationship between women's subordination and the social structure, by looking at the social processes whereby women resist their subordination in the transition from a caste to a class structure.

High-caste women's work in a patriarchal caste society is confined to the domestic sphere, and a return to employment marks a significant rejection of male control over female sexual and economic independence. The desire of women from the middle class to enter paid employment stems from their resistance to the stultifying effects of this control epitomised in the concept and practice of seclusion.

Women's Resistance

There are several important features of the women's resistance:

1) the women's own courage and determination in the struggle against oppression, deriving from their view of themselves as strong and powerful people; 2) the influence of radicalising personal experiences of the system of male domination, and of reformist or revolutionary social movements of opposition to the social structure, which can act on consciousness to effect the change in attitude accompanying or preceding the change in power relations between men and women; 3) the contradiction between women's experience and male constructions of that experience, creating an instability in individual consciousness upon which external factors can act to effect a change. (Women's consciousness is discussed in Part V.) 4) the existence of waged work in the development of a class society, and the possibility of individual women earning an independent wage in the professions, providing the material basis for a change in the power relations between men and women in the family. (The women's material conditions are discussed in Part IV.)

Women's Subordination and Social Hierarchy

The description of how women resist their subordination in the transition from caste to class provides the basis for an analysis of the social processes linking women's subordination to the maintenance of social hierarchy. We have seen that the essential nature of the link between the necessity of marriage and the prohibition on employment for women arises out of the importance of women's seclusion for men's position in the caste hierarchy. The social position of the men derives partly from the status of the women, and the social position of the entire caste group can be ruined by the social conduct of the women. In this way, the women's respectability determines that of the men, the family and the whole caste. In other words, women are not secondary to caste stratification. Gender, in fact, is crucial to it.

Amongst urban communities, where the class system based on wage labour operates, a similar process occurs but in a different form. In the transition from caste to class systems of evaluation, the families at first resist their daughters and wives emerging from seclusion into paid employment. The class system, however, creates opportunities for exceptional individuals to rise, permitting women to break out of the constraints of caste. Such women are able to acquire economic independence, which provides them with the material basis for changing the power relation between them and the dominant males in the family, and for undermining the gender division. But the woman's achievement may be incorporated into the system of class hierarchy, by the family appropriating the social status of the woman's profession for the enhancement of its own class position. The family may discover that the respect which the woman's education and employment took away from them under the caste system, returns to them under the class system, so that the family, specifically the men, again derive part of their social position from the women. When this happens, the family's concern is with the respectability of the occupation: jobs which minimise contact with men and are an extension of women's domestic roles are allowed; low-level jobs are unacceptable, professional jobs are preferred, and high-status professions such as the civil service are most respectable. The actual conditions and practical details of men's control over women changes in the transition from caste to class evaluations, but the control itself remains.

So women are not secondary to class stratification in the Indian class system either. In the urban middle class at least, the class hierarchy is as dependent on the gender division as is the caste structure. The difference lies in the forms of male control over women. The class structure appears to build on the existing gender divisions in the caste structure, modifying their form but maintaining the sexual inequality. The women's personal struggles achieve radical changes in themselves and their families, but limited change in the overall structure, for the class system of social hierarchy adjusts to the women's resistance to the constraints of caste, the women moving from one male-dominated system of hierarchy to another. Women's work, far from being peripheral or incidental to the social position of the group in society, in fact holds a central place in the definition of the group's social identity, in which men derive a significant part of their social position from women. The basis of women's subordination in both caste and class systems is the maintenance of the social hierarchy.

Despite the incorporation of women's resistance to caste into the hierarchy of class, however, women's subordination in the class structure is less stable than that in the caste structure, since the individualism of the class system creates openings for women at the top end of the hierarchy to achieve release from one of the mainstays of male domination, economic dependence. From this basis women are also able to challenge the other foundation of male supremacy, that is, men's control over their sexuality. As we will see in Part IV, concern with female sexuality underlies many of the disadvantages which professional women still have to face in comparison with men, despite their release from domestic seclusion and economic dependence.

Notes

1. Kamala Das, 'The Old Playhouse'. Poem reproduced in *Manushi* (1980) 6, p.52.

2. The Child Marriage Restraint Act was passed on 29 September 1929 to take effect from 1 April 1930. The 6-month interval saw the proportion of married girls under 5 years increase from 11 per 1,000 in 1921 to 30 per 1,000 in 1931, and from 42 to 93 per 1,000 in the 5-10 age group. Gyan Chand (1939) *India's Teeming Millions*. London: George Allen & Unwin, pp.136, 138-9.

3. Heidi Hartmann (1981) 'The Unhappy Marriage of Marxism and Feminism: Towards a more Progressive Union', in Lydia Sargent (ed), *Women and Revolution: the Unhappy Marriage of Marxism and Feminism*. London: Pluto, p.15.

4. Kathasaritsagara, 36, 6-7. Quoted in A.S. Altekar (1956) *The Position of Women in Hindu Civilisation*. Delhi: Motilal Banarsidas, p.174.

5. Khuda Bux. 'Studies Indian and Islamic', quoted in P. Thomas (1964) *Indian Women Through the Ages*. Bombay: Asia Publishing House, p.249.

6. Lalitavistara, Canto XVI. Quoted in Altekar, *The Position of Women*, pp.170-1.

7. Thomas, *Indian Women*, p.247.

8. Altekar, *Position of Women*, p.176.

9. M.N. Srinivas (1977) 'The Changing Position of Indian Women', *Man* 12, p.224.

10. See Sarah Hobson (1978) *Family Web*. London: John Murray, especially Ch.6.

11. Srinivas, 'Changing Position of Indian Women', pp.225-6.

12. Maria Mies (1980) *Indian Women and Patriarchy*. New Delhi: Concept, pp.66-7, 47-9.

13. Dr Rukhmabai (1929) 'Purdah — the Need for its Abolition', in Evelyn Gedge and Mithan Choksi (eds), *Women in Modern India*. Bombay: Taraporewala, p.144.

14. Roushan Jahan (1981) 'Inside Seclusion: the Avoradhbasini of Rokeya Sakhawat Hossain. Dacca: Women for Women', quoted in Kamla Bhasin (1982) 'Rokeya: A Crusader against Purdah', *Manushi* 11, pp.45-6.

15. Mies, *Indian Women and Patriarchy*, pp.47-50.

16. See Nur Yalman (1968) 'On the Purity of Women in the Castes of Ceylon and Malabar, *Journal of the Royal Anthropological Institute* 93, 1, pp.41-2,

and Veena Das (1976) 'Indian Women: Work, Power and Status', in B.R. Nanda (ed), *Indian Women from Purdah to Modernity*. New Delhi: Vikas, pp.134-5.

17. M.N. Srinivas (1962) *Caste in Modern India*. London: Asia Publishing House, p.46.

18. See Ann Oakley (1974) *The Sociology of Housework*. Oxford: Martin Robertson, Ch.1.

19. Andrea Menefee Singh (1976) *Neighbourhood and Social Networks in Urban India: South Indian Voluntary Associations in Delhi*. New Delhi: Marwah.

20. Andrea Menefee Singh and Alfred de Souza (1976) *The Position of Women in Migrant Bastis in Delhi: Report prepared for the Department of Social Welfare*. Government of India.

21. Victor D'Souza (1980) 'Family Status and Female Work Participation', in Alfred de Souza (ed), *Women in Contemporary India and South Asia*. New Delhi: Manohar, p.129.

22. See Appendix, Table 12 for the distribution of religions amongst our women.

23. Amongst the 13 families where the male and female members disagreed over women's employment, only 3 were where the women held radical views and the men held orthodox views.

24. In the UK for instance, 90 per cent of women work in the bottom four grades with none in the highest grade (out of 7), whilst 80 per cent of men work in the top four grades with none in the bottom grade. See J. Hunt and S. Adams (1980) *Women, Work and Trade Union Organisation*. London: Workers Educational Association, p.20.

25. Malavika Karlekar (1975) 'Professionalization of Women School Teachers', *Indian Journal of Industrial Relations* 11, 1, p.55. The importance of this effect can also be seen in the kind of professions which are considered most suitable for women. Blumberg and Dwaraki, and Wadhera found that teaching was considered the most suitable profession for women, and a study by the Shri Ram Centre found teaching, medicine and social work the most popular amongst women. All these professions operate in parallel with, but segregated from, the equivalent male professions, thereby continuing sexual segregation. Rhoda Lois Blumberg and Leela Dwaraki (1980) *India's Educated Women*. Delhi: Hindustan Publishing Corporation, p.55; Kiron Wadhera (1976) *The New Bread Winners*. New Delhi: Vishwa Yuvak Kendra, p.238; O.P. Dhingra (1972) *The Career Woman and her Problems*. New Delhi: Shri Ram Centre for Industrial Relations and Human Resources.

Part IV: Limits to Freedom

16. Class Privilege and Male Supremacy

> One day a turtle decided to emulate the prowess of his legendary ancestor. He challenged a passing hare to race with him and the hare accepted. She was placed at a fifty yard distance, while he was stationed a foot from the finishing line. When the race was done, the turtle had beaten her by a good two inches, which, he said, clearly established the superiority of turtles. The hare demurred, 'You only ran a foot. I ran fifty yards.' But the turtle was unmoved. 'That,' he told her, 'is the luck of the game. You really should learn to be a good loser.'
> Suniti Namjoshi, *Feminist Fables*[1]

We have mainly focused so far on gender as an important feature of social hierarchy. Specifically we have seen women's seclusion as a means to caste privilege, and have examined the way in which men derive their social position from women, suggesting that a similar process occurs in the system of class hierarchy. In other words, we have analysed women's oppression, not for itself, but for the way in which it is mediated by other systems of oppression. In order to understand women's position in a male-dominated class structure, however, we need to examine both aspects: how the gender division mediates the class division, and how the divisions of class mediate those of gender.[2]

An examination of the particular position of professional women, who are dominant in the class hierarchy but subordinate in the gender hierarchy, suggests that the two systems of class and gender dominance are neither autonomous nor identical, but crucially linked. Gender and class hierarchy exist and develop together, each supporting the other. Within a male-dominated class structure, power is both class-based and gender-based. Neither class nor gender oppression is primary or predominant in any fixed way, but the systems of gender and class dominance are linked historically.[3]

The two systems are not identical, for we know that gender hierarchy predates class societies, as in the caste system, and appears to succeed class in post-capitalist countries.[4] Nor are the two systems independent, since the class hierarchy appears to build upon the existing gender divisions within the caste structure, adapting to and incorporating the struggle of high-caste women against the patriarchal constraints of caste. To elucidate the relationship between the two systems we need to look at the ways in which gender hierarchy operates within the class structure and how class hierarchy operates within the gender structure. If we isolate either system, we will fail to understand fully the reality of women's lives.

In Part IV we will look at the conditions of women's lives in the professional class within education, employment and the family. Within each area we will examine the kind of liberation which professional women gain because of their class, despite their sex. These freedoms are the privileges which women share with men at the highest levels of the occupational class hierarchy and which distinguish them from women in lower-class positions. They are indicative of the ways in which class divisions outweigh gender divisions. We will also examine the limits to these freedoms, which professional women suffer because of their sex, despite their class. These limits are the disadvantages which women do not share with men of the same class position, and which highlight the precedence of gender subordination over class privilege.

In Part IV we will show:

one, some of the mechanisms whereby men control the activities of women of the professional class, and through which male domination is maintained within the class structure. This is revealed through an examination of the actual conditions of women's lives;

two, some of the reasons for male control over women in contemporary class society, revealed through the material benefits which men gain from such control;

three, the connections between gender and class, and the specific ways in which each takes precedence over the other for women of the professional class;

four, the ways in which the class structure builds upon the existing hierarchical relations of both gender and caste, and how the institution of male domination adapts to the changes in the structure of the social hierarchy.

17. Education: The Path to Emancipation?

According to the 1971 Census of India, 19 per cent of women are literate, rising to 42 per cent in the urban areas, compared with 39 per cent of males, rising to 61 per cent.[5] Of the literates, 1 per cent of women and 2 per cent of men are graduates and above, rising to 3 per cent and 6 per cent respectively in the urban areas.[6] These figures show what a select group graduates are. They also show that men are four times as likely as women to enter this privileged group.

The women we interviewed are very highly qualified academically. More than two thirds are educated to masters level or above,[7] and more than a third have three or more academic qualifications.[8] The latter figure can be roughly compared with the national figures for qualified doctors, managers and civil servants, which show that only 4 per cent of the total (both men and women) have three or more qualifications.[9] Figures available for *women* doctors, lecturers and civil servants show that 12 per cent have three or more qualifications.[10] The comparisons cannot be precise, since different professions are involved in each case, but the general picture is that our professional women are more highly qualified than either of the national groups, although the discrepancy is much greater when male professionals are included, indicating that women are more highly qualified than men in the same jobs. Comparisons within the national figures also show that women are in general better qualified than men, a pattern that is confirmed by the Ministry of Labour who state that 'Women are, by and large, better equipped than men in most of the [professional] occupations.'[11]

A significant number of our women studied abroad.[12] Well over half were at or near the top of the class at school or college.[13] Most came from financially well-off homes.[14] A quarter of their mothers and four-fifths of their fathers were graduates.[15] Many of them were positively encouraged by at least one member, if not all, of their family.[16] Despite this extraordinary array of privileged circumstances, more than a third experienced difficulties of various kinds in their education.[17]

Effects of Economic Resources

The inability of the women's families to pay for any further education, or to pay for a long, expensive course such as medicine, made it difficult for some women, or meant that they couldn't study what they wanted. We have already met Shikha Munshi, in Part III, who had to delay her academic career for 15 years, studying in the evenings and earning a living as a secretary by day. Some overcame the financial problem by getting scholarships and loans. Others, like Manju Malik, had to content themselves with an area in which they were not really interested.

> After finishing my undergraduate degree in medicine I wanted to do a clinical subject, and I got admission, but I hesitated to ask my father for more money, so I took a non-clinical job in bacteriology. I shouldn't have done it, because without contact with patients there's no job satisfaction. There was no open pressure from my parents, but I felt the financial constraints nevertheless.
>
> My father was a business man and not too well off. I was working at a doctor's as well as training, so I could get some money.

In Neelam Bhatia's case, we can see how financial control is tied up with social control.

> There can be pressures in the joint family. My father wanted education for all the members of the family, boys and girls, but my grandparents were very much against education for girls. They thought it would be a waste because I'd just get married. My father was short of money at the time, for education fees, so there were great difficulties and we suffered because of it. They *had* money, but it was joint family finance, and as they disapproved of me doing fieldwork, they were unwilling to pass it on.

It is difficult to do anything independently of which the family disapproves when the money is controlled jointly. Social control within the joint family has a sound economic basis, and is one of the mechanisms whereby girls' education is limited regardless of income. But where income is low, the financial constraints can affect girls more than boys. If the family can't afford to educate all the children, priorities will be assigned, and many of our women agreed with Ankita Chandra's view: 'Preference is given to boys' education if there are financial constraints.'

The problem of individual families' financial difficulties, however, needs to be seen in the context of India's position in the international economy.

Effects of Imperialism

Education was greatly expanded after Independence, and India now provides schooling from the ages of 5 to 17 (classes I to XII). In most of the states, education is compulsory to class VII, but it is not enforceable because of the economic position.[18] Education is free to class VIII, after which a small fee is charged, depending on family income. 22½ per cent of places are reserved for scheduled castes and tribes (untouchables) in state and central government schools. Central government schools are of high quality, but are designed primarily for the children of government servants.[19] The state schools are considered inadequate by people who can afford to pay for their children's education,[20] because the standard of teaching is low, and the teaching medium is not English but the local language. English is needed to move into higher education, since only English is used at that level.

All higher education is fee-paying, although a few subsistence grants are available[21] and 25 per cent of students receive a full or half concession on fees. All members of the scheduled castes receive fee concessions and government scholarships regardless of merit or income. But historical and contemporary imperialism requires education in English at the higher levels rather than in the languages of India. English is not used in state schools, so higher education is virtually barred to ordinary people, for cultural if not financial reasons. And India cannot enforce compulsory education at primary level because the level of poverty demands children's labour in domestic, agricultural and waged work.

Despite deliberate policies to reduce the discrepancy between men's and women's education,[22] women remain disadvantaged. A government report of 1965 acknowledged that the relative backwardness of women's education was caused by the paucity of state resources[23] and an earlier report found that girls were kept away from school because of the need for their domestic labour.[24] Despite policies to encourage girls' education, and the importance of single-sex education in a segregated society, less than a quarter of primary and middle school teachers were women in 1968-9.[25]

Many of the problems of the education system stem from the effects of imperialism. The poor quality of the teaching was felt by a number of the women. Puja Shukla:

> I gained nothing from school or college, only from reading outside college and from my own experiences. I wrote a book at school, but I was *not* encouraged. 'You can do that sort of thing when you leave', they said . . . I've published 6 books now.

Puja also complained bitterly about cultural colonialism.

> The Western influence is so powerful that Indian culture has nothing to do with my day-to-day life now. At work I have to communicate in English even though I'm teaching literature in my own regional language. We have to do everything in English. I would prefer not to speak English, but there's no practical alternative.

Neelam Bhatia was concerned with India's dependence on the West:

> It's very frustating because of the lack of facilities, we can't get equipment, the library's not good enough. It depends on the political situation; for instance, Ford Foundation grants depend on relations between India and America. It's taken 7 years to get any money for geological research in the department.

The greatest awareness on this issue came from the lecturers, who had to work within the colonial structures set up by the British. Apart from economic considerations, part of the reason for the poor quality of education was that, as Priya Gupta pointed out: 'The British educational system put pressure on knowing, not understanding.' This was in keeping with the British aim of creating 'a class of imitators, not the originators of new values and methods'.[26]

Some lecturers were angry about this heritage. Mira Mitra, for instance.

> I'd like to build up a genuine institution in the department, one not steeped in the colonial set up. The colonial heritage means that, for example, a PhD from Delhi is inferior to a PhD from Massachussets Institute of Technology. We've inherited problems from the West: for instance, even people who were nationalists feel good if they're referred to in a foreign journal. They like praise from the West. They always debate with Oxford and MIT but never with Benares or any of the Sanskrit or Hindi colleges. Choices are not made in India. Academic fashions come from the West. For instance, the sociology of religion relates to Christian theology rather than Hindu or Buddhist thought . . . it may become a little better, but in the end, you have to use the colonial system.

The impact of this heritage on the students is described by Promilla Khanna:

> Most students are exam oriented, therefore they're not ready to go into depth. It's also the teachers' attitudes. They don't attempt to rouse student interest. It's related to the social structure; what can students do after the exams?

A science lecturer, Rama Tyagi, also saw the poor quality of education as related to the high graduate unemployment rate.

> Teaching is dissatisfying because the student response has been very poor in recent years. There are no job opportunities for science graduates, and it's getting worse because of the general economic conditions in India. It might become better if we had more industrialisation.

Of course, these problems affect boys too, but they have a special impact on girls, for despite educational policies designed to improve women's education, priorities are still given to boys when resources are limited. The recommendation in 1966 to open separate girls' schools at the higher primary stage was qualified by 'wherever possible',[27] and men school teachers still outnumber women even at junior levels.[28] Shaleen Sharma's story illustrates some of the most common problems.

> I went to the mission school in Almora, but there were few subjects for girls because there were few women teachers. My cousin had to go to the boys' school for maths teaching. Subjects were still limited in the VIII class and there was no science.

In some areas, the lack of segregated education for girls prevented them from training as teachers or doctors even when there were no financial constraints. Nirmala Verma is a professor of medicine now, but her sister's plans to be a doctor were thwarted for this reason.

> My elder sister also wanted to be a doctor, but there was no women's medical college in Lahore and my father wouldn't allow us to go to the co-ed college.

When *I* wanted to go to college, it was after Partition and we'd already moved to Delhi. So I could go to the women's medical college in Delhi.

The shortage of segregated teaching for girls and the poorer quality or non-existence of science teaching in girls' schools and colleges reflect sex-biased educational policies when the pressure of economic stringency demands the assignment of priorities, despite government attempts to improve female education. Only the state of Kerala has positively implemented recommendations to encourage women's education, with dramatic results,[29] as Marie Raj pointed out.

In Kerala, girls' education is actively encouraged. When I was at school, there were half price fees for girls and the state paid the tuition fees — for girls only. Kerala is atypical. It's partly the influence of the matriarchal system. Women are emancipated, accepted, there's nothing hampering them. Women in Kerala get the most education and have the highest age of marriage in the whole of India.

Within the family, the encouragement of family members, especially parents and husbands, plays a crucial role in facilitating our women's education as we saw in Part III, but when money is short, support is more ambiguous. In general the lack of resources reduces women's education more than men's, both from the point of view of educational policies, and from the assignment of priorities within individual families.

Effects of Gender

We want to look now at the particular impact of being female on a person's education. One of the problems is that of personal safety. This is Kiran Singhal's story:

My state was ruled by a Muslim prince. There was no high school for girls, the girls had to go to a co-ed school. But they weren't safe from sexual assaults because of the prince's power. So I was sent to my uncle's house in another state, where I could get a proper education. My younger sister was the first girl in the family to go to that school, after the ruler of the state went to Africa, because of the social stigma of a certain event connected with his sexual activities.

This was 40 years ago. Only drastic arrangements could procure an education for Kiran under such circumstances. And the reason for the constraints on girls was unambiguous: the fear of sexual assault by powerful males. In an overt or covert way, this problem which some men cause for women is often used by other men in authority as an excuse for actively discriminating against women. Neelam Bhatia:

Everyone at school advised me to think carefully about studying this subject. They tried to dissuade me because of the fieldwork. It's not considered proper for a middle-class woman. My father had to argue with the lecturers at the university in my home town, to get them to give me a place. The Head of Department refused me admission, but he had no grounds, so he had to take me on my father's insistence. But he laid down the condition that I had to be escorted to fieldwork because it was mainly men . . . As a student I really felt the difference in how men and women are treated because of this fieldwork business. Fieldwork is against the cultural traditions for women. When I started the job at this university, they were initially against me supervising students because I was a woman, but I fought against it and won.

This was in 1960. The problem was that physical mobility was not respectable for women. Arrangements had to be made to ensure Neelam's safety — a more veiled version of Kiran's problem. A problem which men do not have to face, but which they create, either by assaulting women or by discriminating against women on the grounds that other men might.

The other problems are less physically violent, but stem from the same assumption that women are the sexual possessions of men, and should lead a secluded, purely domestic life. This is reflected in a number of approaches to women's education. For instance, many women are steered if not harassed into traditional girls' subjects, and away from subjects in which they have an interest or aptitude because they are considered unsuitable. Usha Khanna:

> I wanted to do technical drawing at school so that I could be an engineer. I did 2½ years, but I got so much negative reaction and cruel treatment from the master, that I eventually gave it up six months before the exam.

Indrani Vijayalakshmi didn't even get that far:

> I wanted to do a chemistry degree, but the principal said I shouldn't because I'd be taking up a scarce science place. 'Girls can't pursue a career', he told me. He forced me into humanities. Now there are women even in engineering. I was born 25 years too early.

Many of our women reported that their education was not taken seriously, whether they were interested in 'girls' subjects' or not. In some cases very little encouragement was provided either by parents or teachers, and no guidance was given for selecting subjects or careers. Padma Unnikrishnan: 'The teachers had no expectations of me. When I said I wanted to do medicine, everyone laughed. They couldn't imagine that I could be a doctor.'

Even women who wanted to study literature were not taken seriously. Puja Shukla and Mumtaz Ahmad both wanted to contribute to their own literary heritage, but Puja was told by her teachers 'You can do that sort of thing when you leave', and Mumtaz's parents wanted her to have education 'only for show'.

The 'show' in question, of course, is marriage. An education is increasingly regarded as an asset in the marriage market — not valued for itself or for women's development, but as a commodity. A study in 1972 found three major reasons for women taking professional training: the parents were unable to arrange a marriage for the daughter and preferred her to do something worthwhile until this occurred; the parents or the daughter perceived that professional training would increase her marriage potential; and poorer parents saw the possibility of escaping excessive dowry demands.[30] Rupali Sinha related girls' education to position in the social structure: 'Girls get a degree but they don't go on to a job . . . They get married into high status families because of the degree, but they aren't respected.' This can result in a certain ambiguity towards education, for there is a limit to how far it can go without becoming a liability. Mira Mitra was subject to pressures against continuing her education:

> When I was younger, before I got married, the women members of the family wanted me to stop studying. They applied moral pressure. But my brothers encouraged me. I overcame it by ignoring them and also by moving out and living in hostels.

Moyna Ghosh:

> At Law School, it was a great help to get the first or second place in the exams, because those people were absorbed into the faculty. I did that, then I went to do my PhD at Cambridge. When I got my PhD my aunts wrote to my mother saying how worried they were: how would I get a husband?

But education for marriage creates its own contradiction. Vimla Gupta:

> When women are educated but given no outlet for their talents, this has a bad effect on them and the family. You can't give glimpses of the future then shut off the possibilities. Women must be able to use their education, with all the problems.

All the problems — sexual harassment, stereotyped girls' subjects, the trivialisation of women studying, and education as a commodity for marriage — stem from the same cause. They are the result of a male power structure which defines women as sexual and economic possessions, fit only for a life of secluded and dependent domesticity. They are also problems which are not generally confronted by men. India's inability to provide universal free education at all levels affects girls more than boys. Boys receive a greater share of educational resources despite government policies to improve girls' education. Within the family, boys' education is given priority where money is short. Women's subordinate position as sexual object and domestic dependant inhibits women's education even at the top levels of the class structure, compounded by the effects of cultural and economic imperialism.

18. Employment: Women's Professional Work

It is difficult to present an accurate picture of women's employment, because the definition of 'work' is different in the Censuses of 1951, 1961 and 1971. The 1971 definition particularly underestimates women's contribution to the economy for it defines a worker as a person whose *main activity* is economically productive work.[31] As a result, the work participation estimates fell for both men and women: for men by 4 per cent but for women by 15 per cent.[32] This is a prime example of how women's work is hidden from the statistics. Leela Gulati has concluded from this that there are as many women participating in the economy as a secondary activity, as there are as a primary activity.[33] Given the particular character of women's work, therefore, figures based on the 1971 Census grossly underestimate female employment, excluding all part-time workers and any worker not defining employment as her main activity. This criticism casts doubt on general female employment rates, although its impact on rates for women in full-time professional jobs is likely to be less severe.

Bearing this in mind, women were estimated as 17 per cent of the workforce in 1971,[34] although the figure was 30 per cent in 1961.[35] The total number of women workers in 1971 was given as 31 million, of whom 10 per cent were in the urban areas.[36] Slightly more women were employed in the private than in the public sector,[37] within the organised workforce.[38] The unemployment rate in 1971 for people actively seeking work was in the region of 14 per cent for women and 3 per cent for men.[39] The Ministry of Labour's conclusion that 'Unlike men, women employees were concentrated in relatively few occupations',[40] is shown by the fact that only 12 occupations account for over 80 per cent of women employees, suggesting a high degree of job segregation for women.[41]

In 1970, 17 per cent of professional workers were women,[42] and they comprised 22 per cent of women employed in the public sector, and 10 per cent of women in the private sector.[43] The number of women in the professions has been rising since 1960, although their proportion to total female employees has remained the same.[44] A clear picture of lower pay compared with men appears amongst qualified employees in the 1971 Census.[45] Job segregation occurs, with women having a much greater chance of entering the medical and teaching professions (21 per cent and 18 per cent respectively) than management and

124

executive jobs in industry or the civil service (2 per cent and 9 per cent respectively).[46]

We saw in Part II that the professional class developed from the upper castes, and that the upper castes still dominated the professions 20 years after Independence, despite government policies to raise the lower castes. Amongst our Hindu women (who comprised 84 per cent of the whole group[47]), 38 per cent were brahmins, 33 per cent kshatriyas, 13 per cent non-brahmins (equivalent in rank to kshatriyas[48]), 12 per cent vaishyas and 1 per cent sudras.[49] The sole sudra woman was from a scheduled caste which has achieved a high position in terms of the socio-economic class hierarchy in its area.

The Census of India does not break down the population into castes, except scheduled castes, which comprise about a fifth of the population, and are accordingly given 22½ per cent reserved places in education and government service. We can therefore only compare the distribution of castes within the Hindu population with estimates made before Independence, although it is not certain how reliable these are.[50] The Simon Report of 1930 claimed that brahmins constituted 7 per cent of Hindus.[51] Hiro claims that, in 1931, property was mainly in the hands of the upper castes and a section of the middle castes, comprising 31.5 per cent of the population.[52] These figures are not sufficiently accurate to make a statistical comparison, but they do indicate that the upper castes are in the minority, with sudras and vaishyas comprising around two-thirds of the population. The caste distribution amongst professional women in Delhi suggests that the upper castes still predominate, scheduled castes are hardly to be seen, and although the middle castes are gaining access to the professions, the proportion of each caste still declines with decreasing caste status.

In terms of class position, the education and occupation of our women's fathers indicate that they come from a very select group of families.[53] 82 per cent of the fathers were graduates,[54] compared with 1 per cent of the population and 3 per cent of urban males.[55] 74 per cent of fathers' occupations were in the top two categories, with none in categories V to VII.[56] Comparable information is not available from the Census, but a study of Chandigarh city in 1968 showed that 13 per cent of heads of household were in the top two occupational categories, with 27 per cent in categories V to VII.[57] The figures suggest that although women's professional employment is affected by both class and caste, socio-economic class is a more stringent barrier than is caste, since all the castes are represented in our group, whereas only women from the most highly educated families with fathers in the top half of the occupational hierarchy have succeeded in entering the professions.

The picture that emerges is of a formidable array of structural barriers to women entering the professions, particularly from caste, class, job segregation and high female unemployment. We want now to examine the specific advantages and disadvantages that arise from professional women's particular structural position in the hierarchies of gender and class.

Class Privileges over Non-professional Women

The women experienced certain advantages over women not working in professional jobs; privileges which they share with the men of their class. Two of these are material in the broadest sense; the economic benefits of financial independence, and the social benefits of increased autonomy and control over their own lives. The other two are psychological, and concern self-identity, and increased esteem from others.

It is important to expose the myth that the majority of women in employment are adequately supported by their fathers or husbands, and work in paid jobs only for extras. In our sample, out of 120 women, only 37 per cent were not and never had been dependent on their job for survival. Because women's life-cycle is different from men's, it's important to look at how women's economic circumstances change. Some of our women who were not economically dependent on the job at the particular time we did our study, had nevertheless been entirely dependent on it at other stages of their lives, such as before marriage, at the start of marriage, after the husband had retired, or deserted, or the women had left the marriage. 63 per cent of the women were dependent economically at some time on the job. At the time of the study, 55 per cent relied fully or partially on the job for their income. A full third of these have no other means of support. They include single, married, separated and divorced women, and some of them have dependants to support too.[58]

Sunanda Rao is 54, single, and works as a lecturer. Now she stays with her younger brother, but previously she lived alone.

> I'm fully dependent on this job economically . . . In our family everyone is independent. I like the work too, but I work to have an independent life — economic independence I mean. You don't have to depend on anyone — father, husband or son. You can do whatever you like.

Kusum Gupta is married, and works in the civil service, but at 55 has become the main breadwinner.

> In the beginning I had to work for money. I didn't go into this line out of choice, it was by accident, I was influenced by a friend. I would have liked to be in business or something more lucrative. Since my husband retired — he's 13 years older than me — we've had separate establishments. We live together, but I became economically independent, and my husband and mother-in-law became dependent on me.

On take home pay of Rs1,000 a month (about £70) in 1977, she supported not only herself but also her husband, mother-in-law and three daughters aged between 16 and 26. Kusum is a good example of how women's economic position changes throughout the life-cycle.

Preeti Sohoni is 24 and lives with her mother and younger brother. She contributes Rs900 a month (£60) to the family finances, constituting half the family income. They rely to a great extent on her job, since her father died recently. The other half comes from her older brother, who is in the army. The average contribution of our women to the family income over the whole group is 50 per cent.[59]

The worsening condition of India's economy means that it is not only families with no male breadwinner who have financial problems. 'Conventional' middle-class families are also finding it impossible to manage on one income. Others need the money for many varied and equally substantial reasons. Leela Das is single, 56, and supports her mother and sick brother. Rupali Sinha is 39, married, and needs a second income to send money to support her parents-in-law. Rohini Kapur is 24, single, and doesn't really need the money, in the sense that her parents would suport her if she gave up her job and lived at home. But she doesn't want their support, she wants to be independent. This raises an important issue. Whilst more than half of the women actually need the money, and even those who are supported by men often find that one income is insufficient to support a family, a lot of the women consciously want economic independence.

Vijaya Ambujam is 42, single and works in management consultancy. 'The major advantage of being a professional woman is that I have personal freedom. I have learnt to value it, and . . . I realise I have it more than others.' Minoti Sharma is 29, married and works in industry. 'I don't have to work for the money, but money *is* independence. Independence is *the* reason I work . . . I can spend without reference to my husband.'

Ambika Roy saw clearly the relationship between economics and freedom of action. She's an under-secretary in her late 20s.

> The advantage of a professional job is economic independence and general independence. Most women are subject to their husbands . . . It's because women are economically dependent and *can't* live apart. They can only leave if they have a job or money. You have to *earn* to get respect and identity.

The experience of work and the motivation for employment of professional women has to be seen within the context of the middle-class woman's position in the family and the traditional ideal of women living a life of secluded domesticity. When a man tries to raise his standard of living above subsistence level, and rises up the class structure, part of the meaning attached to this action is his experience as a lower-class man, subordinate to men of the higher classes. In a class sense, a man's rise up the class structure can be seen as an attempt to increase his power of self-determination, and to reduce his subordination to and dependence on men of the higher classes.

With women of the middle class, the desire for an income can also be seen in this way, but there is an additional factor exclusive to women: their subordination and dependence on men. A major part of women's economic motive to work beyond subsistence level is to achieve independence from men. Half of our women who are not economically dependent on the job at all, work for economic independence. 64 per cent of the entire sample work for this reason, regardless of their actual need for the money.[60] This is important for women because of the association between economic and social independence. Economic power over another person is a powerful weapon of social control;

the dependant usually has to pay for her support in social terms. Economic independence provides the material basis for the professional woman's increased control over her own life.

The material benefits discussed above have an impact on the women's sense of self. In terms of recognised benefits, the vast majority of the women raised at least one issue under this heading, discussing how the job encouraged the growth of self-confidence, enabled them to achieve some kind of self-identity apart from being the daughter or wife of a man, how they could keep in touch with the world, meet other people and avoid a vegetable existence through the job.

Anjana Vishwanatan is 30 and works in the civil service.

> I like to be in the thick of things. It's a personality demand — to assert myself and be aggressive. People don't see or hear you if you don't work and have a place or a job of your own. Merely being a daughter or wife doesn't consume your energy and potential. Work is necessary for your own satisfaction. It gives you the confidence to face people.

Bhavna Kharbanda is an under-secretary of 32: 'I have my own status, I can do things the way I want. I'm at par with men in all fields. I'd like all women to have jobs, it makes them more independent thinking. They can be what they are, not what their husbands are.'

A professional woman is accorded increased social standing; her views are given more weight, and she gets recognition and respect from family and friends. Marie Raj is 54. She's a medical practitioner working for a government department. 'You command equality and respect from the community which you wouldn't otherwise have.' Lalita Jayaraman, a civil servant of 32.

> I married young, and started to work after the children were grown up a bit. My husband gives some respect to my views now. And other people assume I have some depth of knowledge.

Namita Iyengar is 39 and works as an anaesthetist. 'I like doing the job, but I also like the fact that I can be on an equal footing in the house dealing with my husband.'

The benefits of social esteem, self-respect, economic independence and autonomy are shared by both men and women professionals. They are the privileges of class which outweigh the disadvantages of gender.

Gender Privileges over Professional Men

Being a woman in a professional job does have certain advantages that men in the same position do not share. Some client groups prefer women, women are not bound by the same conventions as men, and male colleagues, superiors and subordinates often behave better with women than they do with other men.[61]

Women in business sometimes find that being a woman is an advantage when dealing with clients. Sushila Banerji is an engineering manager of 39.

With clients it's an advantage being a woman! I can get more out of them — easier terms than men can achieve. Is it because women are still a novelty? Or because they think I won't bluff or cheat?

Sheela Sarvaria is 29 and works in industry. 'Many people say that women are more dependable than men.' This applies in government service too. Bharati Kapoor is a civil servant of 31.

The public accepts women in India. Many women are working now in many professions. Opinions are changing. I used to feel people hesitated to come because I was a woman. But I don't now. They realise they may get a more serious hearing from a woman.

Women clients in particular are pleased to be able to deal with another woman. Kapila Ahuja: 'Clients prefer women especially in the field as district officers. They're more independent and objective. Women used to come out even in purdah to get an audience.' The same response occurs in medicine, according to Parvati Sahni: 'Once a patient has been to a woman doctor, they won't go to anyone else. The attention is far superior.' Sarah Gonsalves, a doctor of 27, pointed out: 'In obstetrics and gynaecology, women do want women doctors.'

It's not just that the professionals themselves think that the attention they give to clients is superior, more objective and independent than men's. There are solid reasons for it, arising from women's specific structural and cultural position. Kalpana Kunnur, a 43-year-old civil servant, explains.

Clients like the fact that I'm a woman. Men are aloof, less understanding, women are more patient, more conscientious. They try to find a solution, because of having to show results.

And those women whose primary reason for working in a paid job is not financial can have a different approach to the work than most men. Gita Ralhan, 38 and in the civil service:

As a woman choosing to work, I'm working not to earn a living, but to achieve something. A man who works has to earn. Women who come into these careers have a slight edge over the average man, because she opts to make a contribution.

Many women find that they can behave in ways that their male colleagues could not. This expresses itself in a number of different ways. Moyna Ghosh is a professor of 54.

I've been able to get away with more, I could be more impertinent because I'm a woman . . . Men are more willing to compromise. Compromise equals promotion. I value my independence more than increased status. But also I'm better known *because* I'm a woman, and because I don't compromise. My behaviour is motivated by non-dependence on a salary, but men as breadwinners think they have to conform. Women can take a stand, because they're less concerned with ambition.

Women can be more independent politically. Aruna Sharma: 'Women are less subject to political pressures because they're not financially dependent on working.' And they can be more honest. Komal Khanna, a civil servant of 54:

> When clients see a woman, they know there won't be any 'hanky panky'. Women are more honest. They have no financial pressure to make money corruptly and they're not interested in internal politics.

The freedom women experience to act in unconventional ways compared with men is partly a result of the different cultural expectations of women, and partly a result of women's different structural position in the labour market. Women are not expected to perform as well as men in professional jobs,[62] so they often find they have to put more effort into the work to prove that they are competent. In terms of women's position in the labour market, 37 per cent of our women are not economically dependent on the job.[63] They have income from other sources, usually father or husband, and therefore more freedom to be independent, conscientious, honest and risk-taking in the face of political, economic or social pressures. The same advantage applies to men whose wives have jobs. Moyna Ghosh again: 'My work has given my husband the freedom to give up his job when he was dissatisfied with it, and I can earn the money', which suggests that men in this position can also behave unconventionally and take risks.

The other advantage that women have over men in the same class position is that they are often treated better by the men with whom they come into contact. Uma Sudha, a 49-year-old manager:

> If anything, everyone is more helpful and cooperative if you're a woman. It's a terrific advantage . . . Men are very officious with each other, but not with me.

And women are protected from unpleasant aspects of work. Reva Sabhorwal, 23 and in management.

> People are more polite. We're taken care of because there are only four women in this export company, and we're not given dirty work in industrial towns. Colleagues are more polite, they don't criticise so much or push. They help more and they're chivalrous.

Asha Paul, 31, a civil servant:

> Women do get easier jobs . . . Women don't have to work as hard. They're treated favourably to some extent. We're a minority, still a novelty. People think, if she does *anything* then it's good. There's more publicity for the work a woman does. Colleagues don't look upon you with such rivalry. Superiors are very considerate — more so than to men.

Male superiors are more circumspect in their criticism, as Sumitra Kaushik discovered.

> Attitudes vary from company to company, but here I've had nothing but respect. If it were a man in my place he would be at a disadvantage because they'd tell him

off. They won't fight with me if they disagree because of age old chivalry.

Kalpana Kunnur was concerned that men's reactions to women are unpredictable, sometimes treating them worse, sometimes better than men.

If you do the same things as a man, arrive late for instance, you get more criticised. But the opposite is also true. People can be nicer to you . . . The traditional male attitude is not to shout at women.

Not having to do unpleasant work and being treated with more respect are certainly advantages, but at times they can be double-edged. Not being regarded as a rival may mean that a woman's work is not taken seriously. Thinking that *anything* a woman does is good may mean that nothing is expected. Chivalry can be used to devalue a woman's achievements, as Ambika Roy found.

Women have to work harder than men to get the same recognition, because men belittle women's successes . . . They tend not to recognise your merit. For example, I mentioned a very good woman and they all said, 'Oh, anyone would say that of a woman, it would be unchivalrous not to.'

For women, both success and failure can be attributed to femaleness. Kamla Tandon, a 26-year-old doctor: 'If you make a little mistake, they say, it's because she's a woman, but for men, they don't say, it's because he's a man.' Vimla Gupta: 'My colleages are jealous of women. They never attribute promotion to your work. It's always because you're a woman, through a personal contact you've made because you're a woman.' So the advantages of gender can sometimes be turned round and used against women. The gender-based explanation has the cunning effect of undermining even a woman's successes, degrading her sexually, and perpetuating the idea that femaleness is a liability. But equally, the preference of some client groups for women, the tendency for men to behave better in women's presence, and women's freedom to behave unconventionally, can all be used by women to improve their work conditions.

Gender Discrimination

Discrimination against women is found in every area of work that we examined: medicine, education, government service, and manufacturing and service industry. Two-thirds of our women believed that women had to work harder to receive the same recognition and reward. Significantly, over half of those who believed that there was no such discrimination at work were either unmarried women or worked in areas where there was no competition with men, such as gynaecology.[64] Many of the women had experienced discrimination themselves, and we want to look at some examples of the specific form of discrimination in each profession. The examples are illustrative of a wider pattern.

Teaching is one of the most acceptable jobs for women, especially since it is possible, as in medicine, to work only with women, in girls' schools and colleges. Their acceptability is significant, since both professions represent an extension of women's domestic nurturing roles. But there is job segregation even within subject areas. We have seen in the previous chapter how women students are steered into women's subjects. It is not surprising then that few women teach science, maths or engineering at university level. Only five out of our 30 lecturers taught these subjects. The rest were in the 'female' subjects of arts, social science and humanities.

Sridevi Choudhury lectures at the university, is 56, and has been teaching since her early twenties. At the age of 35 she got her PhD from the USA. She was therefore more privileged and more highly qualified than most of her male colleagues, but she still experienced problems.

Have I experienced discrimination? Very much so, especially in the USA. I have a file full of job applications where I was refused purely because I'm a woman. In the US and in India. Jobs, promotion, everything. Even now jobs for women are treated as a part-time thing. Equal promotion? No! The unwritten rule is: no women . . . But only the most candid people will admit it. In my present job I was prevented for years from being reader for that specific reason. It takes you all your life to prove you're good enough, and then you're too old.

For Moyna Ghosh the problems only began when she started getting more highly qualified than the men. She had no difficulty getting a job: the discrimination came later.

At Law School, it was a great help to get first or second place in the exams, because those people were absorbed into the faculty. I did that, then I went to do my PhD at Cambridge. Initially there were no problems. I took leave from the faculty to do my PhD. I extended my leave to 4 years so that I could complete it before coming back, but before I returned to India with my PhD, the faculty terminated my employment. I had to apply again for my job.

The Vice Chancellor said he was pleased to have me back but the new Dean, he was very orthodox, and he specially put on the selection committee a judge known for his bias against women. I was kept waiting two months for an interview. They gave me a very hard time, but I still got the job. I was reckless!

The Dean was against other women because of me. *They* didn't get on because *I* was so independent. For many years the Dean overtly objected to women because 'This one has caused me so much trouble'.

It took me a long time to get the Readership and then the Chair (professorship). I had to have three interviews, even though I had been appointed as Dean. (That's *why* I was held back) . . .

My colleagues have accepted me as an equal. In fact I was offered the Deanship, but I refused it and my colleagues were upset . . . But after I'd been offered it, the Vice Chancellor announced in the newspaper that I'd been made Dean on a purely temporary basis. This never happened with men. So I refused it. The assumption is that everybody is *desperate* to become Dean. He had a very discourteous attitude towards me because of this assumption.

Moyna Ghosh's uncompromising approach is shared by others in higher education. Sunanda Rao, for instance. She studied at an oriental university for four years, before getting her present job. She's 54:

> I've never been subjected to discrimination. Wherever I've tried I've got the job, although I've tried for very few jobs. But if *I* had to face discrimination, I would have made such a row, everyone would know about it. My case is exceptional. There is much discrimination in general. Even if women work harder, they can't get the same recognition. Constitutionally, yes, but actually, no. Sometimes difficulties are made, for instance with Professor Ghosh. In our department there are injustices, but I'm not sure if they're on the grounds of sex. In the University it's difficult to pin down, but in factories and the public field, there's a very great deal of discrimination. The influence on me of China is very great. There's no discrimination there generally. There are women factory heads even.

In medicine there is a fairly high degree of job segregation. Many women go into gynaecology and obstetrics, which has its advantages, both for practitioners and patients. No gynaecologists in Delhi are men, so women in this specialism can work without being barred from the top posts. Many women go into paediatrics since it is concerned with children's diseases, but there are few women surgeons, neurologists or cardiologists.

Anaesthesia was formerly a male preserve, but a few women are now entering it, such as Namita Iyengar. 'Patients used to think that women couldn't be anaesthetists. Now they're getting used to it. I was the first woman anaesthetist in Kashmir, and I've encouraged other women to do it.' Jasminder Surjeet at 47 is a senior surgeon, but was nearly held back at the very start.

> There was discrimination all through. At postgraduate level I passed first time. I was later told by my tutor that one of the examiners said, 'Don't let a girl pass at the first sitting'. I was the one girl in 13 boys and I always had to work harder than them.

Other areas of job segregation are the non-clinical jobs, because women can work from 9 to 5 in them and do not have to be on call. These areas include pathology, bacteriology, radiology and dispensary work. These jobs allow women to do domestic work on top of their paid work, but they are often unhappy in them if they have chosen them for that reason. Shantha Menon is 41.

> I specialised in gynae, then I took up a non-clinical subject because it's less time-consuming. To begin with I was unhappy through not having contact with the patient directly. Now I don't mind. It's just a job now, not a career. It was difficult making the adjustment from clinical to non-clinical. I enjoy the sense of responsibility but there's no intrinsic satisfaction. I work because I get paid for it.
> . . . Clinical work is challenging . . . It was a choice between marriage and a challenging job. It was my conscious decision — I could have refused to marry. But the monotony is very dissatisfying. Non-clinical work is boring.

Even in areas where women are to be found in greater numbers, discrimination occurs. Mohini Sharma is a 38-year-old radiologist.

My appointment letters have been withheld several times on account of pressure from a higher authority, and a job as Medical Officer at Ranikhet was refused me because I'm a woman. A Registrar, that is, a person with only two years experience, has been promoted to a specialist post here, while no such promotion has been given to me despite having more experience and qualifications.

In government service, the main problem for women is that they tend to be assigned to desk jobs within the secretariat. Superiors are reluctant to give women district jobs with sole charge of a subdivision. But without having done the districts, promotion is limited. Gita Ralhan is a deputy secretary in the civil service.

I wanted to do something active and with authority, so I wanted to work in the districts, not desk work. The districts are a round-the-clock headache but I love it. In Uttar Pradesh (my state) they tend to keep women in secretariat jobs, when I particularly wanted a field job for job satisfaction and career prospects. Without certain experience, your promotion is hindered. For instance, you can't get to be joint secretary if you haven't done the districts. So I had to keep asking for a district job. It took longer to get than a man — 5 years longer. Objectively promotion is the same, but . . . from above and below, you have to prove yourself better than a man. When I was a young Joint Magistrate, the district judge said 'Even though she's a woman, she writes good judgements'!

Kalpana Kunnur, at 43, is at one of the highest levels of government so far reached by any woman. When asked if she had ever experienced discrimination, she was unequivocal:

Plenty. I always wanted to be the District Collector. All the men went in turn. They never gave me a chance to go. I asked, they said I could go for a month. I pleaded for a long-term vacancy. I went to the Governor of the state and finally got it. They weren't sure how a woman would cope. I also pleaded *not* to be sent to HQ — I wanted to be independent of them. But they didn't allow it . . . Promotion has not been strictly done in the past. It's been done unfairly. But it's not just promotion. You can take them to court for that. It's the 'plum jobs'. They're decided on discretion not seniority. Women don't get them.

Some women are developing a militant approach to such discrimination. Lakshmi Mitra, for instance, is a deputy commissioner.

Discrimination is on a continuum of degree and kind between different assignments. It's very male dominated. There's a basic reserve in bosses' minds — can she deliver the goods? Queries wouldn't arise if it were a man . . . Things are changing, though. Every year more women join the Indian Administrative Service, the male chauvinist pigs are realising they have to put up with women. On assignments so far they always said, 'She won't be able to do it', but I've always proved I could.

It is in the area of management that the most widespread discrimination occurs against women. Many companies, both Indian organisations and foreign multinationals, reject women regardless of suitability, experience or qualifications. Some companies are quite explicit about their 'no women' policy, including American and British multinationals, who would not be so overt at home. Many of the foreign banks are known not to accept women above a certain level. ICI have refused women for management jobs, and IBM specifically exclude women from engineering. In terms of women's employment, the multinationals are far from being progressive representatives of Western individualism.

Job segregation occurs in specific areas such as operations research and engineering. In engineering, some companies will not take women for jobs in marketing, sales, project work and on-site jobs. Women are not welcome in marketing in general, supposedly because travelling is involved. Even in personnel, women are not trusted in labour relations and dealing with workers. Women's jobs are regarded as temporary and part time. It's assumed they will marry and leave. Women emerging from college with postgraduate degrees in management (MBAs) find themselves at a disadvantage in getting jobs. Ruchira Jang was offered a job by a leading business house, following their policy of offering places to the top two students out of 120 on the MBA. When they realised that one of these students was a woman, they withdrew their offer and changed the company policy. Ruchira is now a successful consultant.

Companies impose conditions that women can't fulfil (such as mobility), refuse to send their women employees on outside training courses or abroad, and sometimes pay them less than men. The doctors, lecturers and civil servants all received equal pay, but 12 per cent of the managers did not. Promotion is generally agreed to be equal up to the lower levels of management, in those companies which take women at all, but at higher levels women are considered unsuitable. These are just a few of the women's stories. The experiences are very common.

Shashi Misra, a 29-year-old junior manager with a state-owned engineering company:

There's plenty of discrimination. One: after BA and before I did my MBA, I applied for a job with a very large company as a management trainee. I had 7 or 8 interviews, including one with the directors. I got through all the interviews and satisfied everyone, then they offered me a *lower type* of job than the one I'd applied for. I asked why. They said, 'Because it's not our policy to offer these jobs to women'. Two: at MBA time we had campus interviews. Many firms, including international ones, refused to interview me because I was a woman, even though I had higher marks than many of the men they did interview. Considerably fewer interviews were offered to me than to the boys. Promotion isn't equal either. I appeared for interviews here recently and they asked me many irrelevant questions not related to the job. A woman has to prove herself *more* capable than a man.

Rohini Kapur, at 24 an assistant personnel manager in the public sector:

Discrimination is so much part of the system, it's difficult to do anything about it. One very large company in North India has an unwritten rule that no women are allowed in executive jobs. At another very large company, I was told they would not take any women, and I should come back in two years time when maybe they would. EPI (Engineering Projects India Ltd) is unique in encouraging women. Promotion to lower levels is equal, but not higher. I have to prove myself all the time. Sometimes my boss says 'Don't send her there because she's a woman.' I argue about this. I'm not allowed to deal with the apprentices in Cawnpore, even though I deal with them here.

Finally Vimla Gupta, whom we met in the last chapter as a young widow, embarking on her career at the age of 33 in the lowest-paid executive job in line management. She is now, 20 years later, chief marketing manager of one of the largest and most powerful state-owned organisations in India.

Women have to work harder, and be better, just to be treated equally. Two of my colleagues in import and export, who were involved in tens of millions of rupees *loss* were promoted. My record is tens of millions of rupees *profit* — but I was not promoted.

My superiors — it depends on my attitude. I am the leader of the officers' trade union. I gave them a lot of trouble with the pay award. We had a go slow for 3 months and won. They will never forgive me. I've been aware of the problem for women throughout work, but mainly in the last few years, since I became number one, Chief of Division. They gave me the division, but not equal pay, and not officially. They made me the Division Manager, but without the title or equal pay until I proved myself.

Apart from direct discrimination in employment, women experience certain other disadvantages which indirectly affect their position at work. These are the problems of physical mobility and social interaction. They are both specific to India in the way they affect women's employment.

Physical Mobility

Women are less mobile than men, they can't travel so easily, they can't go out at night, they can't stay away from home, or go on tour, take fieldwork trips or work on-site in the way that men take for granted. The restrictions on moving around adversely affect women's ability to do their work in most of the professions. Anita Shukla is 30 and works in the civil service.

Some superiors have an overprotective attitude towards women. For instance, if you're the magistrate, the district magistrate will tell you not to go out at night. Colleagues do it too sometimes, but they're less protective because there's an element of competition.

It is easy to see who will fall behind in the competition if a woman magistrate cannot go out at night to solve a problem. Alternatively, women may have to suffer the indignity of being chaperoned. Riti Burman is a 25-year-old junior executive in a large public sector engineering firm.

The boss won't give women mobile jobs. We can't get around as easily as men. I like on-site jobs best, creative research work out in the sun on-site. If a man is given a job on-site, he'd go alone. If I'm given one, I prefer to go alone but they always send someone with me.

If women cannot travel alone, it is not surprising if some firms will not take them for on-site jobs. But the ignominy does not stop here. Ragini Nanda is a lecturer. She is a married woman of 41, but she is not considered able to look after a group of students: 'When I want to take students on fieldwork, the committee says I cannot go alone. I must go with someone who can look after the party properly. I can only be a helping hand.' The restrictions on travelling do not only affect women's ability to do the job, but the resulting appearance of women's incompetence is used to bar them from certain courses and professions. Let us now examine why it is that women may not travel freely.

Four main reasons were put forward by the women in an attempt to find some meaning to their restricted mobility: lack of facilities, the call of household duties, lack of safety and a notion of morality. The problem of women's restricted mobility is expressed at its most concrete level in the lack of facilities for women in public places away from home. Arrangements are made for male visitors — sanitary facilities, a safe place to sleep — but rarely for women. This is a good reason for women not wanting to travel, but the lack of facilities itself needs explanation.

The women also see domestic duties as a problem. It is not just that they are worried about getting behind with the domestic work. Their mobility is actively constrained by the men. Indrani Vijayalakshmi, a civil servant of 41: 'Women can't do tours and my husband wouldn't allow it. I avoid jobs requiring my presence out of the city.' Sarla Kaul is 25, a design engineer in the public sector: 'If I go on tour, my husband will have problems because we live in a nuclear family, and there's no one else to do the housework. So I try *not* to go, which adversely affects my career.' Because of a woman's position in the family as household worker and organiser, the household ceases to function in her absence, and the men suffer. The material benefit that men receive from women's restricted mobility helps to explain their attempts to control women's presence in the house.

The third reason is that it is often unsafe for women to travel around. Bhavna Kharbanda is a civil servant:

I often have to stay late at night in the office. Women shouldn't do that — how to get home at night? Lack of mobility is a problem for women. They can't move around as easily as men, it's not safe to drive or take a taxi at night.

And Sushila Banerji: 'You get uncomfortable feelings in India, although it's basically a safe country. But it's difficult to travel.'

What does it mean, this lack of personal safety for women? It means, of course, not being safe from the unwanted attentions of men. India *is* 'basically a safe country' for men. But not, like most other countries of the world, for women. For the same reason that Kiran Singhal could not go to school in her own state, these women are apprehensive about travelling alone, about staying away from home overnight, about meeting strange men, because they fear sexual assault. The problem may no longer be expressed as clearly as in Kiran's story, where all the females in the state, no matter how young, went in fear of one powerful man. But this is still the underlying theme. Of course, most men are not attackers, but actual assault does not have to occur very often to keep the pressure on women. As long as the threat is there they will restrict their activities. The threat is one of the most effective mechanisms by which men can control women's sexuality, encouraging them to restrict their own movements and to confine themselves to the home.

And finally there is the notion of a moral prohibition. Veena Goyal is 25 and works in financial management:

> Women aren't suitable for marketing because they have to travel, so I chose an office job in finance in a housing company. The touring aspect is the most satisfying part of the job; when you see work being executed and people living in the houses. But mobility's a great hindrance for women. For instance, on tour they don't see women's motive as work, only immorality.

Some women refuse to be bound by the physical or moral prohibition on women's mobility, but are still aware of it, and its consequences. Uma Sudha, 49, is a marketing manager.

> Sometimes men have an advantage when things have to be done out of normal hours, working at night and so on. I don't want anyone to be able to score over me so I make sure I'm equally mobile. If you're not mobile they take advantage. There's a latent idea in men's minds of the things women shouldn't do. You're always aware of it.

What connection is there between women being *unable* to travel about freely for practical reasons, such as lack of safety, no facilities, being responsible for the household, and the idea that women *shouldn't* travel? The idea of what women should and shouldn't do is the embodiment of what actually happens in practice but in more abstract form, simply reflecting the reality in the form of a moral prescription. But it has an additional component, for its very abstractness enables a neat trick to be played, in the form of a complete reversal of reality: although it is men who threaten women with sexual assault if they stray too far from home, it is the women who are accused of sexual immorality, not the men. The idea of immorality justifies the sexual control by men over women, and the idea is used by men to persuade the women that it is *their own fault* that they are subjected to this harassment.

Social Interaction

A similar process occurs with the problem of social interaction. Women have to walk a narrow path between being forced to mix with men at work, but being unable to mix freely. The problem has all sorts of repercussions on women's work, particularly affecting their access to information. Indira Mamtani is a director in one of the ministries: 'Socialising is a handicap for women. Colleagues are not so free with me. It affects work because there's no opportunity for informal discussion.' Kamla Tandon works in paediatrics 'You always feel men become more advantaged. Most of the teachers in medicine are men, so male students can approach them better'.

A consequence of this is that women can't (and don't want to) cultivate a relationship with their superiors, as men do, which can affect how they are assessed. Kaveri Goswani is 50 and works in the civil service:

> Men can try to please their seniors, while women have reservations. So men get better reports. It affects your professional chances. Men can make themselves liked: going round to his house, doing things for him. Women can't have these personal contacts. Inequality has nothing to do with women's objective work, it's because of prejudice against women.

And because there are so few women, and the women who are there cannot talk with the men, the women's position is an isolated one. Shaleen Wahi is 29 and works for an engineering firm: 'There are so few women in engineering. No one will help. You must rely on yourself.' Shikha Munshi is a lecturer of 43: 'The problem is that there is no group with whom I can have a dialogue. I have to work on my own. I can't get any feedback.'

The narrow path that women must tread in their dealings with men affects their work. But if they ignore the path and try to behave in a more natural way, as men do with men, then the ill effects impinge, not on their work, but directly on themselves — on their characters and reputations. Rohini Kapur, a young personnel manager:

> For women, a close relationship with the boss is difficult because friendliness is seen as cheapness . . . There's a lot of gossip about women. You can't be free with males. It's taken for granted that any woman taking a professional job is brash and aggressive. They also talk about me living on my own. Attitudes have not changed. I used to feel very bad because of the horrible things people would say about me and my future husband. I've cried many hours to my parents. Now I don't take any notice. I get support from my parents and my fiance. It would be okay if we were living with my parents because people would think it was a temporary arrangement until we got married. But because I'm living on my own, people think there is some other motive for it, and gossip.

This is not an isolated occurrence. Many women experience the same thing. Some, especially the older ones, are angry about it. Mohini Sharma is a radiologist of 38:

> At the last hospital I worked at, a lot of discrimination and disrespect came my way only because I was a woman. At times even the subordinate staff were instructed to disobey and misbehave by the then Assistant Medical Director and Director. Here, colleagues are jealous, they have an attitude of letting women down, and fooling around. Some superiors are very good, others are definitely mean and indecent. I dislike the way girls are talked about behind their backs. People don't talk nicely about working women, especially relatives. They're jealous. It makes me feel bad. And men don't want to be bossed around by women, so they talk filth about you.

Both these women are unmarried. Some women feel that being married modifies the hostility of their reception into professional life. Lotika Choudhury is 27 and works in sales and marketing:

> The attitudes of men at work towards me depends on the kind of person. If he's from a similar background to me, there's no problem, but there is with the more orthodox men. The way I dress is important, for instance if I wear trousers at a meeting, I'm not taken seriously. Clients may accept or reject proposals because I'm a 'pretty woman'. Occasionally men get ideas — they think I'm a loose woman because I'm a career woman. But it's better because I'm *Mrs* Choudhury.

Married women have at least conformed to the requirements of male domination by placing themselves under the control of a man, legally and ritually, despite their non-conformity in having a profession. In treating a married woman with more respect than a single woman, the men are recognising, not the woman's humanity, but the husband's property rights over her. Unmarried women are a particular target for male slander because their singleness symbolises their independence from men. Separated and divorced women are an even bigger target, as Shikha Munshi found in her teaching post: 'Initially men in the department tried to drive me off, but they had to accept me, so they've learned to live with me. They engage in a lot of political slander and character assassination. Now I have a thicker skin.' But even married women have to be circumspect. Minoti Sharma:

> My superiors always remember I'm a woman. Sometimes I feel slightly insulted, I find myself swallowing certain comments just because I'm a woman, if I dress up for example. You must always be careful to avoid gossip.

The gossip to which professional women are subject is another mechanism whereby men control women's sexuality. It covers all aspects of their lives, from dress to living arrangements. And, as we saw in the discussion on mobility, the moral prescriptions — the ideas of what women should and shouldn't do — justify what happens to women on the ground that it is their own fault. This is what actually happens.

Promilla Khanna, 33, a humanities lecturer:

> Some colleagues are very vulgar. They're brought up sexually repressed, they try to make friends in an objectionable way. The students too sometimes. For instance, when I went on maternity leave, the woman who replaced me was very friendly with the students, and it was misinterpreted by staff and students alike.

And Kalpana Kunnur, 43, a high-ranking civil servant:

> This job in the Women's Section is good for a woman. In other jobs, people are sometimes too familiar. You have to watch out if you're a public person. Or they will be nasty to you if you're not friendly. Many times women have come to me saying they were denied promotion because they haven't made themselves available to their superiors.

Women who refuse to seclude themselves at home as private sexual property may come to be regarded instead as public sexual property, available for any man to degrade or proposition. This is a problem for women in many countries. The particular way in which it is experienced in India is through the constraints on women's physical mobility and social interaction. Although in the West the problem has only recently been named as sexual harassment, India has had a concept for the phenomenon for some considerable time. It is known as eve-teasing.

Eve-teasing occurs even at the highest levels in the professions. The examples indicate that it is a recurring problem for women in all the professions that we examined. It is often associated with positions of male power, but perhaps its most interesting feature is the way in which subordinate men can use the mechanism to exert power over their women superiors, illustrating one of the most powerful ways in which gender privilege can be used to overcome any other system of hierarchy and power.

We have identified a number of problems in this section for women's professional work. Discrimination at selection and in assessment, training and promotion; job segregation; restrictions on physical mobility and on social interaction, and sexual harassment: all of these are problems which men do not have to face in professional life. All combine to disadvantage women even of the professional class compared with men.

19. Family: Women's Domestic Work

Any discussion of the relationship between women's professional and domestic work has to be placed within the context of the different forms of family organisation in India. The traditional North Indian joint family is composed of a group of patrilineally related males having equal rights to property, sharing a common budget, residence and hearth.[65] In a joint family there is segregation of sexes and a general subordination of woman to man; woman's life is characterised by self-control, reserve, modesty and respect for the female hierarchy.[66]

There is some dispute over how far the structure of the family has been affected by urbanisation. The general view is that the migration of young educated males from the villages to take employment in the cities has begun to erode the traditional joint family structure. However, many of the resulting nuclear families (husband, wife and children) subsequently became joint families, with married sons, daughters-in-law and their children staying together. Studies on kinship, urbanisation and family change have provided evidence that joint family living is still largely conformed to even in the urban areas.[67] Other studies have suggested that the prevalence of the large joint family has been overestimated, both in the rural areas, where it was supposed to be most in evidence, and in pre-British India, when it was supposed to be the norm.[68]

Family structure varies in different regions of the country. For instance, amongst the matrilineal Nayars, even those who do not live in traditional taravads but who marry and live with their husbands, have not adopted the patriarchal joint family structure of north India.[69] Family structure also varies with time, the particular composition of the family changing with the development of its members, so it is important to look at family composition as a stage in the developmental life cycle, rather than using a static approach.[70]

A further complication is definition. Kuntesh Gupta points out that there is no agreement between researchers over which form is dominant in India, how many types of family there are, or what criteria should be used to differentiate them.[71] Many of our women found it difficult to define their family organisation if it did not fit into the two or three major types. For this reason we have extended the categories in this discussion on family structure to include alternative family forms.

Amongst our women, 60 per cent were living in nuclear families (as either daughters or wives) and 19 per cent were living in joint families (as daughters or daughters-in-law). The remaining 21 per cent were living alone, with another relative, as single-parent families, or had parents or parents-in-law living with them.[72] None of the women lived with women friends. A third of the women had lived in different forms of family structure at other times of their lives. For instance, all the 21 per cent living in other than joint or nuclear families, had previously lived in different forms of family organisation, and 10 per cent of those living in conjugal nuclear families (that is, as wives) had either lived in joint families until the parents-in-law had died, or had strong ties with the joint family and hoped one day to return. About two-thirds had come from another state to Delhi for employment,[73] and a large number were in transferable jobs or their husbands were in transferable jobs. Geographical mobility affects joint family living so that a family may only live together for limited periods, but still identifies itself as joint.

Because of these effects, the dominance of nuclear families in our sample should not be taken to mean the adoption of a Western model of family organisation by women of the professional class. As Veena Das argues, the Western nuclear family has its own problems, isolating and circumscribing a woman's world in a unique way and curtailing her influence on public affairs to a far greater extent than is true of the traditional joint family.[74] Aileen Ross reports that young modern women desire separate homes more than men do, for this enables them to become independent from their mothers-in-law.[75] Our study suggests that it is this rejection of the female authority structure rather than the imitation of a Western model which prompts women of the professional class to form nuclear families. The move to a nuclear family is not the only way to achieve this, nor is it necessarily the most effective. Other methods, as we shall see, involve changes in the authority structure within the joint family itself.

Women's Work in the Joint Family

When we are looking at women's position in the traditional, patriarchal joint family, we have to distinguish between the natal family (into which they were born) and the conjugal family (into which they are married). The primary relationship of a man is with his father, and of a married woman, her mother-in-law, not her husband.[76] As Kalpana Kunnur points out, 'You don't just marry the man, you marry the family.'

The new wife has to adapt to the existing organisation of the household and, within a traditional joint family, has little power to demand reciprocal adjustments from the family. So the woman's work in a conjugal joint family involves the obligations of a wife, a daughter-in-law and a mother. This includes bringing up the children, looking after the husband, being responsible for all the domestic work such as shopping, cooking, cleaning, washing, under the supervision of the mother-in-law, and caring for any old people in the household, preparation for and organisation of rituals and festivals, and social obligations such as looking after guests, paying social visits and attending social functions.[77] Even when a woman is working full time in a job she is still expected to do all the housework. Kamla Tandon is a newly married doctor: 'In marriage women do the housework whether they're working outside or not. Relatives and husbands expect working women to do the same as women with no paid work.'

Sometimes the mother-in-law is unable to help with the work. Neera Atreyi is 43, her mother-in-law is in her eighties.

> The joint family has no effect on my work. I had to adjust to it according to need. It was an added responsibility. I had to work harder, be more tolerant and make sacrifices. I was and am expected to look after my husband, the children and the older dependants. I had lots of difficulties after graduation. I got married, my husband is in government and we had to move about. But with hard work I maintained work and family. Now my first aim is for my children to be educated. My future is secondary now . . .
>
> But this one thing dissatisfies me: the family/job conflict. There's not enough time for the family. At times I'm desperate that I can't satisfy the old people and the children when they need me; my mother-in-law feels neglected.

Apart from the practical difficulty of having too much to do, the other problem is that in the more orthodox families, they may not be free to organise the work as they wish. Minoti Sharma works in a large public sector company. She is 29, her father-in-law is 64 and her mother-in-law 45. Her parents-in-law benefit financially from her employment, but still exert greater authority in the household.

> My husband's family had traditional attitudes at first, but now due to the increased economic benefits, they've accepted my work and they're much happier. I live in a joint family. The joint family hinders my work very much. It's *absolutely horrible*. Everyone likes a home of their own. Now I have to take instructions from my parents-in-law. I resent this strongly.

Husbands do not participate in any of the duties. The sexual division of labour is particularly reinforced in the joint family by the cultural traditions and the authority structure. Padma Unnikrishnan married late and had her first child at 47. She prefers the joint family because her son is looked after, but:

> I have no time to do both things . . . I want to read research work for some hours, but I can't leave the house for the library when I'm not at work because of the dual role. This is men's advantage. They can devote more time to work and do better. I feel it's unfair. It's an advantage also for unmarried women. From childhood women are psychologically trained to be housewives and not to leave the house. Women have more patience so they do the house job better. Men can't do it. You have to change and adjust throughout life. I'm different with my in-laws. Even if you're older, like I was, when you get married, they are still older and you have to help them and do what they say to some extent. Women have to make adjustments. If people feel satisfied with changes, it's okay, but if people don't want to change it creates conflict. If you want a peaceful life, *you* have to change.

Shashi Misra is 29 and works in management. She lives in a joint family with her 90-year-old father-in-law and her mother-in-law of 70. She prefers the joint family for the same reason as Padma but there are problems.

> The joint family helps because the child can be looked after. In the nuclear family I would have *had* to give up. But there are also problems of looking after the family — the obligations of a wife and daughter-in-law. Work sharing in the family is very uncommon, especially in the joint family. Even if the man is willing to help, he is prevented by other members of the family. Men are ridiculed for domestic work. It's unfair, but part of the culture.

Interestingly, young single women living in their natal joint families (or indeed in nuclear families), experience none of these problems. In fact their mothers are often very encouraging and carry out all the household work themselves. Jaya Misra, 22, is a lecturer in arts.

> I'm the youngest in the family. They felt that I should carry on a profession, not marriage. The joint family helps greatly. I was always pampered. I have no domestic duties. When I have any problems, everyone can help.

Women like Jaya are the only ones whose position at home and work can be compared with that of men. However, when these women enter a conjugal joint family at marriage, they often experience the greatest problems with household chores. Traditionally a young daughter-in-law came into the husband's house in a subordinate position, with the mother-in-law having complete control over her.[78] Today, not only is a daughter-in-law older, but she has more self-confidence, knowledge and experience, and no longer requires the mother-in-law's guidance and advice. This challenge to the mother-in-law's supreme position as adviser and source of knowledge can lead to friction, and hostility to the daughter-in-law's employment. This accounts for some of the married women's certainty, also reported in other studies,[79] that they would not like to live in a joint family. Aruna Sharma: 'In the joint family you can't arrange your own affairs between husband and wife. You have to do what the in-laws say or get nagged.' But in the nuclear family a woman still has to do the housework, care for the husband and attend to the children. As we shall see, the nuclear family solves some problems but creates others.

There is some evidence amongst our women that far from disintegrating in the urban areas, the joint family is adapting to changed circumstances. One of the biggest changes is the increase in women's employment amongst the middle class, which causes domestic problems because of women's responsibility for the household. One of the major ways in which our professional women solve the problem is by living in a joint family that differs from the traditional form in one important respect: the authority structure of the female hierarchy has broken down to a considerable extent. Manjari Seth is a management consultant at 29:

> I live in a joint family. Sometimes my mother gets frustrated because I don't spend enough time with the children. I feel this too, but my husband's family don't. They always encourage me to work. My mother-in-law is mine and the children's 'mother'. It's a very big help.

Kasturi Verma is 50, an additional director in the civil service. She compares the joint family favourably with the nuclear families of the West.

> Family life is always a problem, except where it's one person in a single unit. The joint family definitely helps. In the West you're always worrying about the children, how to go out and so on. Here you can offload some of the responsibilities onto the in-laws. You lose some control of the household, but there are definite advantages and it gives the mother-in-law a place in the household.

Traditionally of course, the mother-in-law's place in the household would have been a powerful one. But this has changed in the 'new' joint families. Many treat their sons' wives as their own daughters, and seem to have adjusted to the daughter-in-law's needs. This is contrary to the stereotype of the mother-in-law/daughter-in-law relationship which is one of tension and conflict, as well as dominance and subordination.[80] In these families, women's solidarity helps both women. As Vimla Gupta observed, 'Joint families are coming back for economic reasons, but now on a more communal basis that's less autocratic.' Another way in which the change in authority structure has come about, also noted by Aileen Ross amongst her respondents,[81] is through the younger married couple inviting their parents or in-laws to come and live with them, rather than the new wife going to live at her parents-in-law's house. Although this arrangement looks the same as the traditional joint family on the surface, it clearly entails a dilution of parental authority over the younger couple. Other unconventional living arrangements have been organised by the women. Kalpana Kunnur:

> I was lucky, my mother lived with us for 10 years and helped with the children. It was unusual, it was because my father was dead. People don't like to go and live with their daughter, it hurts their dignity and pride. Widows are supposed to go to their sons. I had a lot of criticism because my mother lived with me.

Deepti Parukutty did the same thing, but being a Nayar from Kerala, she received no social censure for having her mother to live with her. Nor did Ruth Jacob, whose own parents continue to look after her children in Bombay, whilst Ruth and her husband are temporarily posted to Delhi. Ruth is Jewish, so again the constraints of orthodox Hinduism do not apply. Devaki Chakrabarty lives in a nuclear family, but has all the advantages of a joint one, since her in-laws live nearby, and take responsibility for her son if she's ill or away on tour.

The way in which women have solved their domestic problems marks a change from the conventional relationships between women in the patriarchal family, where the authority structure contributed to antagonism between them. In the new joint families the more democratic relationship between the women relieves the younger women from some of the childcare and household responsibilities, and gives the grandmother a 'place in the household', as well as maintaining the strong bonds of affection between grandparents and grandchildren. It is not surprising that some of the single women and some of the married women living in nuclear families saw the advantages of the joint family structure, like Gita Ralhan. Her children are 7 and 1. 'A joint family would have helped. I'd have had fewer domestic problems . . . I need a reliable ayah, servants, I can't get them. I'm managing without and it's affecting my health. It's a very tough job. Domestic responsibilities along with official work is a strain.'

Women's Work in the Nuclear Family

The work women have to do in the nuclear family is the same as the work in the joint family with the exception of taking care of the in-laws. However, this exception also means there are no in-laws to share the work in the house or look after the guests and the children, do the shopping, the washing, the cleaning, the cooking and the rituals. The entire burden of the house falls onto the wife. Sushila Banerji has a daughter of 12. 'I live in a nuclear family. For a working mother the nuclear family is impossible. The joint family encourages and assists working women.' Some women think that their children have suffered. Although Kusum Gupta's mother-in-law lives with her now, she did not do so when the children were younger. Her daughters are 16, 19 and 26.

> The nuclear family means you have liabilities for the children. There have been problems. The children get neglected. One of my daughters hates working women. It's a permanent problem . . . They don't get enough love. The joint family makes it easier because the in-laws can look after the children. Now it's changing to nuclear families and it's harder for women because there are no creches or anything.

Many of them agree on the problems of women's domestic work in the nuclear family. Charu Thakur is 37 and an under-secretary. She has two children of 5 and 3.

> My husband expects me to be first a good housewife, second a good worker. I'm professionally competent but I can't give my whole time to it. I can't go home late. It creates tension and a lack of concentration. My memory has deteriorated because I have too many different things to get hold of. I used to have a fantastic memory. There's pressure from the children's sickness and the demands of my husband. I haven't resolved the husband problem — I just work harder, to resolve the conflict. It's too hard — I'm straining myself. It's my sacrifice and it's taking something out of me.
>
> The money from the job is extra, but it's no comfort to the individual earning it, it just gives greater comfort to the family. Before marriage, I used to work only for working's sake . . . Now I work to avoid confrontation and unpleasantness, for escapism. If I'm not able to give 100% to my husband, I can use work as an excuse and vice versa.
>
> In the morning I'm irritated because there are so many jobs in the house. By the time I come to work I'm absolutely worked up with the physical strain. The advantage of paid work is the financial freedom — I have a say in the management of the house which I wouldn't have otherwise. And escaping confrontation at home.

Charu is forced into giving the minimum of time and attention to her paid work because her husband is generally unsupportive. She is fully aware of the mental stress she is under. Jasminder Surjeet's husband, by contrast, was always supportive of her work, which is the only reason she was able to compete in the male-dominated specialism she chose. She's 47 and has been head of department for 5 years. Her children are 18 and 15.

> We live in a nuclear family. When the children were small it was difficult to carry on, but I managed somehow, I got servants. It's hard work for a mother. Personally I think the joint family helps a lot. The nuclear family is a great hindrance. There's too much strain. What with dual roles and social visits for work. More than half my money goes on the kitchen and running the house. A housewife can cut down, but I can't because I'm not there to do it myself. Moneywise it's not much advantage except that I don't ever need to ask for money from anyone.
>
> I wanted to do more academic work, I've no time to publish like I used to. These days work is routine almost. I can't even read an article in three or four days. The patients keep coming. I'm overworking; I wish I wasn't working. Lately I've had more strain than I could cope with. I have big responsibilities and it's affecting my health. My contemporaries were rising, I wanted to rise too and I have done so but I'm paying the price and I've worried the family.
>
> I won't say you shouldn't marry because I'm happy and content. It's good for patients that I can share the burden with my husband. He shares the housework, does the shopping, takes responsibility and so on. He's a doctor too. There's no conflict between us. But women can't compete in the academic world. Once my husband and I were attending different sessions at conference. The grandparents were staying with the children, but one of us had to go home. I went. I didn't want my husband to feel I was rising more than him. I keep myself back and he knows it.

The strain Jasminder was under was apparent to any observer. She had sacrificed her physical health trying to compete on unequal terms with men.

Living in a nuclear family can be at least as problematic for a professional woman as living in a joint family. There is no evidence that women establish nuclear families in imitation of Western family forms, rather that they wish to extract themselves from the authority structure of the joint family. Other women have achieved the same end by developing more egalitarian relationships between the generations of the joint family.

Women's Work in Alternative Forms of Family Organisation

Women who remain unmarried do not necessarily escape the demands of servicing and caring for other people. Leela Das is 56. Her mother and brother live with her and she supports them financially as well as caring for their needs. She never married, but is a deputy director in the civil service.

> My father was killed at Partition. After that the whole responsibility for the family fell on me . . . I now take responsibility for my mother and my other brother who can't look after himself. I have to look after them. I keep them, this is my house through the job. As I get older and mother gets ill, I wonder whether I

should still go to work. I'm dependent on servants. I'm despondent because of dissatisfaction with these circumstances.

Leela is not the only woman who took responsibility for dependants because she is unmarried. Vijaya Ambujam is also unmarried. She is 42, a manager, and although her parents do not live with her, her relationship with her parents is unusual by traditional standards.

My parents have become more positive about my work, probably because the other children aren't with them . . . I'm the closest one: an emotional prop. They are very dependent on me emotionally. I've replaced their son.

So unmarried daughters, although anomalous (and none of the families liked the fact that their daughters did not marry), still have domestic and emotional responsibilities for their natal families.

Finally Reeta Rao, now living alone since her sons left:

I'm the only person in the department with everything to do at home . . . Men have much more time . . . My sons shared the household jobs; they learnt to because there was no one else.

Reeta Rao's sons are unusual by any standards.

Men's Domestic Work

Most males do not look after themselves or others, they are looked after by women. Satinder Singh has been doing this for 18 years. She's 44 and a manager in a large state-owned company. Her husband's a civil servant and their children are 14 and 11. 'It's a matter of organisation for women. She always has to think of the family. A man . . . doesn't have to compromise. I would like men to take more responsibility on the home front.' In the joint family, the women who have solved the problem of domestic work are those who have achieved a more democratic relationship within the female hierarchy, and negotiated work-sharing arrangements. In the nuclear family, there is no female hierarchy. The only other adult who can share the work is the husband. Husbands benefit financially when their wives go out to work, but few of them reciprocate by sharing the domestic work. It seems that the very thought of domestic work undermines their masculinity.

Indrani Vijayalakshmi is an under-secretary of 41 with two children, 12 and 8.

I have to compromise between family and career. I have to stay late when there are strikes and so on. There are family problems even though my husband is supportive. My husband's not keen on me working because it means I'm away from home for a long time. Now he's reconciled to it . . . Housework should be shared, but men expect working women to do housework as well. They feel inferior and unmanly if they help.

Promilla Khanna, whose husband is one of the men most anxious to share the domestic work, finds there is a problem of knowledge. She's a lecturer of 33.

I'm trying to evolve a new pattern now the child has come. I'm upset and depressed because of this change and conflict . . . It's a physical strain. My husband's enlightened, but there are still certain influences on him, so that the burden of the house falls on *me*. He doesn't know how to do things. He tries to be helpful but it's still my responsibility.

Only five out of 77 women who are or have been married have been able to enlist their husband's help with the domestic work. All five live in nuclear families. For the majority of men, as confirmed in other studies,[82] domestic work does not exist.

Domestic Work and Class

The problem which the nuclear family solves for women is the problem of the female hierarchy, which is, of course, predicated upon the gender hierarchy. That is, the female hierarchy is a means whereby the men delegate control over the women to women themselves, the older ones having authority over the younger ones. It is the female hierarchy which has broken down in the new communal joint families. The sexual division of labour has changed for women, in that women contribute significantly to the family finances, but it has not changed for men, since few men contribute significantly to the domestic labour.

The problem which the disappearance of the female hierarchy creates for women in the nuclear family is that the domestic work becomes the entire responsibility of the sole adult woman in the household. This is the case with most of the women. Few have succeeded in eliciting any domestic labour from their husbands. The way in which the majority of our women solve this problem of gender disadvantage is by using their class privilege. Those who can afford it employ servants to do some or all of the domestic work, as Kapur also shows.[83] But the women's use of class privilege is predicated upon their gender subordination. Because the men do not do their share of domestic work, the only solution for a professional woman in a nuclear family is to buy the domestic labour of lower-class men and women. This arrangement ensures independence from the joint family hierarchy, but not from the class hierarchy, although Kapila Ahuja does not recognise that her dependence on others has only been transferred, not eliminated. Kapila is 50, an additional secretary and commissioner.

I never used my mother or mother-in-law for the children. I refused help, I wanted to be independent. We had good servants and brought the children up ourselves. The nuclear family helps working women. It encourages independence provided there is an understanding between husband and wife.

Paramjit Caroli does recognise her dependence on lower-class women. She's a social science lecturer in her late twenties:

Our ayah is part of the household. Without her, the nuclear family *would* have hindered my career. But the nuclear family is an advantage because I can take my own decisions about our social life rather than having to see in-laws and visitors.

This helps my work. Teaching's a good job for women because it leaves a lot of time for home. When my child was very young I just taught and ran back home. I couldn't do any extra. But I had help. I couldn't have done without my ayah.

Some women recognise not only their dependence on servants, but that the dependence is only possible because of the privileges of their class position. Kalpana Kunnur:

> When I was first married there was pressure from children, relations, guests, in-laws. It's resented if I go to work when guests come. It's difficult to combine. In my job I'm not too badly off, I have a car, I can rush off at the last minute . . . If I were a clerk I'd have to get the bus. We're also dependent on good servants, especially since the emergence of the nuclear family.

The privilege of class is indeed the reason that some of the older women wanted paid jobs. Satinder Singh: 'My parents would have preferred me to get married first. The woman's role as I saw it wasn't enough for me. Everyone had servants. There was nothing to do.'

Things have changed in the last 30 years. The continuing decline of the economy affects the middle class too now, so that middle-class families cannot afford to employ as many servants as they used to. But for professional women who cannot negotiate the assistance of the joint family or the husband in the domestic work, hiring servants is the only solution. In addition, the inhibition of the economy by Western imperialism is the major reason that a large surplus of unemployed 'free' labour exists, as we saw in Part II. Without the domestic work offered by professional women, many working-class men and women would be destitute, since there are few alternative sources of employment. So middle-class women's use of waged labour for housework and childcare is predicated upon both imperialism and male domination. Until imperialism ceases to create chronic poverty, and until men do their share of childcare and domestic work, women of the professional class will continue to exploit their class privilege to cope with their gender subordination.

Paid Work and the Family

The organisation of domestic work adversely affects women's paid work in a way that does not impinge on men. Ambika Roy: 'If the home is well kept, people say she must do nothing at work. If the home is not well kept, they say look what happens when women work.' Far from receiving credit for carrying this enormous domestic burden, women find that it is often used to *dis*credit them. The fact that women *do* all this work, sometimes at great cost to themselves, is barely recognised by families or employers. Within the family women's primary job is regarded as domestic work, regardless of the benefits her paid work might bring. This fact impinges on her paid work and puts her at a disadvantage compared with men. It means she is stressed and overworked. She can't put in overtime on the paid job. She can't move to another part of the country at will for the sake of her job, but she may have to move for her husband's job. It is partly because of these aspects of women's position in the family that women are steered into traditional women's occupations — not because they are more suitable for women, but because they can more easily incorporate women's domestic burdens.

Employers recognise women's domestic work only as a problem for themselves. The male employee constitutes the standard. Women's domestic work prevents them from measuring up to this standard. So female employees are presumed to be less suitable, less stable and less successful than men, as confirmed by other studies.[84] This presumption, as well as her actual position in the family, adversely affects a woman's selection, training, evaluation, promotion and performance in a job. Ragini Nanda, a lecturer of 41: 'Employers think you will give more attention to the family. They think the job is just to pass time. They try to make conditions they wouldn't ask of men, for instance they ask, "Will you stay?" '

The demands on women's time by the family and the demand for their physical presence in the home by the husband, are taken into account by employers only to brand them as poor workers. Bharati Kapoor:

> Some superiors are very anti-women. There's great prejudice. You can even get an unfair assessment. For example, if a man takes leave because his wife is ill it's okay, but if a woman takes leave because her children are ill, she gets complaints. They can't or won't understand the problems.

The organisation of paid work similarly impinges on women's family life. The emphasis may be different but generally the patterns of work organisation are the same for medicine, industry and the civil service. Education is the exception, although it is by no means unproblematic. The problem is that paid work is organised with men in mind. It assumes that employees can put in unlimited amounts of time, that they have other people in the background, at home, to deal with their children and older dependants, and to perform all the necessary domestic work for the employees themselves. It assumes that everyone who lives in the employees' house can be uprooted and move at any time to another part of the country. It assumes that most employees can work full-time hours and will never need to take a break from paid employment. In other words, paid work is organised around men's lives, not women's. The demands of paid work make it very difficult for *men* to have any share in childcare or domestic work. Yet women in paid jobs do all three jobs with little or no assistance from men.

Lecturing is the only profession with flexible hours, regular holidays and no job mobility. For these reasons, many women found teaching a good profession for a woman. But this doesn't mean there are no problems. Nita Madan, a lecturer of 33: 'Academic life makes more demands — less specific demands, like reading and research. It's not a nine to five job. It also requires more pure attention.'

The problem of working hours is probably worst in the medical profession. Hours are long and unsocial, particularly for young doctors. Davinder Gill is 25, recently married, and a senior house surgeon in obstetrics and gynaecology at a private hospital in Delhi.

> We have too much work. I get only every third Sunday off. There's no time for the family. You have to stay away from home, sometimes overnight if you're on night duty. We have very heavy duties. You can't run the home properly. I would like to work only four or five hours a day. I won't leave my job altogether, but I may have a gap in between, when I have children.

Part-time work and fixed hours jobs are available in medicine, but only dedicated doctors get on in hospital work, and jobs with fixed hours are also the least interesting and satisfying. Nina Singh is 41, a paediatrician at a state hospital.

> My husband was very cooperative — unusual for a non-medic. He understood a doctor's problems. Otherwise I would be in the dispensary now, because there are fixed hours. I never wanted that work. I did it for four years when the children were young. It's just like being a clerk.

It is possible to leave work and join up again after a few years in medicine, but seniority would be lost. Maternity leave is available, but many superiors and employers regard it as a nuisance rather than a necessity, as Wadhera also found.[85] Although maternity leave is begrudged, job transfers are less of a problem in medicine. Most posts are tied to one place.

Conditions of employment in government service are normally good. The problems for women in the organisation of the civil service are connected with hours, leave and transferability. Lakshmi Mitra has a small son.

> I *would* like a five-day week. Six days is very tiring. The hours are too long. What is bad is the cumulative physical and mental effects of over work and strain . . . We get no exercise, no annual leave, and it's bad for the family.

Many women would like to take some years off when the children are small, like Ankita Chandra, 38, with children of 12 and 5:

> Lately I want to devote more time to the children. I would never give up my job but I would like leave. Women should have a couple of years off or work part-time . . . We need more flexibility in society, and flexible working hours. There's disruption in the family life when husband and wife are both working . . . I miss seeing my children growing up. If the children are poorer because of me, I will lose all happiness.

But the age bar prevents taking some years out, and then returning. If a woman leaves the service, it's for good. The other major problem is transferable jobs. Indian Administrative Service officers have to move between the capital and their own state (a state of their choice). This can cause difficulties for working women whose husbands are IAS officers, for women IAS officers who are married, and for married couples who are both in the IAS, although the problems of couples have been acknowledged. Husband-and-wife teams are often given postings in the same place, but this doesn't always work out. Bharati Kapoor's children are 2 and 6: 'When my husband was posted to Chandigarh, I stayed in Delhi and we lived separate for a year. I couldn't transfer to Chandigarh because the district boss was very anti-woman — great prejudice.'

In industry, hours of work depend on the kind of job. Renu Deb works in a small printing manufacturers that's run by a woman, with about 75 employees, a job she couldn't do if she were married.

> Now I'm working very hard. It would be very difficult for a married woman to do this job. I'm still working at nights and at weekends regularly. I really enjoy it. I have total control of production, partly also finance and personnel. If I got married I wouldn't be able to keep this kind of interesting job. A man might *have* to keep that sort of job.

It's often difficult to get leave, as Seetha Jayalakshmi found. Seetha is a deputy marketing manager in her late twenties. 'It's dissatisfying when you want leave, and you can't take it. You arrange some holiday, then you're called back for important work. This happens quite often.' But part-time work is available in industry, and it's possible to take a few years off to have children, despite problems of getting back in, and the length of maternity leave — unpaid, of course.

Paid Work and Class

The organisation of paid work around men's lives is based on the assumption that every woman is economically supported by a man. The gender division is built into the structure of paid work at all levels of the occupational hierarchy. Amongst working-class women, the lower rates of pay compared with men assume at best that a woman has no family to support, at worst that her subsistence requirement is lower than men's. Amongst the middle class, the degree of discrimination against women in professional employment suggests that women have less right to paid work than men.

The organisation of paid work further assumes that the men in the family are able to earn enough adequately to support women and children. Even amongst the middle class, many men are no longer able to do this. The decline of the economy, combined with ideas of women's dependence, has led to women being criticised for taking paid work because of men's priority in the labour market, even though at the same time families need women's economic contribution. So women are blamed for a problem created by the organisation of work under imperialism.

The complications of this position are described by Sarabjit Kalia, a trainee manager of 26.

> Men feel it's not necessary for women to work, because many men are out of work. And then you may leave in a few years. Male typists may be supporting an entire family. *Class* keeps many women down. Many people think women shouldn't work.

Parvati Sahni described how the primacy of women's domestic work is used to give priority to men in paid work. 'In our country, with the economic depression, a woman in a job deprives a man who has to support a family, and it's a rationalisation that women can't put in enough work because of their domestic duties.'

The economic problems are forcing middle-class men to change their views on the sexual division of labour. Riti Burman, a young manager: 'Men think women shouldn't work outside the home. But now due to economic tension, even men want women to work because of the money. Things are changing.' Women want to contribute to the national economy too. Lalita Jayaraman: 'If girls are educated, it's a national waste if they don't work, especially in India where there's so much to do.'

Rekha Rohtagi is 50. She works as a lecturer. She was born 20 years before Independence. She describes the changes she has observed in her lifetime.

> When we were young, women going into paid service was considered below the dignity of the family. It was a social taboo, it meant that the family was poor and contemptible . . . Later, in the lower middle class, girls worked to pay for their dowry when the family couldn't afford it . . . Even when girls worked the money wasn't touched . . . It was considered a sin to use the daughter's money. Now with the economic pressure, the attitude is changing. When the wife's working the money goes into a common pool, and the daughter's money is used to support the family. It's not looked down on in the middle class any more. The rising expectations of living standards and the economic situation have led to a change in attitudes.

And nowadays, as other studies also show,[86] being a professional woman can be a valuable commodity on the marriage market, just as education is. Sheela Sarvaria, a manager in her late twenties: 'Marriage was foreseen in the past as a problem, but in the present economic climate, many men *want* wives who can work.'

This is evidenced by many of the matrimonial advertisements in the English language newspaper, *The Times of India*, January 1977:

> Beautiful Preferably Lecturer or medico for brilliant boy, 29½, 167 cms, earning over Rs. 30,000 P.A., working as chief electrical Engineer with reputed consulting engineering firm. High well-to-do Khatri family having properties in Delhi. Caste no bar. Write *The Times of India*.

That this is a phenomenon of the middle class, not the upper castes, is seen by the use of the employability criterion amongst the Scheduled Castes (S/C):

> Beautiful Bride for Jatav (S/C) IAS Officer, 30 yrs., drawing Rs. 1600/- p.m. Medico or girl well placed in Govt. job shall be preferred. Caste no bar. No dowry. Write *The Times of India*.

Although paid work for women was once a mark of poverty and a target for contempt, a professional wife now brings not only social status to men (as we saw in Part III) but material benefits too. A working woman no longer identifies her family with the lower classes, but distinguishes it from them. In this way, the social hierarchy of class has adapted to changes in women's work, using professional rather than domestic work to maintain class divisions. For women, although professional employment brings certain advantages and releases them from seclusion and economic dependence on men, the constraints under which they have to work and the limitations on their freedom of action are such that employment even at the top of the occupational class hierarchy cannot be said to constitute liberation.

20. Winning and Losing

The barriers to women entering the professions are formidable. They are such that those women who do get professional jobs are an extremely privileged group. The privileges they gain from being members of this elite group help to liberate them from many of the constraints with which less fortunate women are still burdened. They can develop their talents through education. They receive the material and social benefits of economic independence and an interesting occupation. They are given greater respect and social esteem by family and friends.

Yet they do not share all the privileges of the professional class, simply because they are women. The freedoms which they gain are limited by the institution of male domination even at the top level of the occupational class hierarchy. Teachers, employers, fathers and husbands continue to control women's lives in education, employment and the family, and to receive material benefits from this control. The forms of control have changed in the transition from a predominantly caste-based society to one which is predominantly class-based, and are the result of a struggle between men and women, the women resisting male control, the men adapting to their resistance and incorporating it into a changed system of male domination, and the women further resisting. The connections between the gender system and the class system can reveal these social processes as they occur in the social structure.

Mechanisms of Male Control

Male control over female education is continued by not taking girls' education seriously, by directing girls into female subjects, especially those that are associated with domestic roles, by assigning priority to boys, particularly when resources are limited, by sexual harassment, and by using girls' education as a commodity on the marriage market.

At a general level, female employment is controlled by segregating women into a narrower range of occupations than men, especially into occupations that are an extension of domestic roles, by giving women lower pay than men, and by giving priority to male employment especially when jobs are scarce. Amongst our professional women, women's employment is controlled by job segregation within each area of education, medicine, government service and management, and by discrimination in selection, promotion, training and assessment. Women are controlled in employment by the restriction of their physical mobility and their social interaction with males, by sexual harassment at work, and by 'gossip', affecting all aspects of their lives from dress to living arrangements.

In the family, women's lives continue to be controlled through the male and (in the joint family) the female authority structure, by imposing the entire burden of domestic work upon them in addition to their paid work, by defining women as primarily domestic workers and sexual and reproductive property, and by assigning priority to the man's paid employment and the woman's domestic labour in any conflict of interest.

Men's Material Benefits

In education, men gain a greater share of scarce resources spent on education, training and development and are better educated than women as a result. In the transformation of women's education into a commodity for marriage, fathers acquire the social honour of a higher-class son-in-law for less dowry, and husbands gain the prestige of an educated wife.

In employment, thanks to the way work is organised under imperialism, men receive a greater proportion of jobs, and benefit from reduced competition from women of the same class. As a result, men gain a greater degree of economic independence than women, especially when there is high unemployment.

At home, men can relax, continue their professional work, or pursue other interests, whilst receiving the benefit of women's domestic work and personal services, and can raise a family without contributing to any of the labour involved in such an undertaking. And they can gain an increased standard of living through the wife's paid work, at no cost to their benefits from her domestic labour.

Connections between Gender and Class

Amongst our women, the privileges of class precede the subordination of gender to the extent that middle-class women are able to afford higher education; that only women from the highest occupational class categories are able to enter the professions, and such women are able to be economically and socially independent, to have interesting work, and to acquire their own identity and social status aside from their relation to men; and that they can hire the services of domestic labourers to help with childcare and housework. In these ways, professional women are freed from their traditional seclusion, dependence on men, and domesticity. Here the privileges of class outweigh the subordination of gender, helping to break down the gender divisions in one strand of the class hierarchy.

But these freedoms are limited by the ways in which the disadvantages of gender take precedence over the advantages of class. For women, gender disadvantage is paramount inasmuch as education is used to improve their marriage chances and to maintain them in domestic dependence, as well as to provide men with material and social advantages; inasmuch as women are offered fewer opportunities and less choice in employment, are segregated, have access to fewer resources, are compelled to comply with higher standards and are hampered from performing their professional work through restrictions on their movements and interactions and through sexual harassment; and insofar as women have to do all the domestic work on top of their paid work, that paid work is designed for male lifestyles and therefore inhibits women's family life, and that domestic work is organised for male benefit and therefore inhibits women's professional work. They are compounded by the scarcity of educational and employment opportunities imposed by imperialism's inhibition of the economy, and the competition over these opportunities imposed by the capitalist organisation of work, in which men are given priority over women. These privileges and disadvantages, which are associated with women's particular position in the systems of gender and social hierarchy, demonstrate the intricate way in which the two systems of power are linked together. We want now to analyse some of the social processes which occur in the change, maintenance and adaptation of each system in relation to the other.

The Social Processes of Gender and Social Hierarchy

In the first place, the class structure appears to have built on the traditional divisions of caste in that education was offered to the upper castes by the British for administrative posts, and the middle class developed from this group. Brahmins dominated the Indian Administrative Service in the late 1960s, although not exclusively, and a similar pattern was found amongst our professional women; the higher the caste, the greater the chance of professional employment. The relationship between caste and occupational class is not complete, however, for not all professional women are from the top caste or even the top two castes, and more people from the middle castes seem to be rising in class terms compared with ten years earlier, but there is still a direct relationship between the two systems of social hierarchy. The class structure retains the hierarchical system of rewards and occupations from the caste structure, which is now individually rather than group based. The class system also retains the idea of middle-class women as primarily domestic.

The resistance of upper-caste women to the constraints of their particular form of oppression was facilitated by the change from a caste to a class society. Women demanded education for themselves and took advantage of the opportunities for professional employment, rejecting seclusion, domesticity and dependence on men. The development of the class structure built upon the existing gender divisions by segregating female education as far as possible and by confining it to 'women's' subjects. In employment, too, women were steered into segregated professions considered suitable for women, particularly those that represent an extension of the traditional nurturing roles. Even employed women continue to be seen as the sole domestic workers, and as primarily home-centred, despite their economic contribution to the family.

Certain forms of male domination that prevailed at the top of the caste structure are also maintained under the class system. For instance, segregated education and medical practice reinforce seclusion whilst allowing women access to knowledge and health care. Job segregation in general reinforces the gender division. The difficulties of living a single life independent of the family perpetuates women's position as men's sexual property. And employers use ideas about women's primary domesticity to deny them access to the labour market regardless of individual women's specific circumstances.

There are also, however, changes in the forms of male domination in the transition from a caste to a class society, which constitute adaptations by the institution of male supremacy to women's resistance. Male supremacy is no longer maintained through a ban on women's education, but through controlling the kind, quantity and purpose of the education. Nor is it upheld through women's seclusion and economic dependence, but through controlling women's access to paid work, and by insisting that she continues to perform the domestic, personal, sexual and reproductive functions within the family as well as her economic function in the workplace.

The institution of male domination not only adapts its forms to women's resistance, it also incorporates aspects of that resistance into the system itself. Women's education is incorporated by making it a requirement for acquiring an educated husband, thereby restricting women's education to a moderate level and using it for a different purpose. Women's resistance to seclusion and dependence is incorporated by using their employability and earning capacity as commodities for marriage too, fathers paying less dowry and husbands increasing their income, at the same time as doubling the women's work load by their refusal to share domestic work.

Male domination in its new form in the class structure maintains women's subordination in a different way from its form under the caste system. For instance, the educational requirement for marriage must not exceed the husband's education, reinforcing male supremacy in the family. Discrimination in the labour market continues to control women economically, and sexual harassment at work maintains men's sexual control over women, as well as inhibiting women's movements and behaviour. Women's responsibility for both domestic and paid work not only worsens the conditions of their lives and demands twice the labour of men, but also prevents them from being able to perform either job adequately except at great cost to themselves, reinforcing male supremacy both at home and at work. The organisation of paid work around men's lifestyles, and the organisation of domestic work, particularly childcare, around the assumption that the woman will be permanently available in the home, add to these difficulties.

Finally, the new form of male domination also helps to maintain the social hierarchy because having an educated wife, or a professional woman in the family, brings material benefits and social status to the men of the family, helping to distinguish them from lower-class men both socially and economically. Women's rebellion against male domination, economic dependence and domestic seclusion is incorporated not only into an adapted form of male supremacy, but also into the new system of social hierarchy, the class system. Nevertheless, although women's struggles become incorporated into the institutions against which they are directed, we should not underestimate either the degree to which these institutions have to adapt, nor the persistence of women's resistance, for women do use their education for their own purpose rather than purely for marriage, those who are lucky and determined enough do get jobs to maintain their economic independence, and many ignore the constraints which are imposed to control their movements and their behaviour. Where they can, they negotiate more democratic relationships within the family, and they may withdraw from the family if the other members are not willing to adjust. A few women even manage to negotiate the husband's participation in domestic work, as we will see in Part VI. Not that any of these measures is enough on its own. But women know what they need, and many of them are fighting for it.

Notes

1. Suniti Namjoshi (1981) *Feminist Fables*. London: Sheba, p.68.
2. Diana Leonard suggests that the precedence of gender subordination over class privilege shows that the gender hierarchy exists independently of the class hierarchy. Diana Leonard (1982) 'Male Feminists and Divided Women', in Scarlet Friedman and Elizabeth Sarah (eds), *On the Problem of Men*. London: The Women's Press, pp.165-70. See also Zillah Eisenstein (1979) *Capitalist Patriarchy and the case for Socialist Feminism*. New York: Monthly Review Press.
3. Contrary to Diana Leonard's view, the connections between gender and social hierarchy in our data suggest that whilst the two systems are not identical, nor are they independent. We prefer Michèle Barrett's formulation of the gender division as built into, and a crucial element of, class relations, historically, but not necessarily an essential pre-condition for them, logically. Michèle Barrett (1980) *Women's Oppression Today*. London: Verso, p.138.
4. Carol Ehrlich (1981) 'The Unhappy Marriage of Marxism and Feminism: Can it be Saved?', in Lydia Sargent (ed), *Women and Revolution*. London: Pluto, p.110.
5. Department of Social Welfare (1978) *Women in India: a Statistical Profile*. New Delhi: Government of India, Table 4.2, p.120.
6. Ibid., Table 4.3, p.122.
7. See Appendix, Table 1.
8. See Appendix, Table 2.
9. See Appendix, Table 3.
10. See Appendix, Table 4.

11. Directorate-General of Employment and Training (1971) *Occupational-Educational Pattern in India (Public Sector)*. New Delhi: Government of India, p.23.

12. See Appendix, Table 5.

13. 68 women (56 per cent) had consistently been at or near the top of the class during their education.

14. See Appendix, Tables 6, 7.

15. See Appendix, Tables 16, 17.

16. See Appendix, Table 8.

17. 38 per cent experienced difficulties of some kind in their education.

18. Department of Social Welfare, *Women in India*, Table 4.35, pp.181-2.

19. Y.B. Mathur (1973) *Women's Education in India (1813-1966)*. Delhi: University of Delhi, pp.116-17.

20. Rhoda Lois Blumberg and Leela Dwaraki (1980) *India's Educated Women*. Delhi: Hindustan Publishing Corporation, pp.27-9.

21. For example, Science Talent scholarships provide Rs 125 per month at undergraduate and Rs 250 per month at postgraduate level. Approximately one student per year in Delhi will win such a scholarship. Approximately 10-15 students per year in the University of Delhi (undergraduate and postgraduate) will receive a university scholarship. At postgraduate level, the University Grants Commission provides MA grants of Rs 150 per month and PhD grants of Rs 500 per month in arts subjects and Rs 800 per month in science subjects. About 4 or 5 are available annually in each subject. Other grants come from institutions such as the Indian Commission for Social Science Research, the History Association, the Education Ministry, as well as private trusts and industrialists' endowments. See Department of Social Welfare, *Women in India*. Tables 4.36-4.40, 4.43-4.44, pp.183-6, 188.

22. Mathur, *Women's Education*, Ch.7.

23. Bhaktavatsalam Committee (1965) Report of the Committee to look into the causes for lack of public support, particularly in rural areas, for girls' education and to enlist public cooperation, New Delhi: Government of India, p.42. Quoted in Mathur, ibid., p.110.

24. Report of the National Committee on Women's Education, May 1958-January 1959, Delhi: Government of India, pp.40-55. Quoted in Mathur, ibid., p.112.

25. Directorate-General of Employment and Training, *Occupational-Educational Pattern*, Table VI, p.19.

26. B.B. Misra (1961) *The Indian Middle Classes*. London: Oxford University Press.

27. Report of the Education Commission 1964-66 (1966) Delhi: Government of India, p.164, and Report of the National Committee on Women's Education, May 1958-January 1959 (1959). Delhi: Government of India, pp.40-55. Quoted in Mathur, *Women's Education*, p.112.

28. Directorate-General of Employment and Training, *Occupational-Educational Pattern*, Table VI, p.19.

29. See Chapter 7, Note 11.

30. O.P. Dhingra (1972) *The Career Woman and her Problems*. New Delhi: Shri Ram Centre for Industrial Relations & Human Resources (unpublished). Similar findings were reported by: Rama Mehta (1970) *The Western Educated Hindu Woman*. Bombay: Asia Publishing House, pp.36-7.

31. Leela Gulati (1975) 'Occupational Distribution of Working Women', *Economic and Political Weekly* 25 October, pp.1692-3.

32. Ibid., p.1693.

33. Ibid., p.1698.

34. Department of Social Welfare, *Women in India*, Table 5.4, p.212.

35. Kamla Nath (1968) 'Women in the Working Force in India', *Economic and Political Weekly* 3 August, p.1205.

36. Department of Social Welfare, *Women in India*, Table 5.4, p.212.

37. Indian Council for Social Science Research (1975) *Status of Women in India*, a synopsis of the report of the National Committee. Bombay: Allied Publishers, Table 28, p.164.

38. Department of Social Welfare (1974) *Towards Equality. Report of the Committee on the Status of Women in India*. New Delhi: Government of India, para 5.146, p.183.

39. See Appendix, Table 9.

40. Directorate-General of Employment and Training, *Occupational-Educational Pattern*, Table VI, p.19.

41. Directorate-General of Employment and Training, *Occupational Pattern in India, (Private Sector)* Part I. New Delhi: Government of India, Table VIII, pp.26-7.

42. Department of Social Welfare, *Towards Equality*, para 5.226, p.206.

43. Directorate-General of Employment and Training, *Occupational-Educational Pattern*, Table VIII, p.22.

44. Ibid., Table VII, p.21 and Directorate-General of Employment and Training, *Occupational Pattern*, Table IX, pp.29-30.

45. Department of Social Welfare, *Women in India*, Table 5.12, p.259. Reproduced in modified form in Appendix as Table 10.

46. See Appendix, Table 11.

47. See Appendix, Table 12 for distribution of religions.

48. See footnote to Table 13 in the Appendix.

49. See Appendix, Table 13.

50. R. Palme Dutt (1940) *India Today*. London: Victor Gollancz, p.261, writes: 'With regard to caste restrictions and untouchability . . . [it] is impossible not to appreciate the benevolent desire of the representatives of imperialism to magnify and multiply the numbers of the depressed classes and untouchables. A generation ago, before the political situation was so acute, the number of 30 millions was commonly given . . . The semi-official symposium "Modern India", published under the editorship of Sir John Cumming in 1931, hovers "from 30 to 60 millions". The Simon Report tries to fix the figure at 43 millions.' It is not clear whether a similar process occurred with the estimated number of brahmins.

51. Indian Statutory Commission (1930) *Report of the Indian Statutory Commission* (Simon Report), Volume 1 — Survey. London: His Majesty's Stationery Office, p.35, states that the brahmin caste contains seven or eight million males; p.24 states that there are 216 million Hindus. 15 million brahmins out of a total of 216 million Hindus is approximately 7 per cent. The uncertainties of such an estimate are obvious, and whilst it should not be taken as accurate, it does suggest that brahmins constitute quite a small minority.

52. George Rosen (1966) *Democracy and Economic Change in India*. Berkeley: University of California Press, p.3, quoted in Dilip Hiro (1976) *Inside India Today*. London: Routledge & Kegan Paul, p.53.

53. We are not suggesting that class is *defined* by education and occupation, since class refers to a set of social relations within the system of production, but we are using education and occupation as an index of social and economic position within the system of productive relations. Such indices are meaningful only in comparison to other groups. For this reason we have not used income as an index, and although the information is provided in the Appendix, Tables 14 and 15, because there are no figures with which to make comparisons. Income data is available, but it is not sufficiently specific to compute averages, and inflation makes it difficult to compare income bands across different years.

54. See Appendix, Tables 16, 17.

55. See Appendix, Tables 18, 19.

56. See Appendix, Table 20.

57. Victor D'Souza (1968) *Social Structure of a Planned City: Chandigarh.* New Delhi: Orient Longman, p.324. Reproduced in Appendix, Table 21.

58. See Appendix, Table 22.

59. The computed mean contribution of our women to the family income was 49.9 per cent.

60. See Appendix, Table 23.

61. Kiron Wadhera (1976) *The New Breadwinners.* New Delhi: Vishwa Yuvak Kendra, p.209, confirms that employers thought women were more honest, and that men behaved better in their presence.

62. Dhingra, *Career Woman.*

63. See Appendix, Table 22.

64. See Appendix, Table 24.

65. Indian Council for Social Science Research, *Status of Women*, p.19.

66. Rama Mehta, *Western Educated Hindu Woman*, p.13.

67. M.S. Gore (1968) *Urbanisation and Family Change in India.* Bombay: Popular Prakashan; R. Mukherjee (1969) *Family in India: a Perspective.* Calcutta: Indian Statistical Institute (mimeo).

68. H. Orenstein (1961) 'The Recent History of the Extended Family in India', *Local Problems* 8, 4, pp.41-50 Spring.

69. Maria Mies (1980) *Indian Women and Patriarchy.* New Delhi: Concept, p.89.

70. Meyer Fortes (1958) 'Introduction', in Jack Goody (ed), *The Developmental Cycle in Domestic Groups.* Cambridge: Cambridge University Press.

71. Kuntesh Gupta (1973), 'Structure and Organization of Indian Family: the Emerging Patterns', *International Journal of Contemporary Sociology* 10, 4, pp.163-82.

72. See Appendix, Table 25.

73. See Appendix, Table 26.

74. Veena Das (1976) 'Indian Women: Work, Power and Status' in B.R. Nanda (ed), *Indian Women from Purdah to Modernity.* New Delhi: Vikas, pp.144-5.

75. Aileen Ross (1961) *The Hindu Family in its Urban Setting.* Toronto: University of Toronto, p.50.

76. Mies, *Indian Women*, pp.75-6.

77. M.N. Srinivas (1977) 'The Changing Position of Indian Women', *Man* 12, p.226.

78. Pandita Ramabai (1888) *The High Caste Hindu Woman.* Philadelphia: Jas. B. Rodgers, pp.43-8.

79. Ross, *Hindu Family*; Dhingra, *Career Woman*, p.193.

80. M.N. Srinivas (1942) *Marriage and Family in Mysore*. Bombay: New Book Co.

81. Ross, *Hindu Family*, p.172.

82. Dhingra, *Career Woman*, p.193.

83. Rama Kapur (1969) 'Role Conflict among Employed Housewives', *Indian Journal of Industrial Relations* 5, 1, July.

84. Dhingra, *Career Woman*, and Wadhera, *New Breadwinners*, p.209.

85. Ibid., *New Breadwinners*, p.210.

86. Blumberg and Dwaraki, *India's Educated Women*.

Part V: Women's Consciousness

21. Conflicts and Contradictions

She was very beautiful, no one denied it. Every morning she would walk to the lake and look at herself. The shepherd, Narcissus, would follow at a distance. When she was done, he would go to the lake's edge, and stand where she had stood. He would look for her image, but all he ever saw was a reflection of himself. One day, as the shepherd, Narcissus, was staring at his face, the beautiful woman returned to the lake. 'What are you doing?' she asked the shepherd. 'Looking for your image.' But I live on the land, not in the water,' the beautiful woman said, 'You need not be shy. Here I am. Look at my face.' But the shepherd, Narcissus, declined her offer. 'It isn't you I want', he answered politely, 'only your image.'

Suniti Namjoshi, *Feminist Fables*[1]

We look first at three women who came from very different backgrounds, but who all experienced a contradiction between how they saw their lives, and the social expectations and gender images that confronted them as women. Parvati Sahni is from a conservative high-caste family, Kiran Singhal comes from a liberal Jain background, Promilla Khanna is the daughter of parents who were radicalised at Partition. Of the three, Parvati Sahni's story probably represents the greatest absolute change and the hardest struggle.

Parvati came from an orthodox kshatriya family. She took Matric at the age of 15 in Pakistan. She wanted to study further but was discouraged by school and family. In fact she did no more study until her late twenties, when she did a social science degree. During this time she married. Shortly after getting her degree in 1947, the family moved from Pakistan to India when the two countries were divided. Several more years went by before she could do her medical degree, which she finally achieved at the age of 38. She started her first job immediately afterwards, and within 7 years she was made a professor in a very prestigious medical institution. Later she became a Member, and then a Fellow of the Royal College of Physicians, taking her exams at Edinburgh University. She's now 58.

My mother was idealistic and full of compassion for humanity, but she was very frustrated because she couldn't fulfil herself. Although she was very intelligent, she was loaded with domestic responsibility since the age of 10, when her own mother died. She instilled idealism in her daughter in an attempt to fulfil herself through me. But she still hadn't developed the courage to deviate from traditional social norms. And that led to frustration in me. I had very high ambitions and idealism. I had the idea of women as emancipated and the duties and obligations necessary to fulfil that end, but when I deviated from the social norms to fulfil myself, my mother couldn't stand by me. This led to great conflict between us. The same was true of my father, he respected women, he wasn't dominating, and he was very dependent on his wife, and yet he forced me to marry against my wishes. In spite of all this my ambition was not subdued. Subsequently my struggle was entirely independent.

My husband expected me to be a good wife. I wasn't qualified before marriage, and I married into a very conservative family. They didn't want me to study or to work as a doctor . . . I got my qualifications later by simple defiance. I faced tremendous obstacles from the family, which I overcame by determination and defiance, but associated with a lot of guilt. My husband was the main obstacle. I did the medical course only with a great struggle — I broke away for several years. My husband modified his views later, and came back to me. I accepted it because of the children. Now he's proud of me.

The maximum influence on me was my mother, but she was ambivalent about outside work. She saw me as perfectly qualified to be a doctor, and she had these ideals of helping humanity, but she couldn't stand me working when I was married . . . Because of this ambivalence, we can't have a very close relationship. I respect and admire her but we're not very close emotionally.

Both my own family and my husband's family disapproved of what I was doing, but both families changed markedly, partly because of a change in the social milieu and cultural values, and partly because of chronological events. The young girls from my husband's family took my example and got educated to become better citizens. This unconsciously had the impact of a better social image for the family.

Parvati's mother and father gave conflicting signs to their daughter. Her mother's own experience had taught her that it was right for women to fulfil themselves, but she hadn't thought through the consequences of such a step: that to fulfil her mother's idealism, her daughter wanted to work as a doctor, but to be employed in such a capacity would conflict with the secluded domestic life of a good orthodox wife. Her father gave the impression of a gentle man, not at all the stereotypical dominating patriarch of the family, but he couldn't maintain this approach when his daughter refused to comply with the marriage he had arranged; he was forced to become the stern father in order to uphold the family's social image, little realising that his daughter's shameful behaviour would later add to his pride.

Parvati's husband felt no such ambivalence towards her: he wanted her to be a good wife. Becoming a doctor interfered with this: it allowed her to serve humanity at the expense of serving him, and it threatened to ruin his social standing in the community. He refused to allow it. The only way she could do it was by breaking out of the marriage. He was forced to choose between accepting her as a doctor, or losing her as his wife. In the end, *he* changed, as did his entire family.

The source of Parvati's idealism and striving for independence can clearly be seen in her mother's personal experience of domestic burdens at too young an age. Once instilled, this striving could not be taken back, despite her mother's inability to resist the social pressure which ensued when her daughter did not conform. The contradiction created an enormous strain for Parvati, but her experience of the struggle to break out of the domestic sphere is what gave her the strength of conviction on women's issues that she has now. Both Parvati and her mother experienced the contradiction between what they knew it was right for women to do from their own experience, and what a male-dominated society construed as right for them. Her mother could not put it into practice even vicariously because, being dependent on the family for her survival, she could not but take account of the rules laid down for its maintenance. For Parvati, the possibility of a life independent of the family existed: she could survive even whilst rejecting the family's strictures.

Kiran Singhal experienced a similar conflict, although the family ambivalence to what she wanted to do was much more muted. In contrast to the orthodoxy of Parvati's family, Kiran came from a liberal Jain background. Nevertheless, her parents had reservations about many of the things she wanted to do, despite having treated her as equal to her brothers. She's 53.

My father always thought I should be educated as a boy and not waste time in the kitchen. He was a doctor and had a strong belief in women's education . . .

I was the first woman to take matric in my home town, and the first professional woman from both sides of the family. My parents were always very encouraging. When I had a touring job in the villages, sometimes there was no transport, so I went by jeep, on horseback or on foot. My father gave me freedom and treated me like a son. I never abused the freedom.

At adolescence I felt that women were unequal. I decided I would never marry and I would have a career . . . I wanted to look after my parents, but my parents wanted someone to look after *me*. When I was studying my mother used to be very worried and I used to come home very often, but my father got fed up and said, 'Don't study then, stay in the kitchen and we'll get you fixed up with someone.' That had a great effect, I never came home again whilst I was studying.

I did social work at the Tata Institute. My father preferred me to do voluntary work afterwards, but my teachers said I shouldn't waste my studies. Then he wanted me to get a job in town, but I was willing to work anywhere. I applied for the civil service for fun — and I got in! I came first! So I decided to work, and my father didn't object. My first posting was to a tribal area. My parents were reluctant to let me go, but I went.

I married late, and had my son at the age of 42. My husband was also in the civil service. Ours is an intercaste, interreligion marriage. I didn't want to upset my parents by marrying out of my religion . . . so we had to wait for 2 years till they adjusted to the idea . . . Now I have a conflict of dual ideas working on me. Sometimes I think I'm a revolutionary woman working towards emancipation. But I also think that men are a bit superior, so I do the household jobs and don't mind it.

The conflict in Kiran's family had a different emphasis from that of Parvati's. The dominant feeling was that she should be independent, but each step she took towards that end was met with reluctance, followed by acceptance.

Her father educated her 'as a boy', but preferred her to do voluntary work. She insisted she wanted a paying job, he suggested it should be in the same town. When she got a job working in the tribal areas, he was reluctant to let her go but eventually yielded. He was unhappy about her marrying out of her community, but accepted it after some time. His ambivalence about his daughter's independence shows itself in her honest assessment of her own views now: the conflict of dual ideas, which make her feel that she is a revolutionary woman, but at the same time, that her husband is still superior.

Of the three women, Promilla Khanna is probably the least orthodox in terms of her views on women. She is not only consciously trying to change women's subordinate position in her own life and her daughter's, she has also rejected the divisions of religion, caste and class. In this, her father provided the example, for he underwent radical changes at the time of Partition. But none of this prevented Promilla from experiencing the contradiction between what she wanted for herself and her daughter, and the social expectations she had to contend with because she is a woman. Promilla is 33.

> My father thought I should be well educated and grow up to be a human being with critical perceptions — he was a major influence on me. My mother isn't educated, but she also valued education. The family was affected by Partition; they had been well off in Pakistan but when they migrated to India they had to start from scratch with no money, food or shelter . . . Education was seen as a way out.
>
> I was only 3 when we left Pakistan. My father eventually got a job in the civil service. Everybody in the family wanted to study. Because we were living alone . . . my father wanted us to be independent. He was an enlightened man but restricted by the orthodoxies of the joint family. He found it very difficult to throw off these attitudes. But he had to change because of the circumstances. It might have been different if we'd stayed in Lahore.
>
> Both my father and my mother think it's good for girls to work and do what they want. They both believed in equality. But the social institutions gave preeminence to male children. My parents were trying to bring us up equally, and I resented any unequal treatment from other people. I was always taught to question the social institutions, but I'm the only one in the family who has been unusual. I always rebelled against male-dominated institutions. I also read a lot which gave me a better understanding of society.
>
> My sisters also believe women should be people, but they have contradictions — they say one thing and do another, for instance, they buy dolls for the girls and engines for the boys. I won't have it myself — people buy my daughter dolls, I don't give her them.
>
> My father looks after my daughter now while I'm at work. He's upset that I can't do my work properly, because of domestic responsibilities, so he helps as much as he can. But he still wanted me to have a son. I wanted a daughter — to see how you can bring up a girl differently in a patriarchal society. Even amongst the educated elite, they were sorry I had a daughter.

Promilla's father came from a well-off, orthodox kshatriya family, but found he could no longer uphold an orthodox way of life when he emigrated to India as a refugee, without money, food or shelter. His only asset was his education, which enabled him to get a job to support the family. These circumstances of economic hardship made him abandon his orthodox lifestyle and realise the importance of his daughters as well as his sons being able to earn their own living — an idea completely opposed to orthodox views on women. He was in a better position to change than Parvati Sahni's mother because, unlike her, he had left the rest of the family behind, and he was the 'head' of his own family. Nevertheless, he found it difficult completely to throw off the mantle of orthodox ideology. And he was not alone in this, as Promilla found when her educated middle-class colleagues continued to see males as preferable to females. Promilla herself tries to eliminate the contradictions in her own actions. But in a world where men have power to define themselves as primary, the contradictions for women remain.

22. Woman's Place in a Man's World

We have already looked briefly at women's consciousness in Part III. We saw how the women emerged from seclusion, and how their economic independence provided the material basis for changing the conditions of their lives; and we looked at the psychological basis for the changes, identifying the contradiction between women's own attitudes and experiences, and the ideas and expectations of others, as the stimulus for change.

Even after they have emerged from seclusion into professional employment, the women still have to face discriminatory conditions in education, employment and the family. We saw in Part IV how the social and gender hierarchies co-exist, the development of one affecting the forms of the other so that even after reaching a privileged position in the occupational class hierarchy, women have not achieved liberation from gender roles. We examined the conditions of professional women's lives, and the way the conditions are affected by the divisions of sex and class. Now we want to look at the psychological aspects, consisting of the attitudes, values and ideas associated with professional women's particular position in the social and gender hierarchies. We will examine the attitudes and values held by the women themselves, and the stereotypes they encounter from others.

A large number of attitude surveys have been conducted on employed women in the middle class, but many of these treat attitudes in isolation from the social and economic context, tending to focus on female adjustment and thereby attributing women's problems to their personal 'maladjustment'.[2] In this context, Promilla Kapur's studies are notable for the way in which they challenge rather than perpetuate the myths and stereotypes about middle-class women.[3] This is important, but the stereotypes also need to be related to the material conditions in which they occur. The material and the psychological are not separate. The external conditions have an important effect on attitudes and consciousness, as we saw in Part III, where the attitudes of the women and their families altered along with social and economic changes. But attitudes and values also affect external reality.[4] We have seen this in the last three examples, where the attitudes and values concerning women's position helped to define the gender roles themselves.

The contradictions between women's experience and gender ideology are not to be understood as a dichotomy, for the idea of femininity and the reality of femaleness are not distinct. Ann Foreman shows that the ideology of femininity contributes to female reality, and the two together play an active part in constructing the reality of femaleness itself. She suggests that ideology is real experience arising from different levels of reality, some of which is at a level deeper than conscious thought, and is therefore only partially understood. This allows for women to be unconscious of aspects of their oppression, and for conflicts and contradictions to exist between the different levels of their multi-dimensional reality.[5] An example of women's multi-dimensional reality is described in a political analysis of the representation of women in art: 'Men look at women. Women watch themselves being looked at. This determines not only most relations between men and women, but also the relation of women to themselves. The surveyor of woman in herself is male: the surveyed female.'[6] Thus the contradictions women express are not the result of inconsistent or illogical thought processes, but are real and are rooted in the actual experience of their lives. Srinivas has shown that the contradictions existed as far back as the early Hindu religious literature, with arguments taking place about women's roles, and differences between theory and practice. The literature on women, he says, shows a basic contradiction, and 'abounds in inconsistent if not contrary ideas, rules, beliefs and practices'.[7] Prabhati Mukherjee gives examples of these contradictory views, and suggests that they reflect a struggle between 'pro-woman' and 'anti-woman' groups which remain enshrined in the literature.[8]

We have noted that many of our women find their own ideas in conflict with the views which other people try to impose on them. The women find that in challenging discriminatory conditions, they also have to confront a whole range of expectations which contradict their own ideas. Three of the main themes identified by our women as conflicting with their own experience are those concerning female domesticity, subservience and inferiority.

The first myth concerns women's inferior abilities, mental and physical: women have less intelligence, less common sense and less ability to learn; they are unable to learn certain things, such as science and engineering; they have less strength and stamina than men, and they are less competent at certain kinds of work, such as that involving danger, skill, strength of purpose, or the kinds of jobs which men define as theirs alone.

The second myth involves women's subservience to men: women are submissive and restrained in respect of their own desires, are dependent creatures and deferrent to males. Women are not dominant, assertive, independent or self-confident.

The third is the myth of domesticity: women's needs are primarily, if not solely, domestic. A woman's purpose is marriage, reproduction and domestic labour. A woman has no need for a life or work outside the home; if she does have a job, she is not ambitious, nor is her work of importance compared with family life.

In Part V we will show:
one, some of the stereotypes, myths and ideas which form the cultural supports for professional women's position in the gender and class hierarchies;

two, the context within which the myths have developed, and the relationship between the myths and the social and economic conditions of the women's lives;

three, what happens when women begin to analyse the contradictions and expose the myths.

The data we will use for this analysis is the women's consciousness. We are looking, in other words, at what women know, rather than what they do.

23. Creating Gender

The contradictions women express reflect the contradictions they experience in real life. Even when they deny the contradictions, the discrepancy between the woman's experience of herself and the meanings attached to that experience by the male-dominated culture is often apparent. We will examine these contradictions by looking at what women know about the myths concerning their abilities, their qualities, and their needs.

Inferiority

Deepa Kochhar, a young doctor, expresses the stereotype about women's *mental* abilities in response to a general question about paid work: 'Boys are intelligent, girls are diligent. Men have more common sense, women have less capacity, so women may have to work harder for the same recognition at work.' But when asked about her own life, she reveals quite a different understanding, that women's capacity is at least twice that of men's because they organise, perform and are responsible for at least twice as much work.

> There will be difficulties in the future because running the home is a full time job. My fiance wants us to set up a private practice together, but men don't think housework is a part of their job. The male-dominated family structure makes it harder for women, because they have responsibility for the house.

And she knows she will have to work at maintaining the illusion. 'I won't give up work, but I foresee problems. I will compromise, sacrifice a little for a smooth life. I will have to do two jobs.' Deepa, like most women, has learnt the skill of integrating a contradictory reality, and of hiding the truth in her own life so that her husband's path is smooth, shielded from the shocks of the contradictions in *her* existence. Rama Tyagi doesn't have to do this, since she is unmarried, but 20 years as a lecturer are reflected in her consciousness. In reply to a general question she expresses the 'new' male-centred view, adjusted in response to women's demands for equality: that women have equality already, that the male power structure does not exist.

> There's no reason to feel the general attitude that women are inferior or incapable. It's a great advantage to be a woman. Even if a woman's a housewife, no one feels they should be suppressed. It's more an economic thing of support.

They're not looked down on. In the West, the career woman is branded as abnormal.

But in reply to a question about her own work, she expresses a different reality.

I've put off a few people who don't like intelligent women. You have to work harder, you have to be better than men. You're always really on your guard. Some of the men at work prefer you not to be around. Superiors don't like very intelligent women (and men to a lesser extent). If a woman points out a mistake in a seminar, they don't like it.

Veena Goyal, a young manager, exposes the myth of the superior male intellect: 'The custom of society is that men are a better species than women, and men usually have more education, so they think of themselves as more intelligent *always*.' Veena knows that the men have appropriated *learning* for themselves, and built the myth of men's greater mental *capacity* upon it. Such appropriation is not confined to academic learning in the middle class but extends to practical training in the rural working class, as Devaki Chakrabarty knows from her work in the Ministry of Technology.

We won't progress until women and men work together. Women should work only when they're given due reward and respect. In the villages, women do far more agricultural work, but the men are sent off for training when the opportunity arises. Ridiculous!

Women are often unaware of the myths about what they supposedly cannot do. Sushila Banerji:

There was an engineering college near our house, and two of my brothers are engineers. I had no particular desire to be an engineer, but I didn't realise before applying that women didn't do engineering. On the first day I found I was the only girl in 80 boys.

When women refuse to collude in the myth of men's greater abilities, even men are forced to confront the fact that women's 'inferiority' is constructed, not inherent. Shikha Munshi:

Men often can't handle an intelligent woman. They expect them to be inferior. If they're not they can't be natural with them. Senior colleagues will not talk to me in Japanese because I speak it better. I have to play down my ability, otherwise it creates problems.

Shikha compromises with the men's myths to the extent that she plays down her ability, but she also forces the *men* into putting a lot of hard work into preserving their illusion. The men's responses to her are increasingly defensive. First exclusion, then defamation. Finally, desperate to maintain the illusions, questioning her non-linguistic abilities.

They rationalise that I'm so good at languages because I can't do other studies, like knowledge of the culture, ability to analyse, etc. Initially they tried to drive me off, but they had to accept me, so they learnt to live with me. They engage in much political slander and character assassination.

The view that women are *physically* weaker than men is expressed by half a dozen women. Manju Malik wanted to be a surgeon.

If a woman wants to be a surgeon, it's harder because of physical strength. You may have to stand the whole day and operate. I feel I couldn't do it. I do mind men having more physical strength. They can do more physical things.

But Manju also knows why she wouldn't have the strength to stand and operate all day.

The feelings of exhaustion only happened after marriage and the family. I have problems with ayahs; there are no regular holidays at the hospital. I feel tied down now. I regret these home/work conflicts. Women shouldn't marry in clinical work.

Manju's stamina is drained in trying to maintain her husband's illusion of the professional wife with time to spare, which, as we saw in Part IV, is the one thing that women in paid work do not have:

There is conflict because my husband wants me to continue working and he wants me to spend more time in the family. Doctors have long hours. My husband wanted a professional wife but with more free time. Family life is more difficult because of doing two jobs, lack of efficiency, trying to compromise.

Neera Atreyi *is* a surgeon. She *knows* that she is not inferior in physical capacity or any other way.

I was expected to look after my husband, the children and the dependants in the family. I had to work harder, be more tolerant, sacrifice . . . With hard work I maintained career and family. Sometimes I think of myself as *superior*.

Anjana Vishwanatan knows about the physical abilities of working-class women from her work in the Ministry of Labour. 'Lower-class women work with men as labourers on building sites for low wages, yet they say women have no physical stamina!'

In the civil service there is the belief that women are not capable of doing certain jobs. Bharati Kapoor:

They won't post women in certain jobs, for instance a criminal district, or public posts where there's a lot of political dealing. There are few women on election duty. There might be a law and order problem, and people might take advantage where a woman is.

Aruna Sharma knows that the belief is a myth: 'Clients' response to women is very good, and once you've shown yourself to be good, they have complete faith in you. One particular woman is always posted to my district whenever there's trouble.'

Shaheen Kumari works in the heavily male-dominated profession of engineering. When she exposed the myth of male superiority in physical work, the men retaliated by suggesting she had no right to be doing the work.

> I never thought myself inferior, so the way I was treated affected me more. It doesn't feel nice. I'm very angry. Men can't take it that women work as hard as men, especially physically. So they accuse me of taking the place of a man who could support a family. As I've worked I've become more aware, but also more immune.

Women are rewarded for maintaining the illusion of female weakness as Renu Deb found. 'As a woman I can get work done because I appeal to them as men to do it for me. I put on a helpless act.' Renu at least is under no illusion that her helplessness is an act. Her pretence that it is real is the only way she can ensure men's cooperation.

Within marriage, the relationship between men and women is constructed to sustain the ideology of male superiority. First, in terms of individual income. Ambika Roy: 'There was pressure for me to marry, but not to leave the job. This causes conflict and problems because I would need a man earning more than me.' Second in terms of intellectual achievement. Marie Raj explains why she never married:

> I come from a Catholic family. I was expected to marry someone of high intelligence, and it was hard to find anyone as highly qualified as me in our community.

Third in terms of social position. Sridevi Choudhury: 'Girls' biggest incentive is to marry *above* themselves to a higher income group. That suits the men because they can be dominant.' And some of the most professionally successful women persist in maintaining the illusion within marriage. Both Jasminder Surjeet and her husband are eminent specialists in the same demanding field of medicine.

> I didn't want my husband to feel I was rising more than him. I keep myself back and he knows it. I'm quite happy men should come first in a way. I have to care for the children and shouldn't go ahead.

Not only does Jasminder know that her husband's primacy is an illusion, he knows it too. It is maintained only by her acknowledgement of it. In terms of their professional achievements they are equal. The only difference is that he is healthy whilst she is on the verge of nervous exhaustion.

Subservience

In a male-dominated society, women are submissive to men's needs, restrained about their own desires, dependent on, and deferrent to, men. Vijaya Ambujam expresses this view. 'Women have lots of problems with employment. They have to be posted where their husbands are, they won't work after 5, they're very shy.' But Vijaya knows that *she* is not shy. 'I would like to go into politics. I'm good at speaking and debating and I used to be politically active. I would like political power.'

Aruna Sharma is as assertive as Vijaya. She's an IAS officer. She doesn't need to pretend that she's submissive when she's with her husband, but Aruna maintains the illusion for her husband's family.

> My husband's from a very backward area, traditional and conservative . . . Women shouldn't show their face there. When I go to my in-laws, I'm 'two-faced' about it. I cover my face when I go, but I don't go very often.

Sridevi Choudhury decided to stop deferring to her husband's illusions a few years ago. She gave up several jobs to move with her husband, but eventually decided to keep her job and live apart. She has refuted the myth of female subservience but she continues to collude with it in public.

> Particularly with older groups, where women professionals are few, the husbands always have a bit of a complex. You mustn't 'show off' or try to show up your husband. So you have to be two-faced. At work, I make decisions. At home, I stay in the background.

Sridevi's collusion in the myth of submissiveness to her husband is explicit. She acts out the contradiction consciously. But along with her continued protection of him goes her knowledge of his irrationality. 'Even when your husband will agree with reason unconsciously they object to women being equals.'

At the workplace, Amrit Soni, a civil servant of 29, has discovered that *she* can silence the *men* by refusing to collude in their stereotypes, but she may have to pay for her audacity later.

> They're not used to women at work, only in the house. If you're honest, assertive, outspoken, they don't know what to say! If your superior is not very nice he'll take it out on you . . . When I was in the field I had a male colleague doing the same job. We made similar mistakes. I always got told off, he never did.

When Vimla Gupta refused to collude in the stereotype of subservience, she discovered that it caused her male colleagues problems. Significantly she is the most senior and highly paid of the women working in management.

> Everyone is very helpful at low levels. Only at the invisible barrier is there any trouble. As long as they can patronise you, everything is okay, but as soon as you become a threat, everything changes. You can still get on even with a *feminine* approach, but you must never be independent in your views . . . With women, ugliness is no barrier, you can be fat and 50, but *independence* is the greatest barrier. If you say 'I don't agree' they object. Independence of views is bad. Femininity is good. Feminists do not want those sort of advantages through femininity. I'm too strong a woman for them. Had I been a failure they would have been nice to me. I've been aware of it throughout work but mainly in the last few years since I became number one — Chief of Division.

Vimla recognises that pursuing a career through femininity poses no threat to men, since it colludes with male stereotypes of what a woman is, dependent on and submissive to men. As Seetha Jayalakshmi points out: 'There are advantages of femininity — you can get things done more quickly.' But as soon as women refuse to pretend to be submissive and dependent, thereby exposing the myth, they lose the benefits of femininity. The women are punished for refusing men's protection, for female assertiveness represents a challenge to male authority and control. And it is not only men who punish assertive women. Parvati Sahni, a professor of medicine:

> For a time when I was breaking out into education and a profession, friends and neighbours used to envy and idolize me and seek help from me. Then the women developed mixed reactions of jealousy. They expressed superiority by their acceptance of the social norms, and they isolated me. The men take you to a certain level as long as you don't reach their standard. When you reach or excel them they isolate you by giving you the feeling that you're an odd entity. And some men feel mean and guilty that their wives are not allowed similar status, therefore they put *you* down.

Kamla Tandon knows why she is one of the few women amongst her friends to have got into the medical profession:

> Everyone I know has high ambitions, but hardly any have managed to fight the pressures. They struggle a bit and then give up. Women who struggle too much are considered a bit funny. They're trained from the beginning to do what the head of the family says.

The notion of subservience helps to construct women's dependence and restraint, such that any woman who shows assertive qualities is defined as an abnormal female.

Domesticity

In a male-dominated culture, women's needs are defined as primarily domestic, as Anjana Vishwanatan suggests.

> My mother is orthodox, she thinks marriage is the proper state for a woman . . . My cousins think I should be married too. They look at me differently and suggest that I think I'm better than they are because I won't get married.

Which contrasts with her own feelings and experience on the matter.

> It simply makes me want to do more in my career. They always suggest I settle down, but it has the opposite effect on me . . . Merely being a daughter or wife doesn't consume my energy and potential. I don't conform to the stereotype of women in society. I want to change it.

Madhu Jaikishan, a young doctor, knows that women's domestic needs are defined by what *men* want.

> Men are used to seeing women working at home. They want it too. Indian men are not used to women rising, they don't relish it, and try to hinder them.

What men's needs are is revealed by Veena Goyal.

> Society still sees women in the home, so people don't look up to women working outside. It's because of *possessiveness* by men. There's not much respect for a girl, but there's more respect if she's married.

Veena recognises that women's primary need for marriage is defined by men's desire for property rights over women. Sheela Sarvaria explores what the myth about women's domestic needs leaves out.

Many professional men disapprove of us. On economic grounds, women don't need to work, but they forget the intellectual needs. Also women have to be kept in place. In a man's world you have to accept challenge and hardship. It's based on fear. Fear of women becoming equal and fear of losing women to outside friends and other men.

Satya Bhasin, a young manager, experiences the same contradiction as Sheela, and is only partially succeeding in fitting into the stereotype of domesticity. She is fully aware of who holds the reins of power, and the effect this has on women.

I had a good job offer which I had to refuse because of marriage commitments. I resent this to a point, but accept it generally when trying to rationalise not doing well! Home demands much time and change of priorities over a period. Work is important in the office but not outside. This should apply to me also! It's still a man's world. Socialization from childhood has taught us that. Women are insecure. No matter how liberated, women require security. But some men feel insecure by women working.

Satya knows that acknowledging her extra-domestic needs exposes the fact that men's security is based on women's domestication. Sarabjit Kalia exposes the reality of women's domesticity.

Many people think women shouldn't work. So many young girls are prevented from using their talents. I have doubts about ignoring my daughter, but there are so many things that I can't get from home: independence and the company and stimulus of others and the financial benefits. I did *not* enjoy the months at home doing nothing. I want to avoid the slovenly life of a middle class woman and the emptiness of family existence.

Moyna Ghosh has begun to explore and to change the ways in which she colludes with the stereotypes.

I'm very intolerant of the differences in how men and women are treated, and I wish to change them. Because I experience a male dominated world, I'm becoming aware of my own compromise. It's a hard job of liberation. The greatest enemies are women themselves. It is *not* understandable, except for older women.

What happens when women actively resist the stereotype? Usha Khanna found it impossible to fit her own interests and ambitions into the ideal view of women. She is artistic and has started her own fabric business. She doesn't have any problems with her husband, but everyone else — family and friends — criticises what she has done.

My family used to be very encouraging, but now, they don't like me to be ambitious, self-centred, selfish. They like me to have a career, but they don't really approve of business . . . 'Ambitious' is a derogatory term they use. This is purely because I'm a woman . . . It's more difficult for women because of the culture and family ties . . . It reduces the possibility of ambition. To get ahead you must fight for it. Up to a point they say, 'Fine, good, nice to see you occupying yourself.' But beyond that point, you get criticised.

Usha *is* ambitious, no matter how much the myth defines women as having no aspirations other than domesticity. She wants to use her talents to earn her own living, no matter how much the myth suggests that she should subordinate them to the family. Usha has discovered that she simply does not fit the myth.

Women who have chosen a profession in preference to marriage may find they are socially ostracised, like Vijaya Ambujam.

There are social disadvantages — I've withdrawn from conservative society because many people can't deal with a single professional woman. I avoid contact — I've made no friends since college — I just kept the ones who understand me.

The problem is that there is another category waiting for the woman who does not fit into the stereotype of domesticity. Shaheen Kumari:

If you work in a professional job, people don't usually take you to be simple and ordinary. You're always thought of as being complex and different. You're criticised for social mixing, for being 'improper' — this criticism comes from women who don't work outside, and from all men.

Indrani Vijayalakshmi:

A woman who comes to work can't have a good moral character. Now it's changing. I had to prove I was normal. Initially people at work thought me abnormal. The ideal view of women is domesticated. People think me aggressive and immoral.

Any woman resisting the domestic stereotype of woman as private sexual property is defined instead as sexually available to anyone. The experience of being treated as immoral is widespread amongst women in professional jobs, as Reva Sabhorwal knows.

The relics of the Moghul era, especially in the north, and the tendency to keep women in purdah cause problems for women. Free mixing between the sexes is impossible, therefore a professional woman is regarded in North India as a loose woman to some extent. It's not so bad in the South. The men of the family know how they react to other women, so they tend to be protective. It's a blow to men's pride if the wife goes out to work.

The domestic stereotype defines woman as sexual object and male property, and supports the reality that most middle-class women have no choice but to conform to the stereotype. Men benefit from this reality through the possession of exclusive sexual and reproductive rights and through women's unpaid labour in the home: men have a material interest in maintaining women's domestication. Against this background, it is easier to see why a woman and a professional worker are actually seen as contradictory. Anita Shukla:

> There aren't many women in the civil service. Every one is inspected. If she does well at home, people say she's no good at the office. If she does well professionally, people say she's not feminine.

This helps to explain many of the women's experiences of not being allowed to be themselves, but being persistently placed in a biological category. Anjana Vishwanatan:

> Theoretically we have equal rights. In practice we have to fight . . . If we do well, they say it's because she's a woman. If we do badly it's because she's a woman! They won't let you forget you're a woman . . . being a woman they never let you feel at ease, you're constantly going through turmoil because they won't let you forget. You're not accepted as a *person*. Men either put you on a pedestal or look down on you. There's no balance.

The strict division between the biological sexes can only be sustained if the socially constructed distinctions of gender are a prominent feature, reinforcing the divergence of masculinity and femininity, and confirming the female sex in its subjection to men.

The stereotypes about women's inferior abilities, subservient qualities and domestic needs form part of a gender ideology which makes sharp distinctions between the social constructs of masculinity and femininity. The women who speak here, however, know that men in the workplace and in the family are primary, not because of natural abilities, qualities or needs, but as a result of a social process which constructs male superiority, male dominance and male control over women. This knowledge provides the basis for women to question the myths both in attitudes and in action.

24. The Context of Gender

The ideology of gender is not universal in its form. It is specific to particular historical periods, cultural backgrounds, and positions within the hierarchies of class and nationality.[9] This is true of the gender ideology identified by our women. Its components reveal that it is specific to its class, cultural and national context.

The Class Context

The stereotype of domesticity is experienced differently depending on the women's location in the class structure, for it is only women whose family's economic position allows them to live a purely domestic life, who can put the idea into practice. The idea has its origins in the caste system, where women are increasingly secluded with a rise in caste status. Much as they might wish to, lower-caste women are unable to live in secluded domesticity because their economic position prevents it. The same process occurs within the class system.

Ambika Roy illustrates how the practice changes with social mobility: 'In poorer, rural families, women always work, then when they get some money the wife stops working outside. Men get status if they can support the wife.'

There are differences even within the middle class. Aruna Sharma: 'There's a large batch of middle-class women who *have* to work, like typists for example.' Conditions affect the attitudes on women's domesticity. Paramjit Caroli:

> The conflict of values makes it more difficult for women to have jobs — the Indian definition of a good wife and mother. Some traditional well-off families wouldn't like you to work at all. It's a prestige symbol for the wife not to work. In the lower strata working wives are preferred for economic reasons.

So the domestic stereotype is experienced in a particular way by well-off middle-class women, although women lower down the social hierarchy may aspire to the same practice with an improvement in their economic conditions. Many of our women are aware of this class difference in both the conditions of and the ideas about women's lives. This is at least partly because of the visibility of working-class women labouring in their homes as ayahs and domestic servants. As we saw in Part IV, many of our professional women are heavily dependent on such women. There are, however, differences of approach to the question of class. Some of the women experience contradictions between the relations of class and those of gender. This is more marked amongst women working in management positions, where the power relation with subordinate women is explicit and direct. Manjari Seth:

> I have problems because all my subordinates are girls. They feel, even in the office, that the woman to woman attitude should persist. Because I'm friendly, they expect me to be more liberal workwise. Now they realise I can be friendly as well as a taskmaster.

Clearly women do not have an identity of interest across class divisions: the barriers that separate them are structured into the employment relationship, whether as employers and domestic servants or as superiors and subordinates within an organisation. But other women are more sympathetic towards lower-class women, and more conscious of their own class privilege, like Archana Singh.

> Some colleagues and superiors tend to think that women are no good, they take too much leave etc. There aren't many women in high positions. They don't think women at lower levels work very hard, and generalise to higher posts. But why *should* lower level women work like gazetted officers?

Those like Archana who are aware of their class privilege tend to be the women who are also most aware of women's oppression: Reeta Rao, who had to break out of marriage to free herself from domestic seclusion, is now opposed not only to male privilege but also to the hierarchies of caste and religion; Promilla Khanna, whose father was radicalised by his experiences as a refugee, now challenges both orthodox and liberal approaches to the subordination of sex and class.

The notion of domesticity, then, is firmly rooted in the middle class, and is strongly supported by economic conditions which make it possible for women to be supported within the family by the men.

The Cultural Context

The idea of women's subservience is strongest in the more male-dominated cultures of the North, where the patriarchal family structure persists, particularly amongst the more orthodox groups at the top of the social hierarchy. A number of women pointed out the regional differences in the culture of male supremacy and female subservience, such as Lotika Choudhury: 'Male chauvinism is very strong except in the South, in Kerala and so on where it's a more matriarchal system.' This affects relations between men and women. Sumitra Kaushik was brought up in Bombay, married a man from South India, and now lives in the North: 'The North is much more conservative than the West or the South. If you attended a social gathering in Bombay, everyone would mix. Men and women separate in Delhi — they can't talk to each other.'

As we showed in Part II, the culture of male supremacy, although dominant, is not absolute, and the idea of women's power maintains its potency for women in India, even within the realities of the male power structure. Even women from the North acknowledge the influence of the goddess myth. Shashi Misra: 'The positive things about Indian culture for women are the great women of the past. Goddesses have great power, and women too are possessed of great power and virtue.' And the myth of women's power affects the culture for real women. Indira Mamtani: 'There's an Indian tradition of women occupying high positions, although they're still treated badly in some sections of society. It depends on the cultural background.'

So the idea of women's power persists, stronger in some regions of India than others. Although it appears to contradict the notion of male supremacy, the contradiction is resolved, as we saw in Part II, through the containment of women's power rather than its denial. The stereotype of women's subservience contributes to this containment, and it is this aspect which is stressed in the Northern, patriarchal, orthodox culture. The myth is rooted in the idea of the danger of women's autonomy, and is strongest in the North, associated with the patriarchal heritage of that region and the orthodoxy of caste. Despite the dominance of the idea of women's subservience in this region, many women are still conscious of and influenced by the notion of female power.

The Context of Imperialism

The persistence of the myth of women's power in Indian society suggests that the countervailing idea of women's inferiority may have been imported from the West. This has been proposed by writers from colonised Muslim countries, including Azizah Al-Hibri in relation to Palestine,[10] and Fatima Mernissi in connection with Morocco.[11] Tara Ali Baig has made a similar suggestion about India, noting that Indian culture retains the image of woman as powerful, strong and creative.[12] Certainly the notion of women's inferiority is associated in our study with Western forms of academic learning and ideas of competence in waged employment, neither of which had any place in the traditional organisation of education or work in India. As we discussed in Part II, the idea of women's inferiority appears to have no existence in Hindu or Muslim mythology, where containment of women's power is stressed rather than her inherent inferiority. In contrast, the notions of subservience and domesticity do have their origins in Indian culture, and are consistent with the idea of controlling women's power.[13]

The inferiority component of the gender ideology, then, seems to have been influenced by Western culture, in that the notion of woman as inferior is a Western idea contrary to the view of woman as 'too strong' in the Indian tradition. As we saw in Part IV, the idea has taken a firm hold in the modern organisation of education and employment. This is one way in which Western ideas have worsened women's position by adding a further derogatory component to the gender ideology, with direct effects upon women's conditions of work. The influence of the West has more complex effects too. Women who have travelled to Western countries for education and later sought employment, often find that ideas of gender and race inferiority augment the discrimination they encounter in those supposedly enlightened countries. Priya Gupta is one of these.

> I applied for a number of jobs in the U.S. Many people were just wasting my time. They had to interview me because I was educated. Partly it was because I'm Indian, mainly because I'm a woman. They used the excuse that I would marry and leave.

At home the power relations between the West and the Third World place professional women at a disadvantage compared with their Western counterparts, particularly in their work. Unlike class, from which professional women benefit, within imperialist relations professional women in India are disadvantaged. This is particularly marked in the case of industrial management, where the employer is a multinational company. Elizabeth James works as a manager in IBM.

> It's very frustrating where there's no growth for the company, and therefore for myself. IBM is 100 per cent foreign owned. The government says it must have equity shares, otherwise it won't allow IBM a licence to sell, market or manufacture. IBM won't agree, so it has to live on the rental of pre-1969 manufactures and limited imports. I agree with India's stand, but it has reduced my satisfaction with the job.

Elizabeth is in a privileged position as a manager in a multinational, but she is also aware that her job prospects, security and satisfaction are reduced by virtue of being an Indian employee in a subordinate relationship with a Western commercial organisation.

Women in the other professions experience the contradiction too, although its connection with Western imperialism is less obvious in medicine, education and the civil service. Nevertheless, facilities which would be taken for granted in Western hospitals are not available in India, and reduce women's ability to do the job properly, and their satisfaction with it. Nalini Grewal is an anaesthetist in a hospital that caters for government officers, and is therefore one of the best equipped in the country, but: 'The lack of facilities is dissatisfying, there's no time for research work, no facilities for certain investigations and no Intensive Care Unit.'

Archana Singh finds that the development programmes she works on, funded and controlled by Western governments, are inappropriate.

> The development programmes for the country are . . . not suited to the situation. I want to organise alternative methods — how to change the system within the system? I want to change them at ground level, where they actually happen. You've got to work with people, not just give orders from a desk in Delhi. I want to change the nutrition programmes but I've no power to do so. We spend money to find problems that we should spend fighting them. We know what they are already. There's too much survey work. I hate the objectives of this scheme on which I'm working — it's not useful.

We have already seen in Part IV how India's education system has been affected not only by the country's poverty, but also by the cultural imperialism of using a foreign language as the teaching medium, and the attitude which categorises Sanskrit colleges as inferior to English or American ones.

The context of Western domination imports not only the idea of women's inferiority in relation to men, but also a notion of Indian women's inferiority in relation to Western women. The notion of national inferiority is experienced by Indian professional women abroad in encounters with Westerners, and at home where their conditions of work are inferior to those of Western professional women. In some cases, women experience the power relation between the West and the Third World directly in their work. Less directly, the myth of the Third World's inferiority helps to justify continued Western exploitation of Indian resources, which worsens economic conditions in India. This causes a deterioration of women's educational and employment position, thanks to the gender ideology which gives priority to men in conditions of scarcity. Worsening educational and employment conditions make it increasingly difficult for women in particular to complete their education or do their job properly, since they are already additionally burdened with domestic work, as we saw in Part IV. The effect is to reinforce the idea that women are less capable in education and employment than men.

Women in all professions are conscious of how imperialist relations affect their lives, but the awareness is more marked where the relationship is more directly experienced, such as women working for the multinationals, in the higher education system, on development programmes and amongst women who have travelled abroad. The Western notions of gender and national inferiority affect relations between men and women within India, and relations between Indian and Western women. Clearly women do not have an identity of interest across national divisions, for the barriers that separate them are structured into the economic and ideological relations between the West and the Third World.

The gender ideology we have discussed is therefore specific to a particular historical period of India's culture, arising along with the employment of women in the new middle class, taking in features from the colonial culture and preserving aspects of the indigenous culture. It is specific to its location in the class structure, to its place in the patriarchal Northern culture, and to India's position in the hierarchy of nations. It is this very specificity which draws attention to the real divisions between women of different classes, cultures and nations. The divisions must be acknowledged if women are to make common cause internationally in the challenge to male domination.

25. Exposing the Myths

Many of our women find that the image which others hold of them bears little relation to how they see themselves, or to how they experience their lives. The image is more a reflection of others' needs and desires. The women often find that their own ideas conflict with the stereotypes which other people try to impose, and this conflict acts as a powerful stimulus for change. These images, stereotypes and ideas all contribute to the ideology of gender, which provides the cultural support for professional women's position in the gender and class hierarchies. Our women have identified three major myths which contribute to this ideology of gender, and which conflict with their own experience: women's inferiority, subservience and domesticity.

How the Attitudes Affect Women

The contradictory impact of the myth of inferiority affects our women at the workplace and in the family. Intelligent and competent women who have to prove themselves at work, also find that they have to underplay their abilities in order not to upset their male colleagues. Some of the women find that they are resented if they display equal or superior capacity to men in either mental or physical work. Within the family, marriage partners who are less qualified, draw a lower salary or have a lower social standing are not considered suitable, so some women find that they cannot marry, demonstrating the lack of 'superior' male partners. The ideas our women use to counter these attitudes derive specifically from their experience of Indian culture. They counter the notion of women's inferior abilities by referring to the everyday sight of working-class women labouring on roads and building sites, doing back-breaking work in the harsh sun, breaking stones and carrying bricks. They also use the powerful images in Indian religion and culture of strong female goddesses, images which retain their influence for women throughout India.

The notion of female subservience also affects our women in a particular way. The tradition of female seclusion can lead to the incongruous position of a woman in the highest class of the civil service, responsible for Tribal Areas in the Home Ministry, having to veil her face in deferrence to her in-laws' orthodox sensibilities. Or a reader at the university who is assertive and creative at work, having to stay in the background and defer to her husband at home in order to save his 'face'. Even at the workplace some women find that men do not like their views questioned by a woman. Women counteract these ideas in different ways: by being deliberately and literally 'two-faced', presenting different images depending on the company; or by ignoring the disapproval and being themselves no matter who is watching.

The value attached to female domesticity means that a woman who is unmarried after a certain age is regarded as abnormal. A divorced or separated woman is treated disrespectfully and slandered. The importance of domesticity and the relics of seclusion mean that many people regard any woman who leaves the house for paid employment as a 'loose woman', so that it is impossible, for instance, for a woman to share transport with a male work colleague. Our women regard such attitudes as narrow-minded, and although they may initially be upset by the gossip and the slur on their characters many of them become hardened and ignore the slander rather than succumb to social pressure. To counter these attitudes, our women point out that many families cannot survive without the woman's income, that many women cannot fulfil their needs from a purely domestic existence, and that it is a national waste if women are not usefully employing their education.

The Attitudes in Context

In terms of social structure, the context for the development of this particular form of gender ideology is the location of professional women in the class, cultural and national hierarchies. The attitudes relate specifically to middle-class women living in the North Indian patriarchal culture, under the economic and cultural domination of the West, and at a historical period of Western capitalist expansion into the Third World. The stereotypes of subservience and domesticity can be seen to arise out of the tradition of seclusion in the patriarchal high-caste family. The stereotype of inferiority, however, does not seem to fit with the Indian tradition, and may have its source in the West.

At a more specific level, the local context for the attitudes on woman's place can be seen by comparing the attitudes with the actual conditions of women's lives, as discussed in Part IV. Whilst women are considered less able, intellectually and practically, men in fact have greater access to academic and practical courses and to employment opportunities. Women are often excluded from 'male' subjects and occupations. In particular, women are directed into teaching and medicine because they cater for female needs and can be undertaken separately from men. The idea that women are less competent is created by their active exclusion from many areas of education, training and employment.

The myth of women as primarily domestic reflects the reality that men do not share domestic work, and women find it more difficult to get jobs, education or training because of male priority in these areas. Whilst men are able to draw on women's labour at home to restore their own energy, women are said to have less strength and stamina than men, when the reality is that women's energy is spent doing both paid and domestic work. And the notion of women's subservience reflects the reality of male economic and sexual control over women in education, employment and the family, where women who venture into employment are treated as promiscuous, and assertive or rebellious women are regarded as abnormal.

These attitudes and conditions benefit men through greater leisure time, domestic and personal services, control over women at home and in the workplace, and priority in educational and employment institutions. It is hardly surprising then that many men are unwilling to give up their privileges and the attitudes that go with them, and have no desire to change the organisation of work under imperialism which reinforces male privilege.

Changing Attitudes

None of the women we spoke to accepted their subordination to men. Some, it is true, did not recognise that subordination. They thought women were equal already. They were all young single women who had been brought up in homes sympathetic to women's emancipation. All the others expressed contradictions reflecting their experiences as women in a man's world. Even those who agreed at a general level that women were weaker or less intelligent, more submissive and less independent than men, expressed their *knowledge* that these definitions did not fit with their own experience. Not all the women acknowledged the existence of male power, then, but every single one knew that male superiority was a myth, even if they continued to collude with the myth consciously or unconsciously.

We have argued that women living in a man's world experience a contradiction between their own experiences as women, and the way these experiences are interpreted. The contradiction is experienced at different levels of reality and consciousness, such that for many women and for many experiences, there will be no awareness of a contradiction, whereas for other women and other experiences the contradiction will be sharp. Amongst our women we found several different approaches. Some were unaware of a contradiction at a conscious level, yet expressed it explicitly when comparing their own personal experience with the general view of women's position. Some were aware of contradictions at a conscious level, and held both views simultaneously. Others repudiated the contradictions mentally, but continued to act them out in public, deliberately enacting a pretence. Yet others had stopped colluding mentally or behaviourally with male interpretations of their experiences, and refused to acknowledge men's primacy or to act it out.

So we can see that the contradictions women express in their views and attitudes reflect not ill-thought-out ideas, but an experience which contains many dimensions rather than one single reality. At one level of their experience, our women accept the definition of femininity that is constructed for them by the attitudes and practices of their society. At another level, when their own experience denies the validity of these definitions, they may regard themselves as deficient females rather than reject the definitions, thereby colluding unknowingly in the myths about women. At a third level, women can collude consciously, keeping to themselves the evidence which contradicts men's deficient knowledge of them.

All this requires great skill in integrating the many dimensions of experience, to accommodate the contradictions. But it is these very contradictions which provide the basis for psychological change in the women's consciousness. Many of our women now are beginning to explore the contradictions, by disintegrating them and constructing their own meanings. This process is a powerful force for change in both consciousness and action, leading women to break the collusion and expose the myths supporting the institution of male supremacy. How they do this we will see in Part VI.

Notes

1. Suniti Namjoshi (1981) 'The Disinterested Lover', *Feminist Fables*. London: Sheba, p.113.
2. Ann Patricia Caplan (1979) 'Indian Women: Model and Reality. A Review of Recent Books, 1975-1979', *Women's Studies International Quarterly* 2, 4, p.466.
3. Promilla Kapur (1970) *Marriage and the Working Woman in India*. Delhi: Vikas; Promilla Kapur (1973) *Love, Marriage and Sex*. Delhi: Vikas; Promilla Kapur (1974) *The Changing Status of the Working Woman in India*. Delhi: Vikas.
4. Michèle Barrett (1980) *Women's Oppression Today*. London: Verso, Ch.3.
5. Ann Foreman (1977) *Femininity as Alienation: Women and the Family in Marxism and Psychoanalysis*. London: Pluto, pp.103-5.
6. John Berger (1973) *Ways of Seeing*. Harmondsworth: Penguin, p.47.
7. M.N. Srinivas (1977) 'The Changing Position of Indian Women', *Man* 12, p.223.
8. Prabhati Mukherjee (1983) 'The Image of Women in Hinduism', *Women's Studies International Forum* 6, 4, p.379.
9. Floya Anthias and Nira Yuval-Davis (1983) *Contextualising Feminism — Gender, Ethnic and Class Divisions*. Paper presented to the Conference of Socialist Economists, Bradford University.
10. Azizah Al-Hibri (1981) 'Capitalism is an Advanced Stage of Patriarchy: but Marxism is not Feminism', in Lydia Sargent (ed), *Women and Revolution*. London: Pluto Press, pp.184-5.
11. Fatima Mernissi (1975) *Beyond the Veil*. New York: Wiley, pp.xv-xvi.
12. Tara Ali Baig (1976) *India's Woman Power*. New Delhi: S. Chand, pp.7-9, 65.
13. Susan S. Wadley (1977) 'Women in the Hindu Tradition', in Doranne Jacobson and Susan Wadley, *Women in India: Two Perspectives*. New Delhi: Manohar, pp.118-19.

Part VI: Mechanisms of Struggle

26. Working for Change

Why does a crane stand on one leg? Because if it lifted this leg also, it would fall. Why does the burden of marriage fall only on woman? Because if she did not bear the burden, the institution of marriage would break down.
Kamla Bhasin, *The Riddle of Marriage*[1]

In Part III we saw how women emerged from high-caste seclusion to acquire education and professional employment. The issues over which they fought were determined by the special aspects of their oppression deriving from the economic and sexual control to which seclusion subjected them. The location for their fight was the patriarchal family, but their struggles did not thereby appear isolated, for they occurred within the context of the changing social, economic and political environment around the time of Independence, involving the nationalist movement, the movements for social reform and the women's movement itself.

More recently, however, as the movements began to see their aims established in the new institutions of the country, their political drive receded. This particularly occurred with the women's movement, as we saw in Part I. Yet women's struggles did not stop as a result, rather they became less organised and therefore less visible. Individual women continued to face problems and to fight them. Although our women achieved economic independence through professional employment, they did not achieve liberation from gender roles, and we saw in Parts IV and V the particular material and psychological constraints which professional women continue to encounter. Financial independence did, however, provide the basis from which to make far-reaching changes within individual families, from which women could challenge further the other foundation of male supremacy, control over female sexuality. As observed in Part III, the women's struggles achieved limited change in the structures of society, but often radical changes in themselves and their families.

In Part VI we are looking at how the women resist the controls placed upon them within marriage. We have chosen not to look at conflicts within work relations, because so few women are engaged in workplace issues. Very few women are members of a trade union. Vimla Gupta is a notable exception, an activist in a professional trade union. More common is Ankita Chandra's comment on problems at the workplace: 'We need more flexibility in society, and flexible working hours. I have a grievance against government regulations that women can't have time off. But we haven't done anything active about it.' This kind of activity has not been taken up by professional women who, in spite of their work-related problems, are in a relatively privileged position compared with other employed women. The most significant area in which the women could be seen to be actively challenging their subordinate position was in marriage. This is significant, for middle-class women are still defined as subservient and inferior to men, and primarily domestic in their needs. The struggle against this definition is therefore a major issue for our women, and the predominant location is the family, since this is the place where women negotiate the conditions of their domestic work and a considerable part of their paid work too. Not only may women have to negotiate the undertaking of paid work with family members, but subsequently the effect of women's paid work on the family may entail the negotiation of compromises over domestic work too. The private, personal affairs of the family are political problems for women, over which they must struggle for control.

Although supportive alliances are frequently made with other family members, our women report no collective responses to their subordination. The resistance is largely individual and conducted in isolation from other struggles. There are two reasons for this. One is the particular location of women's subjection within the family, which provides no basis for meeting and organising collectively across families. The other is that when we spoke to the women, there was no active women's movement to provide a context for the resistance. There was the beginning of a renewed interest in women's issues, as we suggested in Part I, but the 'second wave' of the movement had not yet appeared. Instead there was a women's organisation without its previous political purpose, plus the ideas handed down from the time when it was active. A very few women, like Rekha Rohtagi, maintained their contact with women's organisations, but most women pursued their problems individually.

One consequence of the focus on the personal relations within the family is that the struggle between individuals is emphasised. Of course, women do have to make their stand within individual relationships, but the problem is also wider than that, for a whole structure of material and psychological controls is set up to support male dominance as an institution. This means, as we will see, that even when the men of the family are supportive, it is often very difficult to break out of the structural constraints and create a new way of living. The women who have done so are truly remarkable, given that they had at that time no wider supporting structures.

Part VI looks at the women's responses to one particular contradiction in their lives, and examines the resistance incorporated in their responses. The specific issue we have chosen to look at is the negotiation within the family of the relationship between marriage and employment. Amongst our women, the struggle against male controls can be seen not only in outright resistance, but also in the strategies of compromise and sacrifice. Sacrifice of their own interests for the sake of others is the expected response of high-caste or middle-class women to the contradictions of their existence. In that the whole weight of the social structure and ideology lies behind this response, the 'choosing' of it needs no further explanation, although the experience of it needs further exposure, and is discussed in the next chapter.

In trying to understand how the women came to choose a response other than self-sacrifice, we will examine two features of their lives, using the analysis from Parts IV and V. First, their objective conditions, that is, what material power the women had to use as a basis for negotiating a change in the conditions. Second, the women's subjective consciousness, that is, how aware they were of the power structure, of the ways in which it could constrain them, and of their own potential power and how it could be used to achieve what they wanted. In discussing the women's responses we do not intend to suggest that they exclusively chose one form of response over others. Often their responses changed over time, or according to the issue at stake. The point is not to classify the women into fixed response categories, but to examine the effects of different responses and to analyse the circumstances under which they occurred.

In Part VI we will examine the mechanisms by which women resist the constraints of male domination, and their effects; the extent of the changes our women have achieved through their resistance; the specific character of the resistance and the changes they have achieved.

27. Sacrifice

In brahminical Hinduism, the stereotype of the ideal woman is represented by Sita, the heroine of the Ramayana Epic.[2] Sita was abducted from her husband Rama, patiently endured all privations, resisted all attempts at seduction and later undertook without complaint the ordeal by fire to prove her innocence and fidelity. The rite of becoming sati extended this ideal of self-sacrifice to the point of death on the husband's funeral pyre, an act which liberated the husband's soul and brought the woman religious merit for her next incarnation. Gandhi, despite his desire to release women from their seclusion, reinforced the ideal of sacrifice: 'I do believe that it is woman's mission to exhibit ahimsa [non-violence] at its highest and best . . . For woman is more fitted than man to make ahimsa. For the courage of self-sacrifice woman is anyway superior to man, as I believe, man is to woman for the courage of the brute.'[3] He especially used the concept in his philosophy and practice of non-violent resistance to the British, and suggested that he had learnt it from his wife, in her implacable but silent resistance to his own demands on her.[4]

The concept of sacrifice, then, is a powerful concept for women in orthodox Hinduism. It embodies the ideal of what women should be in a male-dominated society — silent, subservient, self-effacing.[5] For women and the lower castes, the principle could be enacted through service to others higher in the social hierarchy, specifically high-caste males. Such service brought religious merit to the giver, and material benefit to the receiver. For high-caste males, sacrifice was practised by becoming sannyasi, that is, leaving the comforts of home later in life and becoming a wandering holy man, dependent for survival on begging for alms. This course was freely chosen for the release of the soul. It brought no material benefit in terms of service to others, but benefited only the self, albeit in a spiritual not a physical manner. In contrast to the choice offered to high-caste males, the sacrifice of women was demanded and often coerced. For such women, the concept of sacrifice was, and is, a powerful element of patriarchal ideology justifying women's material services to men, with the promise of spiritual benefit to themselves later.

However, the ideology of sacrifice is also a means whereby the constant negation of the self can be justified. The concept is appealing because it fits so well with one aspect of the Hindu religious philosophy which aims for the liberation of the soul through the self denial of the body. (This aspect is a feature of patriarchal brahmin Hinduism; the very opposite of 'matriarchal' Tantric Hinduism, which liberates the soul through the celebration of the body.[6]) Self-sacrifice brings religious merit and social approbation. In the absence of any alternative, it can give purpose to a miserable life, it can make a wasted life seem worthwhile through selfless service to others, instead of a purely selfish striving towards personal fulfilment. Nor is this ideology found only in India.[7]

Some of our women use the ideology of sacrifice to come to terms with their own experience. Asha Paul:

> If I were posted apart from my husband I'd have to follow him, but I would try to get posted to the same place. My fantasy is to go to the top of my profession, but in reality I'll have to sacrifice for family life so I won't make it. I don't mind very much.

It's interesting that the highest proportion of women who use this ideology to understand their lives come, not from the group of married women (one-fifth use it), but from women who are engaged to men of their parents' choice (more than two-thirds). Although these women comprised only 6 per cent of the sample, they accounted for 22 per cent of women using that ideology, suggesting that women do try to fit in with men's expectations of them, but that many of them find the reality impossible to implement after marriage.[8]

Almost all the women who have sacrificed some aspect of themselves for their husbands and families express regret. Madhu Jaikishan is a doctor:

> I will take a part-time job in 2 or 3 years. My husband's studying for his MD . . . so we need the money at the moment. He wants me to study MD too. I wanted to become a big woman — to do something with my life — to serve people . . . When I have children it will be a problem. I will take a permanent part-time job until the children are grown up. I wouldn't like to give up work altogether. I'm satisfied with my job, I've no ambitions now. I've done a diploma, not MD. I have the chance to do it, but I don't want to because it would take 2 years, I would have to leave my husband and it would spoil the family life. After marriage and when the children come it's quite difficult for women. Women have to do both jobs.

Madhu's paid work is supporting her husband's postgraduate training. He wants her to do her training next, but she knows — and maybe he does too — that she won't. She has, indeed, already sacrificed her ambitions for his.

Leela Misra found herself in a similar position. The overwhelming impression left by her story is of the confusion over the impossible situation in which she found herself.

> Both my parents were doctors, I was expected to do the same. I passed the entrance exam, but I reacted against it because my mother worked very very hard, and I decided I wanted to work fewer hours in teaching . . .
> I married after I became a lecturer. I think possibly my husband married me *because* I was a lecturer. I was sure I'd continue working . . . I'm married to a foreign office man who may have to go abroad — he *has* gone abroad, therefore I cannot stay at home. His mobility stops the development of my career. He's encouraging and he expects me to continue working, but it depresses me that

when I finish my PhD what do I do?

My husband's in Jakarta now, and I'll be leaving after I finish my PhD. He wants a wife who is interesting, so that we have something to talk about. But his job *prevents* my working. I help his career very much.

I'm not in control of my work at all. This takes a lot of mental adjustment. When my husband went to Japan I went with him, and I was reduced to tears for 4 months around the clock. Then I made a radical adjustment and saw the advantage of the family — it serves as an emotional buffer. I pursued my interests during leaves. But I have to come to terms with the fact that boys who were not as good as me will be professors. This is the major conflict about work. I put my feelings to one side. My aunt who's a doctor was very fussy about a husband, and eventually did not marry. Now she's very lonely, she's given up her career and joined an ashram. It's not accepted to stay unmarried . . . My awareness sharpened very much after marriage, and I had to gradually learn to accept that my career came second. I don't want to give up my work but I will have to. Through working, my own status in society is enriched. I'm not just Mrs Misra, not just an appendage of my husband. It gives you confidence and helps in your marriage. When your partner knows you are emotionally, psychologically and financially independent, it makes a great difference to the partnership. You don't drain your husband emotionally. You have a life of your own, you're not just an extension of your husband. The disadvantage is the strain of doing 2 fulltime jobs. My husband did help in the house, but only when I'm not around and he has to. When I'm around he will not do so . . . There's a lot of potential for marital disharmony. There are pros and cons, but still I prefer the nuclear family for personal development. It's bad enough catering for the whims and fancies of my husband and son without adding to it.

If I had a daughter, I'd still like her to be economically independent despite the problems. There's a woman behind the rise of every man, but there's also a man behind the fall of every woman.

Leela married well. Her parents were from the vaishya caste. She was an only child, very bright, always top of the class. She never faced the kind of problems her mother did over getting qualifications and working outside the home. Nor did she anticipate problems when she married a man of the highest caste, a brahmin, with a very prestigious job in the foreign office. He wanted a wife who could be a companion, not a domestic servant. She was sure she would continue working.

What went wrong with these plans? Having had such an easy time during childhood, she couldn't anticipate the problems marriage might bring. Having found a husband who wanted a wife who could treat with him on equal terms, she could not believe that he would always give priority to *his* work. Nor did she realise what giving up work would mean to her. Only after marriage could she see how important her own work was for her identity, her confidence, her independence.

In Japan she was torn between two mutually exclusive paths: work and marriage. It took four months of anguish before she finally chose the marriage. When she considered the possibility of choosing work, she recognised that life without her husband would not be easy. It was a possibility, but within the present structure it was not attractive. She knew that other people in her community would not accept it; she would be lonely and friendless. Her unmarried aunt had experienced precisely this loneliness. Under these conditions, where companionship can only be found within marriage, and marriage the only approved state for a woman, the decision was not a choice at all. Heavily weighted in one direction, it was an almost inevitable outcome.

Leela justified her forced choice by coming to regard the family as an emotional buffer, even though it was the family which had caused the emotional problems in the first place.

Manju Malik did not have to give up her job, but she had to leave her area of interest. In Manju's case, it was not only her position in the family that forced the sacrifice but also her natal family's financial position. She works as a bacteriologist, dealing not with people but with cells.

> I wanted to do a clinical subject, and I got admission, but I hesitated to ask my father for more money, so I took a non-clinical job . . . I didn't want to ask for more money because I was the eldest, and there were some financial difficulties.
>
> I wanted to do clinical work, but didn't. If I went back I would lose experience and seniority. There is family pressure to stay where I am because of my small son. It's hard to go against the recognised pattern of a career. I might change back in future when my son is 5.
>
> I still have this conflict over clinical work. Clinical would mean more time at work. Occasionally, say every 6 months, I feel upset that I'm not doing clinical. I've resigned myself to it. Before marriage I worked for the job only. Since marriage I work for financial reasons as well — I want everything for my son. Before marriage I was more free to do what I wanted, and change over to clinical, etc. I dislike not being directly in touch with the patients and work that is not of direct benefit to people. I regret these home and work conflicts. You shouldn't marry in clinical work. I can never give up my work – I won't survive.

Manju gets no satisfaction from her work, but she can't survive without it. She's resigned to the sacrifice she's made, but not reconciled to it. For Manju, like Leela, the choice was forced, the sacrifice coerced, but this time by economic as well as gender constraints.

The last three women experienced essentially the same contradiction, although the details may differ. Their work is, or was, important to them, an essential part of their identity. But the gender ideology defined their professional work as secondary both to their husband's career and to their own domestic duty. And the organisation of the family and of employment enforced this definition, making it *impossible* for the women to find any alternatives, leaving them only with regrets over what they have lost. Self-sacrifice is far from 'natural' in women, as Gandhi believed.[9] It is often a learned response to, and a subsequent justification for, an enforced set of circumstances.

A gloomy picture indeed. But there is another side to the concept of sacrifice. For in a very subtle way, resistance can be contained in the sacrifice. In the last resort, when there is no other way out of a powerless situation, sacrifice is sometimes used as a passive form of resistance. It can be turned around and used against the oppressor in a number of ways. One way is to deprive the oppressor of something he values at the same time as depriving oneself of it.

An example of this can be found in a later version of the Ramayana Epic,[10] where Sita is called upon to undergo a second trial of her honour, to which she consents but on her own terms. Instead of being saved from death by her honour, Sita invokes the Earth Goddess to take her into the earth if she is innocent. This happens. Rama is distraught, but Sita has finally resisted the intolerable demands placed on her and punished Rama by depriving him of herself.

The problem is that the only bargaining counter is the self, and depriving the other of oneself achieves, not change, but self-destruction. But some women find that threatening to sacrifice something that is dear to both parties can produce the desired changes. Rupali Sinha did this. She's a university teacher now.

> My parents and elder brothers thought I would continue with my studies because I was brainy at school. They didn't expect me to work. Education was considered mainly for self-fulfilment but not for a job. I'm the only professional woman amongst my sisters, although they are academically qualified. All my sisters are married, only I am working. I'm different because I was always concerned about *what* I studied, not just with taking examinations.
>
> The influences on me came from outside. One important influence was my father. He put a lot of emphasis on my scholastic achievement in my school days . . . I was also very much influenced by my chemistry teacher. I didn't know her very well, but I noticed she was married and that her marital status didn't stop her from being a scientist. I wanted to be like her, and to be a full-time teacher in chemistry.
>
> At school there were high expectations of me, and at college I also did well. I did science, but my family wanted me to change from science to arts, because you couldn't do science honours in the girls' college in those days at Calcutta, and they didn't want me to go to the co-ed college. I mentioned that I wouldn't study at all in that case! I felt unhappy that my family wouldn't let me fulfil my potential. I would have had to do a Pass course not an Honours course, but I had to have Honours to do postgraduate work. I wanted to work in a laboratory, and I had to have postgraduate qualifications for that. Then my brother suggested psychology, in which science background students are given MSc degrees at postgraduate level. I agreed to this. I have no regret today. I enjoy my work.

In Rupali's case, her threat not to study at all gave her family a dilemma, for they had taken a keen interest in her education and encouraged her intellectual development. They too would feel the loss if she threw it all away. Her brother found a solution which pleased everyone. Had Rupali meekly accepted the change to Arts, it's unlikely she would have had a career at all, and it's certain she would not have been working in the area of her aptitude. This form of resistance would not have succeeded had her family opposed education for girls. It would not, for example, have worked for Reeta Rao, whose father thought girls' education 'ridiculous'. It worked for Rupali because she threatened to withdraw something her family also wanted. Rupali also used this form of resistance over her marriage, when she threatened to sacrifice marriage entirely rather than take a husband she did not want.

My marriage was not an arranged one, like the prevailing convention in our society. My mother and brothers objected to this as the boy belonged to a different caste, which was and is a strong consideration for marriages. However, I explained that I didn't want to marry against the wishes of my family, therefore I would rather not marry at all. To this, mother relented as she couldn't think of one of her daughters remaining unmarried throughout. She was basically concerned with the welfare of her children. My 'threat' for not getting married at all really worked, and in fact, my family eventually took the initiative in settling the marriage . . . according to the usual religious rituals!

Another way that resistance can be seen in sacrifice is in the raising of an equivalent sacrifice from the other. The concept of sacrifice implies a conscious subordination of the needs of the self to the demands of others. The resistance is contained in the counter-demands to which the sacrifice gives rise. The person for whom the woman has sacrificed herself is now morally bound to fulfil an obligation to her needs. Padma Unnikrishnan: 'You have to depend psychologically on your son in later life, so you must do things for him when he's young to a certain extent.'

Mira Mitra has experienced this from the position of a daughter having to respond to her mother's sacrifice.

I'd be miserable if I gave up work. Some friends of mine have given up work when they had children. And they expect so much from the children that they resent any independent decisions, because the parents have invested so much of their lives in them. I felt this from my own mother. I felt that my primary loyalty should be to her.

Sacrifice, in other words, can be reciprocal, and in this form, as a last resort, can be seen as a means of resistance, although it may be equally destructive to both parties. It is particularly used by individuals in a powerless position, without allies and unable to organise the support of others. This is often the position women find themselves in within the family. It may be the only alternative to total submission.

The method can also be used collectively. Passive resistance was one of the methods used in the fight against British colonialism. It did not single-handedly free India from British rule, but it contributed to it. The use of the method, however, was not without its ambiguities, since it allowed the political revolution to occur without the accompaniment of a social revolution eradicating caste and class privilege.[11] Or indeed, gender privilege. Sacrifice can embody resistance, and resistance can be seen in many acts of sacrifice. It can be a personal and a political means of resistance to oppression, used individually or collectively. But it cannot necessarily achieve radical changes on its own when used collectively, and its effect may be self-destructive when used individually.

28. Compromise

The inequality of the power relationship between men and women is encapsulated in Kapila Ahuja's comment on the difficulties for middle-class women of breaking out of domestic work and into waged work: 'Much depends on the woman, if she's determined, and the man, if he's broadminded.' If the husband is broadminded, he may be willing to give up some of his privileges for his wife. If the wife is determined, she may be able to negotiate a compromise with her husband. The nature of the compromise and how it will be achieved may differ with each set of circumstances, but there is no doubt who is the more powerful. We can see some of the more common solutions by looking at a few examples.

Clearly, the kind of marriage entered into is important. Some women, keenly aware of the effect marriage will have, make it a condition of an arranged marriage that they will not be pressured into giving up their jobs. Gita Ralhan:

> My husband always expected me to stay in my job. I was in the civil service before marriage. At times he says I shouldn't work, but he knows my devotion. It was all settled before marriage. He hasn't interfered even though we've had to live separately for three years.

Others resist the pressures on them by specifying the kind of man they will marry. Promilla Khanna made a love marriage, but: 'I wouldn't have married unless I'd met someone who thought of me as a human being.' And some women insist that their parents should let them get established in a job first before arranging their marriage, like Satinder Singh:

> I was working when I got married . . . I got my law degree at 21, took some more exams 4 years later, then got my first job at 26. I only got married a couple of years after that. I persuaded my parents not to arrange my marriage until I had a job. Then I wondered whether my husband had married me for the sake of my work!

Those women who are able to achieve a compromise acceptable to themselves and their families have a power base of some sort from which to negotiate a solution. Gita Ralhan secured her husband's agreement that he would not try to persuade her to give up work. Her husband was understanding; had he not been, he would not have agreed to the marriage either. And Gita knew what she wanted. But these attitudes were backed up by the reality of Gita's powerful bargaining base. The fact that she already had a well-paid job which made her economically independent, gave her a secure basis for laying down the conditions under which she would marry.

Despite Gita's determination, her struggle to achieve a compromise was by no means straightforward.

> My parents encouraged me to do the IAS exam, but when it actually came to it, there was opposition from my father. When I got my appointment letter, he didn't like it. He tried to dissuade me because women shouldn't really work. *Now* he's very proud of me.
> A joint family would have helped me. I'd have fewer domestic problems . . . It's a very tough job. I took three months maternity leave at full pay. If I stopped I wouldn't get in again because of the age bar.

Despite Gita's ability her father was still unhappy about Gita's employment. But since she had been offered a post, his opposition was necessarily confined to dissuasion. With her marriage, Gita made sure that her husband would not turn against her job at the last moment. Yet she still finds the compromise less than ideal because, although she negotiated a marriage contract which enabled her to work outside the home, there was no agreement binding her husband to work inside the home.

Kalpana Kunnur took a different course to achieve the compromise with her husband and his family. She made no demands before marriage, although she was already established in the civil service. Instead she engaged in a policy of conciliation: she *persuaded* her husband's family to let her continue work.

> My husband's family weren't happy about my work at the beginning. I put in a lot of effort to show the family came first. They changed their minds because they found I was human. I reconciled them slowly . . . They have accepted me because they know I care for my husband . . . But they still don't like it when I go abroad.
> My husband thinks that if I'm happy at work, I should continue. In the early stages it was thought that I should give up. My in-laws are very orthodox . . . My mother-in-law didn't want me to work outside, but she didn't interfere. Then she saw the benefits when the economic situation made it necessary to have 2 salaries . . .
> My work's never taken seriously and I'm not in control of it. I'm tied to my husband's career. If my husband is posted away, I have to take leave . . . I'm not ambitious, but I'm very interested in my current work — I would like to see the cause of women promoted. I want to say 'we've arrived!' Every woman has to decide for herself whether she should work outside the home. Women's liberation is for each individual.

Kalpana persuaded the family to accept her work by putting in more effort to show she put the family first: to *prove* her priorities were the same as theirs. This was combined with a determination not to give up, despite all the problems.

207

She was able to do all this because of her class position: she could rely on servants to take a large share of the domestic responsibilities, and she could afford to run a car, so cutting down the time spent away from home. She is aware that a woman in a less well-paid job would have none of these advantages. And she was given concrete support in her campaign to convince her in-laws, by the financial benefits her job brought: the economic situation made it necessary for even middle-class families to have more than one salary, a fact which her in-laws could not ignore.

But because she took a more conciliatory approach, she was less successful than Gita Ralhan at getting her job valued equally with her husband's job. Although Kalpana had the same power base as Gita — an established profession giving her economic independence — she used it less effectively. The reason for this was not to be found in the changed cultural milieu of a different time period, for there is only five years difference in their ages, but in the effect of the family's history on the two women's consciousness.

Gita had experienced opposition, and she'd fought against it. She knew it was wise to get an agreement out of her husband, rather than wait and see what happened. Kalpana, though, had been encouraged by her father from the beginning. She'd experienced no opposition. But she hadn't thought anything through for herself either. As she put it:

> My father encouraged me, and I'm indebted to him for that, but I had this dilemma with him because I don't like to argue . . . I can see it now — I was 'obedient'.

Kalpana had never experienced opposition and she hadn't learnt to think independently, so she was unable to use the power she had as effectively as Gita.

The majority of our women were already established in professions when they married, an important power base from which to negotiate the conditions of their lives in both domestic and waged work. But only those who are aware of the impact marriage will have on their lives, either through some experience of their own or by observing others, are able to exploit this source of power to achieve a compromise in their own interests. Some, who are uncommitted to their paid work in the early stages of marriage, are able to retrieve the position later, but less effectively than those who are clear about their intentions from the beginning. After marriage, the kind of compromise a woman can achieve depends much more heavily on the husband's good will. Riti Burman has doubts and uncertainties over her future, but it is impossible to know whether they will be solved in the way she would like. She's a manager in the public sector.

> I've not been married long. I don't think my husband will mind me working, but not at the expense of the family. I don't think I'll leave but I'm not sure. His family don't have anything against my work, but maybe they will later when I have children.
>
> I enjoy coming to work in the morning, every day there's something new and interesting. But now I'm married there's too much to do. I need 48 hours a day. You can't give your whole time to the house — you have to neglect it to some extent. We both have transferable jobs. I'd follow my husband if I could, that

is, if there were a vacancy. Otherwise we would have to come to some arrangement. I wouldn't necessarily give up. I would feel very bad if I had to give up. I wouldn't like to leave. I would revolt if I were forced to leave without a genuine reason.

It is very clear that Riti both enjoys her work and values it as an activity within which she can fulfil herself. Yet she has made no definite contract with her husband on the position of her work within their relationship. Already the pressures are building up.

All three women who have discussed their position in detail in this section are in arranged marriages. A love marriage, however, is no guarantee against any of the problems and may pose problems of its own. Minoti Sharma is newly married, and is as undecided about her future as Riti Burman. She works for management services in a public sector company.

My husband and I were students in the same institute. It wasn't an arranged marriage. He had no particular expectations, but he wouldn't have any objections to my work, except that he does expect the housework to be done.

After marriage, my work required me to go out of town for 6 months. My husband's family objected and so I had to leave that job. I haven't been able to control my career because of family problems. There will be more problems in the future when I have children. I'll have to stay away for 6 months. Then I hope to return but this isn't decided. Also if my husband had to go elsewhere, I would have to move but I would protest. I will eventually return to university teaching; I was originally a lecturer but I left because of the family problems.

Minoti had to give up her old job; may have to give up altogether when she has children; has to follow her husband's job; and has to do the housework. Being in a love marriage has not prevented any of these problems. The only reason she is able to carry on against her in-laws' wishes is that the economic situation has made them value her financial contribution. Neither Minoti nor Riti faced any opposition from their parents, they were encouraged and supported throughout. But something was missing. Regardless of whether they were in a love marriage or an arranged marriage, neither woman was prepared for the problems until they happened. Being unaware of the power structure which made them subordinate in the family, they could not get any commitment on their own work from the husband or in-laws. Of course, some women were able to retrieve the position later, but the attitude and response of the marital family is unpredictable unless the issue is discussed explicitly. The only reliable way of securing an agreement is by negotiating from a position of power.

The system of arranged marriage can make these negotiations easier, because an arranged marriage is explicitly a legal-religious contract. A love marriage is based on the romantic mythology of an everlasting emotional bond tying two people together. No such emotion binds the partners of a prospective arranged marriage together, and both are emotionally free to reject a match which does not suit them for other reasons. Archana Singh for example: 'I've never had any difficulties with keeping my job. I refused a marriage offer from someone who didn't have a Delhi job. I never saw anyone special for whom to sacrifice my career.'

Sumitra Kaushik *was* bound by emotional considerations. She works for a private foreign-owned company in personnel.

I met my husband in the UK, he was a friend of my brother's. It's not an arranged marriage. He wanted me to continue work against my own wishes. I wanted to give up. I had a child and spent 6 months at home, but I got so bored I couldn't stand it and came back. Without a servant I couldn't have worked . . .

I will have problems if my domestic arrangements change. My husband's job is transferable, I'll have to move with him, so I didn't want a job where *I'd* have to travel. There are many constraints to be considered for a job, that you wouldn't have to consider if you were a man — mainly concerned with household duties. This also affects employers — they know there are constraints for women.

I wanted to work in the UK for a year, but I had to choose between that and my husband. He wanted me to go back to India and get married because he was getting on (he was 30), so I chose my husband.

Sumitra has two problems. Her husband's job has inevitably taken priority since she left hers to have the baby. And no matter how encouraging he is about her profession, the very structure of work, including the fact that she will never be able to earn as much as him now she has taken a break, militates against her work having as much importance attached to it as his. If she is less diffident about her career now, she has also jeopardised her power base.

It does appear, though, that women who use their power position to negotiate within a love marriage are able to get a better solution. For it is only within love marriages that some of the women have got concessions and active cooperation from their husbands. In such a marriage, the *husband's* emotional attachment can be used as a power base from which to negotiate concessions. The compromises achieved by the women in arranged marriages involve the women being allowed to take on a job outside the home as well as the one inside. In love marriages, a few of the women are able to get their husbands to give up some of their privileges.

Mira Mitra teaches at the University.

My husband and I met when we were students. He expected me to continue working. My husband's family accept my working more easily now . . .

I would like more time with the children. We try to accommodate by my husband helping, so they see *us* together, instead of all mother and no father. I spend a lot of time with them in the holidays. When I was housekeeping for a month because we had no servant, I spent less time with the children than I do now.

In a crisis, for instance if my child were retarded or something, I would give up work and my husband would retain his job. Or if he were offered a job elsewhere. It happened when he expected to go abroad for his PhD, but he didn't go, he adjusted to my job. There's been no serious conflict yet, and none is expected.

In the morning, at home in the family, I'm thinking I must get on with the housework. Whether women should have jobs or not depends on the kind of work. With children, I wanted a flexible job and I would have given up if I hadn't got one. If I gave up work I'd be miserable. I faced it when my first son was born. There were pressures from the neighbours to give up, but I overcame it. I realised then that I had to continue.

Mira Mitra and her husband established an egalitarian pattern at an early stage, when her husband gave up the chance to go abroad so that she could keep her job at the university. Essentially their jobs are equal, *and* he takes a share in the childcare — not an equal share, and the housework is still her responsibility — but still, she has begun to break down the sexual division of labour in the home.

She is not the only one to have achieved this. Aruna Sharma has a similar arrangement. Aruna got into the civil service only after her sister had waged a long struggle with their father, an orthodox man who did not want his daughters to have jobs. Even after his eldest daughter had gone into a profession, he still had doubts about Aruna doing so, thinking it would be difficult to marry her.

> I made a love marriage, my husband's in the civil service too. He expected me to make a mark . . . He takes my career seriously — he didn't expect me to give up.
> We follow each other for jobs, it's not just one way. I expect it to get easier in the future, the main problem is having a young child. My husband sees the problems . . . We share the duties of the child, but our relatives think we're both odd.

Neither Aruna nor her husband gives priority to her husband's job — both jobs are equally important, and they follow each other when one is transferred. They also share the childcare. Having witnessed her sister's fight with her father, Aruna had no intention of marrying too early or finding herself with the wrong man. She was too well aware of the dangers, for she had seen her own mother's talents wasted. She was therefore able to use her powerful economic and social position as a member of the IAS, to choose for herself whom she would marry, to make sure that he was willing to give equal priority to her work, and to enlist his assistance in childcare.

A small number of women have been able to secure their husband's participation in the domestic work — a significant change in the division of labour in the home. In most cases, this participation is in childcare. Fewer can claim that their husbands help with housework. Rekha Rohtagi is one of these. She is an exceptional woman in other ways too. She is the only woman whose father insisted that his three daughters should find their own marriage partners. She's a lecturer of 50, and was involved in the early women's movement.

> My father . . . couldn't find companionship with his wife, who was a very fine woman, but uneducated. I always felt the incompatibility between my mother and father. I felt that women should have economic independence as well as equivalent intellect . . .
> I always had different ideas from people at college. I was politically motivated and have worked in various women's organisations — I wasn't interested in fine clothes or a rich marriage . . .
> Mine is a love marriage. My father said I should find my own partner in life. All the sisters did, though not my brothers. I was already working and had a PhD when I got married. My husband always helped in the house, for instance, when

I was writing a book recently, he did the housework and looked after the children. I had no problems when the children were small, I had a good ayah and my husband also helped. He's a lecturer in a sister college. He shifted to evening classes when our timings clashed, so that one parent could always be with the children. My husband was so helpful in the house that I seldom felt any pressure.

Working women make better mothers, better companions. In my opinion they *don't* neglect the house and children. I like this job because it's more suited to women, it has limited hours of work. I wouldn't leave my job under any circumstances. I can't think of it. It's necessary for equality and independence. It's not the only thing, but it's the first step. I'm ideologically convinced women should work. If women and men are equal they have to prove it in the professions. It's a challenge which women must take up, and work along with men. I made a conscious decision to work in a coed college in order to prove this. Women were hesitant to join a coed college when I joined. I was the only one in my college for 10 years. I think my example influenced women to come and teach in the coed college. Our male colleagues saw how my husband and I managed to organise ourselves. It broke down some of their prejudices.

Rekha experienced no opposition to her desire for a professional job. On the contrary, her father said she should be economically independent. But what made her aware of how important it was to keep this independence was not her father telling her, but awareness of her mother and father's incompatibility; a thing she always felt keenly, and didn't want to experience herself.

Something else influenced her too. Her father's attitude to marriage was a radical one, arising out of the incompatibility he had felt through not choosing his own marriage partner. Rekha knew her father wouldn't find her a rich husband. This not only made her want to be independent, it also made her question conventional ideas about women's pursuits and women's position within marriage.

Rekha's awareness of what she wanted made certain that she chose a man who was compatible with her own needs. And it enabled her to use her powerful position before marriage of already being established in a job, to get her husband to give equal priority to her work *and* to help with the childcare and the housework — again, not perhaps completely equal participation in the domestic work, but a considerable share. And this compromise was made possible by Rekha's class position, which allowed her to hire domestic servants who could do the work that neither she nor her husband could do while they were out at work.

Apart from Rekha, all the women who achieved a compromise they were happy with had to fight for it; they had to *use* the power they possessed to achieve the bargain. Behind all this resistance was the final sanction that they would remain unmarried if they could not get what they wanted. And in fact many of the women did remain unmarried until quite late. There was a common pattern of women refusing marriage until they were established in a job (by which time they were emotionally and financially independent), then marrying a husband of their own choice in their thirties or even forties. Many had their first child relatively late in life. Kapila Ahuja is a good example.

My husband is also in the IAS. It was an out-of-caste, non-arranged marriage. I joined the IAS before marriage, I wanted to make a career before I got married. My husband never expected me to give up. My husband's family had no objections either, because we were both at a senior level — they looked up to us. I was in my thirties when I got married, and I had my first son at 37 and my second at 40.

I do feel guilty — whether I'm giving enough to the home and family. We give more time, we try to compensate far more than non-working colleagues' wives. But I would never give up . . .

Women working outside is good. It develops her personality — she can be an equal partner — an equal not an appendage. In the Indian system, where the woman is subjugated to her husband, economically dependent and uneducated, she can never be equal. Women will develop if they work and it will contribute to a greater friendship between husband and wife. If she works she will be financially independent — that's better for society and the family — instead of being a curbed personality where she can't function as an independent entity. Even when they're working women are still unequal in many homes.

Kapila did not intend to marry before establishing herself in a job. When she did marry she was already in a senior post, and it was to a man of her choice. From this powerful position, she was able to establish that her work was as important as her husband's and that he would contribute to the childcare. He took his full share of the domestic work. And she was able to continue because she could afford to hire servants.

Kapila's story represents a common pattern of late, own-choice marriage, where the women are prepared not to marry at all rather than agree to conditions which do not suit them. Nirmala Madan, for instance, decided that women were unequal and that she would never marry, then met her husband and married him in her late thirties, having her first child at 42. Shaleen Sharma, an untouchable, didn't want to marry into the village where she would be subjected to caste discrimination, but entered the civil service as a way out. She later met a brahmin man and married him in her forties, having her first son at 48. Padma Unnikrishnan wanted to be a doctor from childhood, and calls herself a self-made woman, because whatever she wanted she achieved. She could not have done so within marriage, but having achieved a position, she met a man from the Far East, married him in her forties, and had her first child at 47. Mumtaz Ahmad, a Muslim and a lecturer, was determined to study literature, refused to be married off and got a job instead. She met a man she wanted to marry in her late thirties, and had her daughter at the age of 40.

Some of the women who have not yet married are quite explicit about their intentions. Sheela Sarvaria is 29 and works as a publicity officer in a public sector company.

I decided *not* to marry in the first three or four years of my career. I feel that I'm largely in control of my work because I took a deliberate decision not to marry for the first few years.

. . . And I would *not* marry anyone who resented my working. So I'm 'prevented' from marrying, but I'm happy enough about this. I'm ambitious, I want to get ahead to as high as possible, and I think I'll be able to achieve it because I won't get involved in a marriage that would prevent it.

A course of action like Sheela's requires not only determination, but also encouragement from others and, especially, knowledge of what different courses of action will mean. As Lakshmi Mitra points out, all the pressure is in the direction of marriage.

> None of my friends influenced me. On the contrary. Most of them from school and college have not opted for a career at all. They all married. They all regret it. They regret they didn't do what I did with the same opportunities . . . For the average middle-class girl it's too easy to slip into marriage. You have to make a conscious effort to 'educate' daughters to avoid easy matrimony. Women have to engineer their way into a career.

Because the social structure and the ideology direct middle-class girls towards early marriage and a life of domesticity, women who want more than this have to be aware of women's subordinate power relationship with men, and have to plan to use what power they have to achieve what they want. Otherwise the very structure of the family and employment will push them inexorably into living out the stereotype of the domesticated woman, regardless of support from husbands or fathers. Marriage is a crucial point in the determination of the conditions of a woman's life. Kasturi Verma suggests with regard to employment that women have to establish their position right from the start and again at certain crucial points.

> You have to exert yourself and show self-determination at the beginning to establish your position. You have to do it early, you can't retrieve the position later. I had to establish myself. There are certain critical periods when you have to do it, such as after marriage.

And this applies to marriage itself too. You have to establish your position within marriage at the start, and if you want more than marriage, you have to establish that before entering a marriage. Then you can negotiate the conditions of your life from a position of strength. This is what the women who married late were doing. There are many other instances of late marriage than those given above, especially of women marrying in their thirties. By comparison, the average age at marriage for women in India is 17, and 19 in the urban areas.[12] Despite the censure that late marriage might incur, these women have not only established themselves in employment, they have also entered marriage, not as a powerless subordinate, but with a power base admittedly unequal to that of the husband, but sufficiently strong to allow them to make demands and achieve compromises with their husbands, in some cases even eroding their husbands' privileges.

29. Resistance

Many women make their resistance, not through self-sacrifice, not even through compromise (no matter how hard a bargain may be struck), but through explicit rejection of a marriage and family structure which largely fulfils the interests of men by imposing physical, mental and economic constraints on women.

A surprisingly high percentage of our women are single — 36 per cent in an age range of 22 to 59.[13] Amongst the urban population, the proportion of single women doesn't rise above 19 per cent even in the 20 to 24 age group,[14] the first that can be compared with our women's age groups. Some of our single women have deliberately rejected marriage, at least in its contemporary form. A revolutionary step by women of the middle class, whose highest calling and social duty is marriage. Ambika Roy at 29 is an under-secretary at the Ministry of Labour.

My parents had no clear idea of what they expected. Women were educated for marriage. They probably would have liked me to work outside, but they didn't *expect* it when I was young . . .

I had a lot of encouragement from my father. My mother was neither for nor against. My father influenced me to do the IAS exam — he wasn't keen on any old job, he liked the status of the IAS. I was a teacher before, I didn't like it much. Possibly they brought me up for a career because there were no sons to take the limelight. I thought it was natural.

Later there was pressure to marry but not to leave the job. My mother wasn't too keen at the beginning, when I went into the IAS. She's more against it now because I'm too independent to marry, compared with what Indian women should be. There are conflicts and problems because I would need a man earning more than me — it's an on-going problem. An arranged marriage is also unthinkable. I can't do what they want, so they'll just have to get used to it. I've tried to reason with her but I can't do anything. I wouldn't like to change my way of life for my mother. I'm quite satisfied with myself.

Women working should be encouraged. Most women are subject to their husbands; daughters-in-law are ill treated. There are few divorces but not because there are better marriages. It's because women are economically dependent and *can't* live apart. They can only leave if they have a job or money. You have to *earn* to get respect and identity. You can't ignore the economic and employment situation . . . Women can't leave even if they're beaten because they can't support themselves and society looks down on them.

Within a joint family, the in-laws help working women to look after the children, but they may not like the daughter-in-law to work outside, it's not considered okay, although it's changing fast. It would curtail my freedom. Personally I would find it a handicap. I work because I'm interested in the civil service, it's something useful to do, I can't sit at home; but mainly it's for independence — financial (that's secondary) and otherwise . . . If you're independent, you don't have to listen to what other people think, or do what they want you to do.

Ambika raises the question of the low divorce rate. This is less than ½ per cent overall, although this may be an underestimate, and the figure is lower in urban areas.[15] Ambika suggests that this is not because marriages are satisfactory, but because there is no alternative. Most women can't leave their marriages even if they're beaten, because they have no other way of supporting themselves and they will be treated with contempt. Ambika's analysis is confirmed by the data from our women, who *do* have an alternative. Although the divorce rate is still small, at 3 per cent it is ten times that of the urban female population. More significantly, the marriage rate is much lower amongst our women. 58 per cent of the women between 22 and 29 were not married. The comparable figure for urban women as a whole is 19 per cent for the 20 to 24 age group, and 4.5 per cent for the 25 to 29 age group.[16]

This startling difference in the marriage rate amongst our group of professional women compared with the urban norm is also reflected in the approach of many of our women, who do not regard marriage as their only goal in life. This suggests that marriage is much less attractive to women who are able to earn a living independent of the family, and that marriage and a life of domesticity are not the fulfilment of every woman's desires. Some of these women recognise that conflict is inherent in marriage because it is built upon the subordination of one sex to the other. Their rejection of it is a mark, not of their abnormality, but of the unequal distribution of power and resources within the family.

Ambika is not the only one to have a critical analysis of marriage. Priya Gupta feels much the same way. She's in her late twenties and a lecturer at the university.

Up to 9 or 10 my parents expected nothing. Then at about 18 or 19 my mother and father's expectations diverged. My mother wanted me to marry, my father wanted me to get a job. My father was always much more serious about my ambitions. Other members of the family expected marriage. My father never *really* expected me to get a job, but he was always supportive. There was some pressure to go into the civil service once it was acknowledged that I was going to work, although this kind of pressure is applied to men too.

When I was very young I wanted to be a professional. It was entirely my decision. I was fascinated with science. At 14 or 15 I realised that for economic independence I had to rely on myself. My mother never worked outside, but one of her female relations, who was widowed soon after marriage did. A job was necessary for her.

My mother experienced a dilemma over my work. She was perhaps the first to articulate for me some of the views popularised by Friedan and Greer. Only in her time it was dismissed as 'housewives' neurosis'. Subconsciously I realised I took it all in and took it seriously enough to revolt . . . My mother is largely responsible for what I am today. I remember her always asserting — 'In my house girls are equal'.

But the normal expectation of a mother is that her daughter should marry. Depending on my age, we had a lot of discussion, odd rows, but my parents always responded to reason. They're both educated people . . .

At first they were vaguely indulgent to me, but the crucial point came after I refused to go into the civil service. Also marriage was in the background. All the time. I went abroad to do my PhD, came back, still there was pressure to marry. But now I'm much happier as I have a *good* job. My mother still has some latent antagonism to my work. She's worried about me being left on my own. My father thinks I should be more hard-headed in my approach to ambition. On the whole he's happy I have a career.

The advantages of a job like this are independence, interaction with people, you can make choices for yourself; belonging to a community that is not all recipes and babies. I've not so much in common with the average housewife . . . This is a disadvantage less of a working woman than of a *single* woman. In the family ambit you have a strange social status. They're always trying to push you in one direction or another. There's a certain pressure because you're not conforming to the social rule. This changes but doesn't disappear when you're married. There's not much I can do about it — I live with it. I find friends with similar values. When I was abroad I learned to live by myself and be self dependent.

The present Indian social structure makes it harder for women to work. It's partly the expectations of home and children. And it's partly the attitude of men; arranged marriages require great adjustment, which usually works against women. *They're* supposed to change.

The structure is for encouraging the dependence of women — mental rather than economic. Women are often stronger emotionally but are inhibited by the rigidly circumscribed environment of women's role. Duty to one's daughter equals getting her married. You have to be strong and stubborn and determined to make it . . .

The only difficulties I have now are that occasionally my parents still pressurise me to get married.

Both Ambika and Priya have so far resisted the pressure to agree to a marriage which they recognise is not for them. They both reached this position gradually, at first wanting to complete their education and get a fulfilling job, by which time the problems associated with marriage were clear to them. Both were supported by the encouragement of their fathers, but sharpened their resolve on the ambivalent approach of their mothers. Ambika valued above all her independence. And she recognised the practical constraints of a marriage system where the husband's superiority to his wife must be maintained at all costs.

Priya also wanted independence. She realised she had to rely only on herself for this. She also knew that marriage does not spell lifetime security, as the experience of many young Indian widows indicated. Then she went abroad and learnt to live on her own, to be self-sufficient. She has recognised that the organisation of arranged marriage encourages the dependence of women, and is not for her. She too is strong enough to resist the considerable pressures.

Both women have gradually come to the conclusion that they cannot enter into an arranged marriage, although they may yet marry a man of their own choice. Marriage is not ruled out, but it would be on their own terms. Other women made deliberate choices which prevented them from marrying. Komal Khanna is 54, a civil servant who started her career in teaching, then did a PhD, got a post as a lecturer, and entered the civil service.

My parents expected me to marry. I had an offer after my MA to teach. My mother didn't approve, my father said she shouldn't stand in my way. My parents kept trying to marry me, but I said I wouldn't marry anyone who wanted dowry. It was a very new idea in those days, so I gave up marriage for my principles.

My father helped me all along, though his parents didn't like me working. My grandmother was very annoyed, but my father was a pillar of strength against her. My father had great faith in me and knew I wouldn't do anything against the family prestige.

I wanted to work for independence and this was strengthened by the fact that I was against dowry, therefore I couldn't marry. It didn't just happen. My approach to life affected my attitude to work.

. . . My mother was annoyed but my father didn't agree, so she couldn't say much. My mother later accepted the whole thing and my success made her think she'd been wrong.

Professional women need help to be successful. The husband would still expect a working wife to do the household duties; he won't share it. He feels that he still has someone at his beck and call. This is a great disadvantage. Women have to stay away when they're ill and when the family's ill and they can't devote the proper time to work. Sometimes the husband helps if he's considerate but his profession is always considered more important than hers.

Komal was born in 1923. At the time of Indian Independence she was 24. The two decades before 1947 witnessed a politicising of the Indian people, not only through the nationalist movement but also through the women's movement. In 1945 Komal took a degree in history, and in 1948 she studied political science. These influences, together with her own desire for independence, led her to question and reject the institution of dowry, as well as the marriage structure on which the system of dowry was based. It was a deliberate step against the subordination of women within marriage.

Mohini Sharma also pursued independence at the expense of marriage, but for different reasons. She was too young to witness the political movements of the 1930s and 1940s, being only 8 at the time of Independence. The influences on her were more concrete and closer to home.

My parents didn't expect anything very specific. Later they wanted me to be a doctor. I was forward in studies, a bright student. I decided after intermediates. It was my own idea, but my father also wanted me to be a doctor. I did it to be independent, to be away from home, because my father used to get very angry and call us all bad names. My father was entirely in control of my career at first, but I have control now. I'm living independently without any interference from family members.

I work to be independent and to spend my time usefully. You don't have to depend on anyone, you are your own master... Now my family members appreciate me more. Their attitude used to be one of indifference. Now they have grown very affectionate and concerned about me, while I have grown totally unconcerned.

Mohini's father was a professor of history. Her predominant childhood memory is of his anger, and the fear he generated within the family when he took his anger out on subordinate members of the family. It was from this aspect of the patriarchal family that she wished to escape. The means to escape lay, not in entering another patriarchal family as a subordinate member, but in earning her own living as a single, independent woman. Mohini's critique of marriage arose from a less theoretical basis than did Komal Khanna's, but both bases were equally sturdy in providing a foothold for the first step away from the subordination of women within the patriarchal family.

The resistance to male control is not only found amongst women who have rejected marriage. It also occurs with women who are in marriages, and who have experienced the contradiction of trying to fulfil their own needs within a structure designed to suppress them, to the extent that the contradiction becomes intolerable and a move to resolve the contradiction is inevitable, despite the power of the male-dominated structure and the ideology of sacrifice. Sridevi Choudhury is 56, and teaches at the university. She has worked outside the home since she was 20, and has been at this university for 17 years.

My mother expected me to have a career, my father too but less so. They wanted me to be *able* to earn, but not necessarily that I *should* do so. My father was a barrister, he influenced me very much. My aunt was the first woman BA in the Punjab — she went to Oxford. All the women in my family work including my mother and my sisters. My parents suggested education. My mother suggested a career for independence. I wanted to be a professional from very early.

My husband encouraged me to work right from the start. My in-laws didn't think the women in the family should work outside. Only women who require money should work. I overcame their opposition through my husband. They let me know they're not happy about it, but they didn't actively oppose me...

Originally we lived in a joint family with my husband's parents, but there was constant friction and I couldn't organise my home life and work life. It's difficult to coordinate in a joint family, and if I complained of tiredness, they always said, 'You don't have to work.' So we left for a nuclear family.

For several years my husband was in a transferable job. In that period I gave up several jobs, and for 5 years I had no job. I had no control over my work, my husband's career had the first priority.

Then I decided... to settle in one place. My husband became a farmer (before that he was an industrial engineer). Now he is 70 miles away at the farm, and I *will* not move and make the same mistake again, until after I retire.

I never took my career seriously in the beginning. It was only treated as security by my mother and others. I only decided gradually to work seriously —

it crystallised much later. I would not give up now unless there was a calamity . . .

Women with high education are unhappy at home. Those who enjoyed their studies are frustrated. The disadvantage is in the family, having to do two jobs. All women have social and home responsibilities. Even if husbands help they think they've done you a favour . . .

Social obligations make it harder for women to have a job. The expectations of the in-laws — work isn't respectable, you're dragging down the family honour if there's no economic need. You can be proud of a son's achievement, not of a daughter's. In all India, 'Good wishes' implies God should give you so much that you don't have to work. 'Raj karna' is a benediction to young girls, and means, 'May you have no work, and staff to order around.' So you go through work thinking of it as a punishment for previous misdemeanours. This is a problem for men as well as women, but particularly for girls. Girls' biggest incentive is to marry *above* themselves to a higher income group. It suits the men because they can be dominant. I tell everyone — every woman must have a mental occupation; whether for earning or not is unimportant — for self-development.

Sridevi has resisted the constraints of marriage within marriage itself, by ignoring the convention and living separately until her working life is complete. Having learnt that accommodation on her part elicited no adjustment in response from in-laws or husband, she consciously rejected her constraints and deliberately removed herself from the bars which held her only by her consent plus the fear of moral censure; first from the joint family; then from the nuclear family.

Nita Madan is in a slightly different position, and at an earlier stage of life. But it is easy to see that she is going through the same kind of friction as Sridevi went through. It is not clear at this stage how she will resolve it. Nita is 33, a teacher at the university. She comes from a liberal family, where women have had jobs for two generations before her. She married a man of her own choice, a Hindu from the kshatriya caste, although she herself is a Christian.

I always assumed I'd work . . . My father was the determining factor — he projected an image of me as a professional . . .

My husband didn't expect me to take work seriously. He expected me to work but only as a sideline. Now he's modified his view to *me*, but not to women in general. He's not very keen on my working. He expects a social role and mobility for *his* job. That's still there to some extent. It hasn't been overcome in any rational way. It's just time. We've had tumultuous arguments and a slight psychological adjustment over time. I'm stubborn. I will not compromise.

I'm not in control of my work because of my husband, although it has improved now. But I'm not happy about this. My husband was seriously against my work; he made demands on my time which I would have liked to spend on my job. I had a very large guilt feeling, now largely but not entirely stopped. A joint family in my case might have helped. It might have meant less demands by my husband on me because there would be more people around. Due to these family commitments I can't devote myself to my career enough to expect promotion. Women do have to work harder to achieve recognition, given the amount of pressures they have to counteract — domestic pressures.

My aspiration is to keep up with my job. I have to be more creative than if I were a man. In the future I fear that I may have to make a choice, if my husband moves his job for instance. For me, work is a necessary part of my personality — it's a deprivation not to work, in human terms. It gives you an independent status. You exist more in your own right, rather than meeting people as someone's wife. I married before doing a PhD. With hindsight I would have done my PhD before marriage. I can't think of giving up work — it would be a disaster. I don't think I could.

Every individual, man or woman, should have a choice. If women don't want to work, okay. But you have an obligation if you've been trained. I'm angry about the differences in how men and women are treated, but I can't see an answer that would arise in my lifetime. Men have far greater expectations, they can't see the advantages of women working, reducing their load and so on. The cause is in basic social and maybe even biological factors. I'm much more aware of it now — recent feminist literature has helped. It's articulated long held feelings.

Both Nita and Sridevi come from liberal families, where women have worked outside before them. Both were encouraged by their parents to work if they wanted to. Neither had any opposition against which to rebel until they were married, when it was too late to lay down demands and make conditions. After marriage, Sridevi's opposition came from her in-laws. Despite the fact that her husband supported her against them, she later found that the very organisation of work, structured around men whose families can move with them at will, promoted his career at the expense of hers. Her determination to be independent resolved the tension through her decision to live separately.

Nita's opposition comes directly from her husband. He expects her to forego all her desires. And this is a love marriage. The conflict between them is 'tumultuous'. He has modified his views slightly, but there is still a great gulf between them. She failed to make her demands explicit before marriage, not expecting her husband to be any different from her parents in his approach to her work. But having encountered the opposition, she is determined not to compromise. She is firmly resisting her husband's attempts to get her to minister solely to his needs and to suppress her own. It is quite possible that Nita will take a firm stand against him if he doesn't make a radical change.

Women who recognise, *before marriage*, that marriage may severely jeopardise their position as paid workers, find themselves in a much stronger position to bargain. They can negotiate a compromise with the husband or in-laws from a position of strength, or if they fail to achieve an acceptable agreement, they can, because of their economically strong position, refuse to marry. And possibly, if the circumstances arise, they can marry later than usual to a man of their own choice. Women, however, who fail to recognise the subordinate status of their employment within a marital relationship until after they are married, find themselves in a much more difficult position. Sridevi managed to retrieve her position later in life, without divorcing her husband, because her husband was amenable to living separately for a considerable part of the time. It may be impossible for Nita to retrieve her position *within* the marriage because of her husband's uncompromising approach.

This is what Lotika Choudhury discovered. Lotika is 27 and works for a public sector service organisation. She married in her early twenties, had a daughter, then separated from her husband because of the difficulties he caused.

> My parents expected marriage and children, generally. But they did think of paid work — they're less orthodox than the other family elders.
>
> My husband resented my working life — he didn't like me to be successful in my job. He didn't like the competition. He wanted me to work for an *income*, but only as a job, not a career. My husband's family were very discouraging too. They always needed my money, but they always resented my work. My husband caused a lot of difficulties for me . . . He was worse when I was expecting the baby, and after the baby was born he was intolerable . . . Because of these problems of doing all the work in the house, and my husband being so critical and uncooperative, I took a year off and did freelance work. When I got a job again it wasn't any better. My husband had double standards: he wanted the money I earned, but he wouldn't help in the house, and he complained that the house and child weren't properly looked after.
>
> In the end I simply couldn't tolerate it any more. I left my husband because of all the problems. Indian men think of women as domestic only. It's *their* problem to accept *us*. I've always been self-willed and tended to rebel against instructions. I must be entirely financially independent from parents and husband. Work is a means to an end for my ambition for recognition and financial independence, and being able to prove my *equality*. I'd be *miserable* if I gave up work. I wouldn't do it unless I really had to, for example if someone in the family was ill. And I would never marry anyone who had that problem — who thought women had no right to paid work. A successful professional woman gets fantastic respect, even from people with double standards like my husband.

Lotika's husband made her life a misery, using her money at the same time as criticising her work. Because of the strength of her financial position, she was able to find a way out: she used the ultimate sanction against his demands by rejecting her relationship with him. Lotika stripped her husband of his power over her, and took power for herself, by the simple but difficult act of defiance. She withdrew from the relationship and refused to allow him to override her human dignity. And she recognises that what she has done, with all its problems, is to abolish the personal power relationship between them. This recognition marks a revolutionary step in women's thinking about gender relationships. First, that it is possible for women to take power into their own hands. Second, that by doing this, the problems that beset women will become men's problems.

The final story is of a truly remarkable woman whom we met in Part III. She survived a mental breakdown caused by her marriage — an experience which revolutionised her thinking and her actions; a success story, despite the sorrow. Shikha Munshi is 43 now and lectures at the university. She began her working life in a job that everyone considered too lowly — a secretary. After six months of marriage, she had a mental breakdown. Her marriage had disintegrated.

> After that I wanted to get away from the past. I decided to study Japanese because it was a challenge and there were not many people in it . . . I couldn't

get a research fellowship after my marriage, so I maintained myself while I did my PhD. Then I got money to go to Japan and in 1970 I got this job. My parents and my brother and sisters gave me very strong moral support for my studies after the breakdown of my marriage. I do not think I would have succeeded without this anchor . . .

I don't like the way women are treated. The attitude of men has not changed very much: there is outward acceptance of women but inward resentment. The cause lies in the sense of fear that women will surpass them. Women can be cowed down by men's attitudes. The old taboos still apply. I've become increasingly aware of this, but my sensitivity is decreasing. I orginally thought I could fight it and change it. Now I ignore and accept it.

Men often can't handle an intelligent woman. They expect them to be inferior. If they're not, they can't be natural with them . . . I have to play down my ability, to keep the peace. There was a big change when they knew I took it as seriously as they did . . .

Working gives you financial independence and a lot of self-confidence. It increases your vision — you see a bigger world than the joint family, and you have a better perspective — more understanding even of family problems. It shifts attention from self to community and country. There are no disadvantages for me now because there is no conflict from the family. Women should work. Teaching and medicine are not against the cultural milieu. Note that voluntary social work for the community is acceptable. But generally women are supposed to be dependent on the family and the husband, therefore financial independence is a revolutionary concept. It's changing: now many girls are expected to work for self-confidence and respect. But all of this only applies to the middle classes — in the working classes, all women must work.

My present position makes my ex-husband's people come to me now for help and advice to go abroad. They seem to have forgotten that they didn't even treat me as a 'human being' when I was with them.

For Shikha, the move to resolve the contradiction she experienced after marriage occurred outside her control; mental breakdown forced a change in her consciousness and her life. The key to her resistance lay in her own strength of purpose, the unconditional support of her own family, and her ability to earn her own living.

Shikha's determination is remarkable. Clearly her breakdown was not caused by weakness of character. She resolved to do what she had always wanted, to get a proper education to the highest level. She embarked on a completely new, particularly difficult, and relatively unpopular subject of study. She travelled alone to study in a foreign country, whose culture had little in common with her own. And she did all this by her old trusted and self-reliant method, working full time to pay for part-time study, eventually winning a scholarship for her PhD abroad.

Shikha still meets with the same attempts by men to suppress her, but she understands the nature of a male-dominated society now. She modifies her behaviour to keep the peace to the extent that she decides. But the men can no longer make her think there is something wrong or bad about her. She knows she is more competent than they, personally and professionally, and they know it too. Her experiences of marriage have heightened her awareness of the power men exert over women both at home and at work. But now the tables are turned, for Shikha's professional position gives her the power to dispense favour to the very people who were the cause of her anguish.

30. A New Beginning

Women do not passively accept exploitation and oppression. Where they are submissive, their submission is often enforced and coerced. Where they have the opportunity to live independently they resist oppression in many different ways, engaging in negotiations to improve the conditions of their lives, or rejecting the constraints of a male-dominated marriage structure altogether. In order to do this successfully, they need both a material power base and an awareness of the power structure if they are to achieve changes in their position within the family *individually*, which is how most women have to negotiate personal issues within marriage. Women *are* exploited and oppressed, but they are also the instigators of radical change, fighting back, resisting oppression and striving for freedom.

Mechanisms of Resistance

Self-sacrifice is the form of response to oppression encouraged in the middle class, since it characterises the ideal woman in a male-dominated society. The ideology is also a means of justifying the negation of the self. But sacrifice can also contain resistance, by depriving the other as well as the self, of something that both value, or by raising a reciprocal sacrifice from the other. Where total submission is the only alternative, it is a form of resistance which can be disguised as acceptable to the oppressor. In this form it is used by individuals in a powerless position without allies and with no possibility of organising the support of others. This is the position in which women often find themselves.

As a method of struggle sacrifice can also be used collectively in the form of passive resistance, as demonstrated by the freedom movement. At its best it can be a truly revolutionary form of resistance, embodying the notion of individual sacrifice for the common good, since it opposes not only the content of oppression but also the oppressors' methods.

The negotiation of compromises is another method which women use to carry their challenge into the family. For this to be effective, women have to have a material power base, particularly if they are unable to mobilise support from other family members, and they have to *use* this power. To use it, they have to be aware of it, and awareness comes from experiencing opposition or observing it. Only women who are aware of the power relations in the family are able to exploit their own sources of power, knowing that a bargaining strategy is required to be sure of achieving a compromise. This is the only reliable way of securing agreement since the very structure of domestic and paid work will force women into the stereotype against which they are struggling, regardless of support from husbands or fathers.

A conciliatory approach is less successful in achieving an acceptable compromise. It may be possible for a woman to retrieve her position later, but she will be much more dependent on the family's goodwill. The most effective strategy is to establish oneself in a profession before marriage, and to lay down the conditions of marriage before entering into it. Marriage is a crucial point in the determination of a woman's conditions of life, and she needs to establish her position both in employment and in marriage from the start, and again at crucial points in the life cycle.

Compromises and negotiations can be more successful in an arranged marriage than in a love marriage because it is an explicit legal-religious contract rather than an emotional bond. The prospective partners in an arranged marriage are theoretically free to reject a match involving conditions with which they disagree. A love marriage is no guarantee against any of the problems encountered by our women. But a woman who bargains from a position of power in a love marriage may achieve more positive cooperation, since only in love marriages have women achieved concessions from the husbands in the form of their active contribution to the domestic work, rather than merely agreeing to their wives taking on paid work as well as domestic work.

The extent of women's explicit resistance to their oppression within the family can be seen by the startling difference in the marriage rate compared with the urban female population. The divorce rate is low, but is still six times the urban rate.[17] Clearly marriage is much less attractive, still less the fulfilment of every woman's desire, when women have alternative means of surviving. Many women reject arranged marriage, some resist marriage of any sort, others resist the constraints of marriage within marriage itself, or else find the experience intolerable and feel forced to leave.

Changes Achieved

The extent to which professional women, from their position of economic independence, have successfully challenged male control over specific aspects of their lives can be seen in a number of ways. A comparison with the education, employment and domestic commitments of the women's mothers shows that a quarter of the mothers were educated only to primary level or below. Less than a quarter were graduates.[18] Only one in six of the mothers was employed during her married life.[19] The average number of children the mothers gave birth to was 4.8, with 45 per cent having four or more children, and 5 per cent having ten or more.[20] By contrast, amongst our women who were married and over 35 years of age, the average number of children was 1.7, and no one had more than three children.[21] Of course, this figure may rise, for the women may yet have more children, but their family size is unlikely to approach that of their mothers. These comparisons give us an indication of how far our women have moved out of domesticity compared with the women of the preceding generation.

The extent to which our women have challenged male control over their sexuality can be judged by their marriage patterns. Control over female sexuality, traditionally required of those groups high in the social hierarchy, necessitated early, indissoluble, arranged marriage, within the caste. The low marriage rate, the prevalence of late marriage, the relatively high divorce rate, and the incidence of non-arranged marriages (half of which are cross-caste or cross-religion)[22] show how far professional women have moved from the orthodox criteria of caste and gender respectability. In fact, women who are single, separated, divorced, and in non-arranged marriages are in the majority.[23]

There has been a very considerable breakdown of the sexual division of labour for women at the workplace, and our women now contribute an average of 50 per cent to the family finances. The same effect has not occurred amongst men in the home, for only 5 per cent of the women receive assistance from their men in domestic work. Nevertheless, those few women who have obtained cooperation rather than passive acquiescence from their husbands have begun to break down the sexual division of labour amongst both sexes.

The Character of the Changes

These changes are not insignificant, despite their individual and isolated appearance. At the end of Part II we pointed to Elizabeth Sarah's question and her comment on India:

> Do we really believe that when all the movements subsided, all the feminists who were involved with them vanished? . . . Maybe the difficulty lies with our definition of what constitutes participation . . . The example of India raises a lot of questions about . . . our categories and definitions.[24]

There are two issues here. One concerns the particular site, methods and form of women's resistance. The other is the myth, arising from a misunderstanding of the first issue, that without an organised movement, no significant changes and challenges can occur.

The methods of resistance used by social movements are, by the nature of movements, collective. The site of the resistance is defined by the source of the oppression. For example, the source of the class conflict is the wage relation, and its location is the workplace. In imperialist struggles, the source is the economic domination of the foreign country, and the site is the various locations of this power such as, in the case of Britain and India, the shops selling foreign cloth and the salt mines producing tax revenue for the foreign government. It is understandable that people involved with social movements see collective action as the only effective means of achieving significant social change, since the primary targets for change are the external social structures and institutions of the society.

Such an analysis, however, neglects the cultural and psychological aspects of change, as well as the particular kinds of change required to eradicate women's subordination in the family. These two are closely connected, as we shall see. One of the major sources of women's subordination is the organisation of the patriarchal family. The family is the place where women have to negotiate the conditions of their working lives with husbands, fathers and parents-in-law, often on an individualistic basis. This applies to domestic and partly to paid work too. By definition, the personal and domestic, sexual and family relations between men and women are conducted individually, and although collective analysis and action give effective stimulus and support to women's efforts, it needs to be recognised that changes in these personal relations are crucial in eliminating women's position of subordination in the family, and can only be made at a personal level. Even when social movements are active, their collective analyses and policies on *personal* politics have to be taken into the family and negotiated by individual women. Even after legal and institutional reforms in family relations have been implemented, as with the Hindu Code and the constitutional guarantee of sex equality, the initiative for enforcing them within the family lies with individual women. So the *form* of women's resistance in the family is often necessarily individual.

The location of women's subordination in the family also affects their methods of struggle. Since the issues which women raise require changes in the domestic sphere as well as in public policy, different modes of resistance may be required. The collective, confrontational methods of conventional political activity for changing institutions and social processes may be of limited effectiveness in altering the personal relations of the family. The recognised forms are important too, on the streets and in the assemblies, but not in the family.

Consequently it is necessary to look beyond the conventional types of challenge such as organised social movements and campaigns for changes in the law. We have to look for defiance in different forms and places, including individual opposition in the family, and in alternative methods: not only in overt rejection of patriarchal controls, but also in negotiated compromises and conciliation, and even in sacrifice. A woman who is subordinate in the family frequently cannot resist force by counter-force, if she has no power base from which to do so; therefore she may not be able to use the aggressive techniques of resistance normally associated with other sorts of political conflict. Although sometimes less effective than other methods, women's more passive modes of resisting should not be seen as submission.

These methods in their particular location may appear individual in form, and it is true that change will not be effective if it is *only* conducted individually. But for women, neither will it be if it is only conducted collectively. *Women's* liberation requires both collective social change and individual personal change, breaking down the barriers between the public and the private in the political as well as the domestic sphere.

The myth that no significant change is occurring unless there is an organised movement arises from the mistaken idea that individual battles within personal relations do not constitute participation in the campaign for women's liberation. Of course, such efforts cannot achieve radical changes in social structures and institutions, but they can achieve far-reaching psychological change in attitudes and consciousness, as well as changes in the conditions and organisation of family relations, as we have seen from our women. Both are essential to eradicate the subordination of women.

In any case, our women's rebellion does not occur within a vacuum. Many of the women form supportive alliances with other family members, of both sexes. Some of the older ones began their fights at the time of the early women's movement, before Independence. The majority struggled on after the demise of the organised movement, without the benefit of the atmosphere for change which such movements inspire. Despite the lack of a movement between the 1950s and the 1970s, the ideas for these individual battles can clearly be seen to derive from the early movement, handed down from mothers and aunts to daughters and nieces.

Our women's opposition occurs within a social context which provides both a history of ideas and a direction for change, and the resistance itself helps to create the social context and to reinforce change. These individuals have kept alive the ideas and analyses of the women's movement through its dormant period and have acted as models for other women. They have continued the challenge and achieved immense changes in their personal circumstances compared with their mothers' times. They form the group out of which the 'second wave' began to reorganise, only a couple of years after they told us their stories. In Delhi in 1977 these women were fighting their battles alone.

In 1979 a new women's magazine called *Manushi* was published in Delhi.

Notes

1. Kamla Bhasin (1982) 'The Riddle of Marriage', *Manushi*, 11, p.38.
2. See Mathuram Bhoothalingam (1964) *The Story of Rama*. New York: Asia Publishing House.
3. M.K. Gandhi (1938) *Women and Social Injustice*. Ahmedabad: Navajivan Publishing House, p.21. Quoted in Maria Mies (1980) *Indian Women and Patriarchy*. New Delhi: Concept, p.125.
4. Madhu Kishwar (1983) 'Attenborough's Version of Gandhi', *Manushi* 3, 3, p.46, March-April.
5. Tara Ali Baig (1976) *India's Woman Power*. New Delhi: S. Chand, p.50.
6. Philip Rawson (1973) *The Art of Tantra*. London: Thames and Hudson, pp.7-9.
7. See for example T. Nichols and H. Beynon (1977) *Living with Capitalism*. London: Routledge & Kegan Paul, Ch.13.
8. See Appendix, Table 27.

9. Gandhi, *Women and Social Injustice*, p.21. Quoted in Mies, *Indian Women*, p.125.

10. Sister Nivedita [Margaret Noble] (1907) *Cradle Tales of Hinduism*. London: Longmans, Green & Co., pp.146-50.

11. Gail Omvedt (1973) 'Gandhi and the Pacification of the Indian Nationalist Movement', *Bulletin of Concerned Asian Scholars* 5, 1, pp.2-8.

12. Department of Social Welfare (1978) *Women in India: a Statistical Profile*. New Delhi: Govt. of India, p.59, Table 2.17.

13. See Appendix, Table 28.

14. See Appendix, Table 29.

15. Ashish Bose (1975) 'A Demographic Profile', in Devaki Jain (ed), *Indian Women*. New Delhi: Government of India, p.156. Ashish Bose points out that the divorce and separation figures may be underestimated in the Census. He does not say why, but it is presumably because of the persistence of unofficial divorce and remarriage amongst the lower castes in the rural areas. This is supported by the fact that even the official divorce rate is higher in the rural than in the urban areas.

16. See Appendix, Table 28 for data on marital state of our women, and Table 29 for data on marital state of the urban population.

17. See Appendix, Tables 28 and 29.

18. See Appendix, Table 17.

19. 17 per cent of the women's mothers were employed during marriage; 83 per cent were not.

20. See Appendix, Table 30.

21. See Appendix, Table 31.

22. See Appendix, Table 27. 23 per cent of the women had chosen their own marriage partner (including engagements). 32 per cent of all the marriages (including widowed, separated and divorced women) were non-arranged. The figure remains the same whether engagements are included or not. Of the 25 women in non-arranged marriages, 6 were cross-religion and 7 were cross-caste.

23. See Appendix, Table 27. Single, separated and divorced women and those in non-arranged marriages constitute 72 women, or 60 per cent of the total.

24. Elizabeth Sarah (1982) 'Towards a Reassessment of Feminist History', *Women's Studies International Forum* 5, 6, pp.520-1.

Part VII: Conclusions

31. Understanding Women's Oppression and Resistance

At the beginning of the book we posed three questions on the basis for women's oppression, the main influences in freeing them from the constraints, and the nature of the social processes linking the hierarchies of privilege and subordination. This chapter summarises the discussion and raises some implications of the answers.

Is Women's Subordination Related to Men's Position in the Social Hierarchy?

From the historical discussion of the development of gender, caste and class hierarchies, and from the empirical evidence of professional women's transition from seclusion to employment, it appears that women's subordination is crucial to men's position in the social hierarchies of both caste and class. We have shown in Part II how the gender division, based on control of women's sexuality, was integral to the formation of the social structure, based on the control of economic resources. The patriarchal upper castes tightened both caste and gender divisions as they consolidated their economic supremacy and defended challenges to that supremacy. These processes reveal the link between female sexuality and the economic position of the community, where female property is removed from the family at marriage but is contained within the caste group by controls on the women's sexuality. One result of this high-caste male supremacy is the persistent association between ideas opposed to caste and ideas opposed to the subordination of women within all the social reform movements over the centuries.

In Part III we showed how women alone pay for the rise in caste position by the loss of their social and sexual autonomy. Seclusion epitomises men's economic and sexual control over women, by withdrawing them from productive agricultural work and by rigidly controlling their sexuality. It is the sexual aspect which explains why the women rather than the men withdraw from outside economic activity when the caste raises its position, for in a patriarchal family system the woman's property goes to the family of her sexual partner. It is significant that it is also from this sexual aspect of seclusion that the hardship entailed in seclusion derives, for the later strictures on women suggest that the control of women's sexuality became increasingly important to men as an issue in its own right. Employment outside the home violates both the sexual and the economic controls on women, requiring physical mobility and providing an independent income. The gender-specific notion of 'respectability' reveals the links between the two systems of gender and caste, for loss of the woman's sexual respectability destroys the man's caste respectability. Amongst the high-caste orthodox groups, the basis for women's subordination is the maintenance of the men's economic and social position.

In the transformation from caste to class, however, women's subordination does not disappear. The class hierarchy is as dependent on the gender division as is the caste structure. Under class, male control over women is maintained but in different form, having incorporated and adapted to aspects of women's resistance under the caste system. As we show in Part IV, women's subordination at the top of the social hierarchy no longer consists in domestic seclusion, a ban on education and employment, economic dependence and extensive control over her sexuality, as it did under the caste system. Instead, it consists in controlling the kind, quality and purpose of women's education, limiting the type and level of employment, the harassment and eve-teasing of non-secluded women in education and at work, and in the requirement that women continue to perform domestic along with paid work. Male domination under class also helps to maintain class itself, through the requirement for educated and employable women for marriage, which brings material and status benefits to men, helping to distinguish them from the lower classes socially and economically. The class structure, however, appears to be less effective in the control of women than the caste system, since some women are able to break one of the mainstays of male control, that of economic dependence, through professional employment. From this position, women are also able to challenge the other mainstay, that of male control of female sexuality, and the evidence on marriage rates in Part VI shows that they do. Parts IV and V show that the concern with female sexuality continues to underlie many of the disadvantages which professional women face despite release from domestic seclusion and economic dependence.

Women's subordination, however, whilst crucial to social hierarchy, is not identical to it. Male domination and caste supremacy are distinct, since male privilege changes but does not disintegrate in the change from caste to class. Nor is male supremacy identical with class, since the relationship between male domination and class privilege is variable, sometimes gender subordination taking precedence over class supremacy, at other times class dominance outweighing the disadvantages of gender in a professional woman's life. The two systems interact with each other, but there is no fixed mode of precedence between them. So the systems of gender and social hierarchy are not identical but they are not independent either.

If the early women's movement in India did not recognise its own concerns as class-specific, in that its demands focused on issues which did not assist lower-caste/class women, it had a very clear analysis of one of the major locations of women's subordination as resting on the personal relations of the patriarchal family. The demands embodied in the Hindu Code fundamentally challenged (in principle, despite difficulties of enforcement) the organisation not only of male dominance but also of the social hierarchy itself. This is why the opponents of the Code feared that women's divorce and inheritance rights would destroy the caste structure, and why they fiercely resisted the introduction of the Code, particularly in the domestic areas of marriage and inheritance. Part VI shows that the women of today continue to challenge their subjection in the relations of the family. Since women's subordination is entrenched in the social hierarchy whether of caste or class, it is essential for women to confront not only male supremacy but also the hierarchies of caste and class. It is not enough to oppose male dominance on its own, since male privilege will remain, bound up with the social structure, if both are not resisted together. Equally, it is not enough to change caste and class systems alone, since the social and economic structures are not identical with the gender hierarchy, and there is no guarantee that the demise of the former will eradicate the latter.

Is Women's Liberation Related to the Influence of the West?

The historical evidence for the British influence on the position of women is contradictory. As we show in Part I, despite the official policy of 1858 not to interfere in personal law, the British government nevertheless claimed credit for liberalising the law relating to significant aspects of women's subordination. In fact, the British were selective in both their liberalising and their non-interference, in some cases destroying the liberal heritage which the women of certain groups had enjoyed for centuries. In their encounters with the early women's movement, the British supported the women on those issues where their interests coincided, and opposed them where their interests conflicted. The dominant motive for the British government supporting women's liberation was to demonstrate that India was unfit for self-rule, in the interests of maintaining colonial control of the country.

The British women who started the women's organisations in India are also cited as evidence of Western influence on the liberation of women, but we have shown in Part II that the British women's initiative was only one intervention within the totality of Indian history. This history demonstrates that women's resistance in India goes back much further than the intervention of the British feminists, and provides the Indian women's movement with its unique heritage.

A further contradictory effect of colonialism on the position of women was the creation of the new middle class, which both maintained many of the strictures imposed on rural upper-caste women, and allowed some women to break free of the strictures by taking advantage of the new economic opportunities in the professions. The latter effect was increased with the *removal* of foreign rule, since Independence expanded professional opportunities that had previously been closed to women. At the same time, the opposition to British rule that developed in the country helped to stimulate the organisation of women to fight their subordination to men and to imperialism. Within the nationalist movement itself, the British influence was again contradictory: British criticism of Indian women's subordination, designed to continue colonialist oppression, put pressure on Indian culture to defend and reinforce, as well as to change, existing caste and gender relations. British criticism also encouraged the alliance between the women's movement and the nationalist movement, a factor which more than any other stimulated the development of Indian women's organised resistance.

The empirical evidence from our women in Part III indicates that the most significant external influences stimulating the transition from seclusion to employment lie in their personal experiences of the effects of male domination or those of their close relatives, and in the social movements which arose against the privileges of caste, class and imperialism. The system of male privilege can on occasions fail those who are meant to benefit from it, and is also liable to raise resistance from women. The support, and in some cases the example, of other family members is an important influence in making the change, as was the traumatic effect of becoming a refugee during the geographical movement of the population at Partition. The social reform movement, the socialist movement and the nationalist movement all played their part in breaking down the constraints on women. Of these, the last two were certainly not associated with the British establishment or even dominant Western ideologies, although both had supporters amongst Western radicals. In the case of the first, Vina Mazumdar has convincingly argued that the more radical elements of the social reform movement took their inspiration from Indian, not Western, education and culture.

But perhaps the most significant aspect of this question is the way in which male domination, whilst being forced to change by women's resistance, has also incorporated women's gains to maintain male supremacy in a different form under an imperialist class structure. These controls are both material and ideological, as we showed in Parts IV and V. They include the priority given to male education and employment, vertical and horizontal segregation of women in the educational and employment structures, sexual harassment and direct discrimination at work, and female responsibility for domestic work on top of employment. In the ideological field, male control over women is maintained under an imperialist class structure through the myths of women's subservience, women's domesticity, and women's inferiority, of which the last appears to be a specifically Western notion, and by the definition of women who do not conform to the stereotype as immoral or unnatural. The important point is that the class structure, created through the introduction of Western imperialism into India but inhibited from full development for the benefit of the Western economies, is no more egalitarian than the caste system in terms of either social hierarchy or gender hierarchy. It is only that the basis of the inequality is different, mobility being collective for caste and individual for class, so that where whole groups rise in the caste system, individuals, including women, can rise in the class system. But the freedom that these women won from their constraints in the change from a caste to a class society does not constitute emancipation, only a different form of control; the transition from seclusion to professional employment releases women from significant aspects of their subordination, but it also presents them with new forms of oppression and exploitation.

So women's liberation in India does not arise from the liberalising influence of British colonialism, since its impact is at best contradictory; nor does it arise primarily from the influence of the British women's movement, although that was one intervention in the history of women's resistance. The influence of Western imperialism and Western culture is harder to assess, but the evidence of professional women in Parts IV and V suggests that its material and ideological effects on them have been negative rather than positive, by inhibiting economic development with consequent effects on male priority, and by introducing a notion of gender and national inferiority. Women's desire for freedom arises from the influence of their own cultural heritage, which gives them a view of themselves as strong and powerful people, from radicalising experiences of the system of male domination and of oppositional movements, and from their position in the social hierarchy which provides a material basis for changing the existing relations of gender, caste and class. As we have shown in Part II historically, and Part VI even today, women's position is a result of struggle, in which women exploit opportunities and contradictions in the social structure, forcing the institution of male domination to change and adapt to aspects of their resistance. The Western idea of gender and ethnic inferiority is insidious because it undermines people's confidence in their ability to act. In contrast, despite the fact that it is associated with strong controls and is conceived of as dangerous, the Indian view of female power provides the psychological basis for women to exert and exercise their power.

The lessons of Indian culture are that women are strong, powerful and active, and are capable of destroying the social hierarchy. The international women's movement can use these ideas of women's power to challenge Western notions of both gender and ethnic inferiority. It can also use the lessons of the early women's movement in India, recognising the importance of imperialism in maintaining women's subordination, and acknowledging the dangers as well as the benefits of any alliance with national liberation organisations. Since imperialism reinforces women's oppression in particular ways, it is essential to confront imperialism alongside male supremacy. But it is also vital for women to organise autonomously, since women's oppression is not identical with Western imperialism, any more than it is identical with caste and class hierarchy.

What Social Processes Link the Structures Together?

We have said that male domination does not occur on its own, but that it is crucially tied up with the social hierarchy. These two systems of power occur within a third system, the international capitalist order under which the Indian economy is subordinate to Western financial interests. When women's individual experiences are placed within the context of these power structures, it can be seen, through an examination of the social processes which link them, that the experiences are not purely individual but are crucially related to the social structure.

Gender under Caste
The social process linking women's subordination to the maintenance of the social hierarchy can be seen in the essential nature of the link between the necessity of marriage and the prohibition on employment for women of the higher castes. This link increases in importance as a caste raises its position, and arises out of the importance of women's seclusion for the maintenance of property within the caste and therefore for men's position in the social hierarchy. Men derive a significant part of their social position from the degree of sexual control held over women. The idea of female subservience reinforces the containment of women's power in the gender hierarchy. In this way, women's sexual respectability determines the social respectability of the men, the family and the entire caste. High-caste women's work in a patriarchal caste society is confined to the domestic sphere, the notion of women's domesticity reinforcing women's seclusion. The economic and the sexual are directly linked through the processes of gender hierarchy, female seclusion, and female to male status derivation, the men of the family receiving part of their social honour from the women.

The Change from Caste to Class
Class does not appear to develop in opposition to caste, nor does it completely break caste down. Rather it builds on existing caste and gender divisions, modifying them to suit the changed circumstances. This was begun by the British, who deliberately chose upper-caste males for middle-class administrative jobs. The pattern continues today, with a direct but not perfect relationship between membership of the professions and caste status, and a heavy predominance of males. Amongst our women, class background is a more stringent barrier than caste to entering the professions, indicating both that caste is breaking down to a limited extent, and that class is no more egalitarian in terms of social mobility than is caste. The appearance of egalitarianism under class is due to its individualist mobility, allowing individuals to rise — unlike caste, where only groups can rise.

High-caste women's resistance to the oppression of seclusion is facilitated by the change from caste to class, since the class structure allows some of them to take advantage of opportunities for education and professional employment. Within the context of a patriarchal high-caste background, women's employment marks a significant rejection of male control. The desire of women in the new middle class to emerge from domestic seclusion and enter employment stems from their resistance to their particular form of oppression in the higher castes.

Gender under Class
The organisation of male supremacy under class both adapts to women's

resistance and retains aspects of women's subordination under caste in modified form. Middle-class men find it increasingly difficult to exclude women from education and employment and confine them to the home, and thereby lose a significant degree of sexual and economic control over women. Whilst being educated, for example, a woman may find her own marriage partner; a job provides her with an independent income.

The class structure retains the hierarchical system of rewards and occupations from the caste structure, which, however, allows individual rather than group mobility, permitting women to enter the field. Gender hierarchy is also retained through discrimination against and harassment of women who enter the fields of education and employment and through the assignment of priority to males. Male priority is reinforced by the retention of the idea of women's subservience to men, justifying the continuation of male hierarchy and control. Women's access to education and employment in competition with men is compensated for by introducing the idea of female inferiority to males in those fields. The organisation of domestic and paid work is retained in accordance with the assumption, now increasingly untrue, of separate spheres of work for men and women. Attempts are made to maintain this separation by segregating education and employment as far as possible in terms of women-only schools, colleges and professions, and of confining women to 'female' subjects and jobs, particularly those which represent an extension of traditionally female nurturing roles such as teaching and medicine. This separation is reinforced by retention of the stereotype about women's domesticity, discouraging any change in the organisation of domestic and paid work. And the derivation of men's social position from the actions of the women is retained, except that now her professional achievements bring honour to the men, as well as her sexual purity. This is reflected in the change from opposition to pride at women's emergence from seclusion to professional employment, and in the demand for educated and professional wives for men of the middle class.

In short, the same social processes help to maintain male dominance in the class system as did so under the caste system, but in modified form. Within the class structure, male dominance is maintained through the process of hierarchy in both gender and class, although modified into an individualist form and introducing the notion of female inferiority; through the process of segregation in spheres of activity and ideology, modified to include women's educational and professional presence; and through the process of men deriving their social position from the women, modified to include female education and employability, not only sexual purity. These processes demonstrate that there is no liberation for women under the class structure, despite the gains women have made at the top of the social hierarchy.

Gender under Imperialism

The British used the women's cause to maintain colonialism and to demonstrate national superiority. They therefore had an interest in liberalising women's position whilst maintaining and emphasising women's subordination, the former to confirm British superiority, the latter to reject demands for self-rule. The gender division is linked to economics by this process, since it was precisely this contradictory approach that was required to protect British financial interests in the colonies. So gender divisions helped to maintain colonialism, and colonialism helped to preserve gender.

A similar process occurs today whereby Indian women are portrayed in the West as abjectly submissive, without any reference to the contrary images and realities of female power. The notion that women's liberation is Western inspired is a further mystification of women's history in India, serving to emphasise the Indian form of male domination over the Western forms and perpetuating the myth of Western superiority in gender relations. On a material level, imperialism maintains the gender division through the association of the West's economic exploitation of India with the gender ideology, giving men priority in scarcity. This contributes to the deterioration of women's educational and employment prospects, which makes it harder for women in particular to complete their education, find a job, and organise their home and work life, because of the additional pressures faced by women in the home and at the workplace. This in turn reinforces the idea of women as less competent and reliable than men.

Ideologically, cultural imperialism has introduced the notion of female inferiority which had no part in Indian culture, where female power and its containment was stressed. Although females were segregated in the upper castes into the domestic sphere, this separation did not imply an inferior evaluation of the domestic, since that arena was crucial to the maintenance of caste purity. The inferiority notion adds a derogatory component to the gender ideology, serving to worsen women's position. It also makes for a degraded position for women abroad when added to the imperialist ideology of Western racial superiority, for the context of imperialism creates a notion not only of women's inferiority to men, but also of Indian women's inferiority to Western women. The construction of ideas about gender and national inferiority, the distribution of disadvantage in scarcity down to the female sex within families, by employers and by governments, and the conflation of male domination with evaluations of cultural difference, are all processes by which imperialism helps to maintain, and is maintained by, the divisions of gender.

Statistical Tables

Note: data refer to our sample of 120 Delhi professional women, unless otherwise specified.

Table 1
Level of Highest Qualification

Graduate	17%
Professional Diploma	14%
Masters	50%
Doctorate	17%
Fellow etc.	2%
Total	*100%*

Table 2
Number of Qualifications:

1	16%
2	47%
3	29%
4	4%
5	3%
6	1%
Total	*100%*

Table 3
Number of Qualifications:
Doctors, Managers, Civil Servants (men and women) in public sector in India

1	70%
2	26%
3+	4%
Total	*100%*

Derived from DGE&T (1971)
Occupational-Educational Pattern in India (Public Sector). New Delhi: Govt. of India, Appendix II, pp.306-7, 320-7, 338-41.

Table 4
Number of Qualifications:
Doctors, Lecturers, Civil Servants (women) in public sector in India

1	34%
2	54%
3+	12%
Total	*100%*

Derived from: DGE&T (1971)
Occupational-Educational Pattern in India (Public Sector). New Delhi: Govt. of India, Appendix IV, pp.354, 356, 362.

Table 5
Country of Education

India only	86%
Europe	10%
U.S.A.	2%
Asia	2%
Total	*100%*

Table 6
Father's income in Rupees per
month

Rs < 1000	17%
1001-1500	26%
1501-2000	11%
2001-2500	11%
2501-3000	6%
3001-3500	1%
3501-4000	3%
4000+	4%
Unspecified	21%
Total	*100%*

Mean = Rs 1989
Note: These figures are for 1977

Table 7
Monthly Emoluments in Rupees
per month:
Male degree holders & technical
personnel in India

Rs < 1000	73%
1000-1999	6%
2000+	1%
Unspecified	20%
Total	*100%*

Derived from: Dept. of Social Welfare
(1978) *Women in India: a Statistical
Profile*. New Delhi: Govt. of India,
Table 5.12, p.259.

Note: These figures are from the 1971
Census of India. The Indian High
Commission estimates an inflation rate
of 81% between 1971 and 1977.

Table 8
Natal Family's Attitude to
Women's Employment

Opposed	5%
Divided	19%
Laissez-faire	55%
Supportive	21%
Total	*100%*

Table 9
Unemployment Rate 1971: Workforce in India

Area	Sex	No. of Unemployed Persons (millions)	No. of Employed Persons (millions)	Total Potential Workforce (millions)	% Unemployed out of Potential Workforce
All	Total	9.0	180.4	189.4	4.8%
India	Males	4.0	149.1	153.1	2.6%
	Females	5.0	31.3	36.3	13.8%
Rural	Total	7.7	148.4	156.1	4.9%
	Males	3.2	120.4	123.6	2.6%
	Females	4.5	28.0	32.5	13.8%
Urban	Total	1.3	32.0	33.3	3.9%
	Males	0.8	28.7	29.5	2.7%
	Females	0.5	3.3	3.8	13.2%

No. of unemployed persons derived from: Indian Council for Social Science Research (1975) *Status of Women in India*. New Delhi: Allied Publishers, Table 27, p.164.
No. of employed persons derived from: Dept. of Social Welfare (1978) *Women in India: a Statistical Profile*. New Delhi: Govt. of India, Table 5.4, p.212.
All figures are from the 1971 Census of India. The unemployment figures are for people actively seeking work. Note that the figures can only be regarded as rough estimates because of the vagaries of the enumeration system.

Table 10
Monthly Emoluments in Rupees per month: Qualified Employees in India 1971

	Males	Females
Rs < 100	0.3%	0.8%
100-499	49.9%	63.4%
500-999	22.9%	14.7%
1000-1999	5.6%	1.5%
2000+	1.0%	0.1%
Unspecified	20.0%	19.2%
Total	*99.7%*	*99.7%*
No.	1,311,374	149,620

Derived from: Dept. of Social Welfare (1978) *Women in India: a Statistical Profile*. New Delhi: Govt. of India, Table 5.12, p.259.

Table 11
Women Employees in the Professions under Study:
Selected professions in India

Profession	Total Employed	No. of Women	% of Women to Total Employed
Doctors (Graduates)[1]			
1977	171,619	36,622	21.3%
Teachers (Higher education)[2]			
1973-4	161,419	28,441	17.6%
Indian Administrative Service[3]			
1977	2,556	218	8.5%
Administrative, Executive & Managerial Workers[4]			
1970-1	695,000	13,000	1.9%

1. Dept. of Social Welfare (1978) *Women in India: a Statistical Profile*. New Delhi: Govt. of India, Table 5.38, p.284.
2. Ibid., Table 5.44, pp.290-1.
3. Ibid., Table 5.28, p.278.
4. Derived from: DGE&T (1971) *Occupational-Educational Pattern in India (Public Sector)*. New Delhi: Govt. of India, Tables VI & VII, pp.19 & 21, and DGE&T of Labour (1973) *Occupational Pattern in India (Private Sector)*. New Delhi: Govt. of India, Table IX, pp.29-30.

Table 12
Religion

Religion	No.	%
Hindu	101	84
Christian	6	5
Sikh	6	5
Jain	4	3
Muslim	2	2
Jewish	1	1
Total	*120*	*100*

Note: 3 of the Hindus gave their religion as atheist, agnostic or humanitarian.

Table 13
Caste by Profession (Hindus)

Caste	Doctors		Lecturers		Civil Servants		Managers		Total	
	No.	%	No.	%	No.	%	No.	%	No.	%
Brahmin	6	26.1	15	55.6	8	32.0	9	34.6	38	37.6
Kshatriya	9	39.1	6	22.2	7	28.0	11	42.3	33	32.6
Non-brahmin*	4	17.4	2	7.4	4	16.0	3	11.5	13	12.8
Vaishya	2	8.7	4	14.8	5	20.0	1	3.9	12	11.8
Sudra	0	0	0	0	1	4.0	0	0	1	0.9
Unspecified	2	8.7	0	0	0	0	2	7.7	4	3.9
Total	23	100	27	100	25	100	26	100	101	100

*Non-brahmins are castes which do not fit into the 4-varna system, but are high-ranking. They are considered to be below the brahmins but above vaishyas. They cannot be classed as kshatriyas, but they are of approximately equivalent rank to kshatriyas.

Table 14
Total family income in
Rupees per month

Rs	
1000-1500	12%
1501-2000	14%
2001-2500	26%
2501-3000	21%
3001-3500	6%
3501-4000	10%
4001-4500	3%
4501-5000	4%
5000+	4%
Total	100%

Mean = Rs 2859

Table 15
Per Capita Family Income in
Rupees per month

Rs < 500	19%
501-1000	52%
1001-1500	21%
1501-2000	5%
2001-2500	2%
2500+	1%
Total	100%

Mean = Rs 938

Table 16
Father's Education

Illiterate	0.8%
Primary	1.7%
Middle	6.7%
Secondary	7.5%
Graduate	47.5%
Postgraduate	31.6%
Doctorate	1.7%
Fellow etc.	0.8%
Unspecified	1.6%
Total	*100%*

Table 17
Mother's Education

Illiterate	5.0%
Primary	19.2%
Middle	7.5%
Secondary	42.5%
Graduate	18.3%
Postgraduate	5.0%
Doctorate	0.8%
Fellow etc.	0%
Unspecified	1.7%
Total	*100%*

Table 18
Percentage Literacy by Sex: Percentage of total population 1971

Area	*Literates*		*Illiterates*	
	Males	*Females*	*Males*	*Females*
All India	39.4	18.7	60.6	81.3
Rural	33.8	13.2	66.2	86.8
Urban	61.3	42.1	38.7	57.9

Source: Dept. of Social Welfare (1978) *Women in India: a Statistical Profile*. New Delhi: Govt. of India, Table 4.2, p.120.

Table 19
Educational Level of Literates by Sex: Percentage of total illiterates 1971

Education	*All India*		*Rural*		*Urban*	
	Males	*Females*	*Males*	*Females*	*Males*	*Females*
Primary	34.6	38.2	38.9	43.8	25.6	30.8
Middle	18.9	15.8	17.7	12.7	21.3	19.9
Secondary	12.3	7.8	8.0	3.4	21.6	13.6
Graduate	2.3	1.3	0.8	0.2	5.5	2.7

Source: Dept. of Social Welfare (1978) *Women in India: a Statistical Profile*, New Delhi: Govt. of India, Table 4.3, p.122.

Table 20
Father's Occupational
Classification*

Class	
I	28%
II	46%
III	25%
IV	1%
V	0%
VI	0%
VII	0%

* The fathers' occupations have been classified according to D'Souza's method, which has been verified for India, and is claimed to have a high degree of similarity to the Registrar-General's classification of occupations in the U.K.

See Victor D'Souza (1968) *Social Structure of a Planned City: Chandigarh*. Bombay: Orient Longman , p.379.

Table 21
Head of Household's Occupation:
Chandigarh City

Class	
I	3.4%
II	9.9%
III	17.2%
IV	42.3%
V	9.3%
VI	15.2%
VII	2.7%

Source: Victor D'Souza (1968) *Social Structure of a Planned City: Chandigarh*. Bombay: Orient Longman , p.324.

Table 22
Economic Dependence on Employment by Marital State

Marital State	*Economically Dependent on Job*						
	Fully	*Considerably*	*Half*	*Partly*	*Not now, but at some time*	*Not at all*	*Total*
Single	15	4	2	6	1	15	43
Married	3	7	7	18	8	28	71
Separated	1	0	0	0	0	0	1
Divorced	3	0	0	0	0	0	3
Widowed	0	0	0	0	0	2	2
Total No.	*22*	*11*	*9*	*24*	*9*	*45*	*120*
Percentage	18%	9%	8%	20%	8%	37%	100%

% of women fully or partially dependent on job	=	55%
% of women not economically dependent on job	=	45%
Total	=	100%

% of women dependent at some time on job	=	63%
% of women never so far dependent on job	=	37%
Total	=	100%

Table 23
Economic Dependence on Employment by Economic Motive for Working

Economically Dependent on job (a)		*Motive for Work is Economic Independence (regardless of other support) as % of (a)* (b)	
		no.	%
Fully	22	18	82%
Considerably	11	9	82%
Half	9	7	78%
Partly	24	13	54%
Not now, but at some time	9	7	78%
Not at all	45	23	51%
Total	*120*	*77*	*64%*

Table 24
Perceived Sex Discrimination in Employment by Marriage, and by Women-only Occupation

Perceive Sex Discrimination at Work (a)		*Unmarried Women as % of (a)* (b)	*Women in Women-only Occupations as % of (a)* (c)
Yes	63%	32%	1%
No	37%	44%	12%

Table 25
Family Structures by Marital State

Family Structures

Marital State	Living Alone	Living with Another relative	Natal Nuclear	Natal Joint	Conjugal Nuclear	Conjugal Joint	Parents living in	Single Parent	Total No.	%
Single	9	3	16	5					33	28%
Engaged (arranged)	2		5						7	6%
Engaged (love)	2			1					3	2%
Married (arranged)	1		1		32	9	3		46	38%
Married (love)					17	7	1		25	21%
Separated								1	1	1%
Divorced (arranged)	1		1	1					3	2%
Widowed	2								2	2%
Total	*17*	*3*	*23*	*7*	*49*	*16*	*4*	*1*	*120*	*100%*

Table 26
Region of Origin

Northwest	37%	
North	20%	
South	13%	
East	13%	
West	8%	
Pakistan	8%	
Bangladesh	1%	
Total	*100%*	

The states were grouped into five regional categories
Northwest – Delhi, Haryana, Jammu & Kashmir, Himachal Pradesh, Punjab
North – Uttar Pradesh, Madhya Pradesh
South – Karnataka, Andhra Pradesh, Kerala, Tamil Nadu
East – Orissa, Bihar, Bengal, Assam
West – Maharashtra, Gujerat, Rajasthan

Table 27
Marital State by Response to Conflict between Marriage and Employment

Marital State		Response				
	No problem	Resistance	Compromise	Sacrifice	Total	
Single	9	19	2	3	33	(28)
Engaged (arranged)	1	1		5	7	(6)
Engaged (love)			2	1	3	(2)
Married (arranged)	1	6	28	11	46	(38)
Married (love)		4	18	3	25	(21)
Widowed	1	1			2	(2)
Separated } (arranged)		1			1	(1)
Divorced		3			3	(2)
Total	12 (10)	35 (29)	50 (42)	23 (19)	120 (100)	

Note: Percentages in brackets

This table is not intended as a fixed classification of our women's attitudes to employment and marriage. As indicated in the text (p.199) we do not imply that the women exclusively or consistently chose one form of response over others. The table signifies our selection of the women's responses to a significant issue or potential issue, where a conflict of interest could occur between marriage and employment.

Table 28
Marital State by Age

Age Group		Marital State			
	Single	Married	Widowed*	Divorced/ Separated*	Total
22-24	11 (100)				11 (100)
25-29	15 (44)	18 (53)		1 (3)	34 (100)
30-34	8 (40)	12 (60)			20 (100)
35-39	2 (12)	14 (88)			16 (100)
40-44	2 (15)	9 (70)		2 (15)	13 (100)
45-49	2 (22)	6 (67)		1 (11)	9 (100)
50-54	2 (17)	9 (75)	1 (8)		12 (100)
55-59	1 (20)	3 (60)	1 (20)		5 (100)
Total	43 (36)	71 (59)	2 (2)	4 (3)	120 (100)

Note: Percentages in brackets

* The figures in these columns are too small for the percentages in each group to be significant. Comparisons should be made only with the total percentage.

Table 29
Marital State by Age, 1971:
Percentage of female urban population (excludes 0.1% 'unspecified' category in some rows)

Age Group			Marital State		
				Divorced/	
	Single	Married	Widowed	Separated	Total
20-24	19.1	79.7	0.7	0.4	100
25-29	4.5	93.5	1.5	0.5	100
30-34	1.9	94.1	3.5	0.5	100
35-39	1.1	92.1	6.2	0.6	100
40-44	1.0	84.9	13.5	0.5	100
45-49	0.9	77.7	20.9	0.4	100
50-54	0.8	60.9	37.7	0.5	100
55-59	0.6	55.1	43.7	0.5	100

Derived from: Ashish Bose (1975) 'A Demographic Profile'. In Devaki Jain (ed) *Indian Women*. New Delhi: Government of India, Table 15, pp.155-6.

Table 30
Number of Children in
Natal Family

Number of Children	% of Families
1	2%
2	8%
3	21%
4	22%
5	17%
6	8%
7	7%
8	6%
9	2%
10	2%
11	2%
12	1%
Unspecified	2%
Total	*100%*

Mean number of children = 4.8

Table 31
Number of Children in
Conjugal Family (Married and sometime married women over 35 only)

Number of Children	% of Families
0	7%
1	22%
2	47%
3	9%
Unspecified	15%
Total	*100%*

Mean number of children = 1.7
n = 45

Bibliography

Acker, Joan, Barry, Kate and Esseveld, Joke (1983) 'Objectivity and Truth: Problems in Doing Feminist Research', *Women's Studies International Forum*, 6, 4, pp.423-35.

Al-Hibri, Azizah (1981) 'Capitalism is an Advanced Stage of Patriarchy: but Marxism is not Feminism'. In Lydia Sargent (ed), *Women and Revolution: the Unhappy Marriage of Marxism and Feminism*. London: Pluto.

Altekar, A.S. (1962) *The Position of Women in Hindu Civilisation*. Delhi: Motilal Banarsidas.

Ambedkar, B.R. (1945) *What Congress and Gandhi have done to the Untouchables*. Bombay: Thacker & Co.

Andrews, Robert Hardy (1967) *A Lamp for India: The Story of Madame Pandit*. London: Arthur Barker.

Anthias, Floya and Yuval-Davis, Nira (1983) 'Contextualising Feminism — Gender, Ethnic and Class Divisions'. Paper presented to the Conference of Socialist Economists, Bradford University.

Asthana, Pratima (1974) *Women's Movement in India*. Delhi: Vikas.

Babb, Lawrence (1970) 'Marriage and Malevolence: the Uses of Sexual Opposition in a Hindu Pantheon'. *Ethnology* IX, pp.137-49.

Baig, Tara Ali (1976) *India's Woman Power*. New Delhi: S. Chand.

Bamberger, Joan (1974) 'The Myth of Matriarchy: Why Men Rule in Primitive Society'. In M.Z. Rosaldo and L. Lamphere (eds), *Woman, Culture and Society*. Stanford: Stanford University Press.

Barrett, Michèle (1980) *Women's Oppression Today*. London: Verso.

Basham, A.L. (1966) 'Indian Society and the Legacy of the Past', *Australian Journal of Politics and History* 12, pp.131-45.

Basu, Aparna (1976) 'The Role of Women in the Indian Struggle for Freedom'. In B.R. Nanda (ed), *Indian Women from Purdah to Modernity*. New Delhi: Vikas.

Beauchamp, Joan (1934) *British Imperialism in India*. London: Martin Lawrence.

Beechey, Veronica (1979) 'On Patriarchy', *Feminist Review* 3, pp.66-82.

Berger, John (1973) *Ways of Seeing*. Harmondsworth: Penguin.

Beteille, André (1971) *Caste, Class and Power. Changing Patterns of Stratification in a Tanjore Village*. Berkeley: University of California Press.

Bhasin, Kamla (1972) 'The Predicament of Middle Class Indian Women — An Inside View'. In Kamla Bhasin (ed), *The Position of Women in India*. Srinigar: Arvind Deshpande.

Bhasin, Kamla (ed), (1972) *The Position of Women in India*. Srinigar, Arvind Deshpande.

Bhasin, Kamla (1982) 'The Riddle of Marriage', *Manushi* 11,p.38.

Bhasin, Kamla (1982) 'Rokeya: A Crusader against Purdah', *Manushi* 11.

Bhatty, Zarina (1976) 'Status of Muslim Women and Social Change'. In B.R. Nanda (ed), *Indian Women from Purdah to Modernity*. New Delhi: Vikas.

Bhoothalingham, Mathuram (1964) *The Story of Rama*. New York: Asia Publishing House.

Blumberg, Rhoda Lois, and Dwaraki, Leela (1980) *India's Educated Women*. Delhi: Hindustan Publishing Corporation.

Bose, Ashish (1975) 'A Demographic Profile of Indian Women'. In Devaki Jain (ed), *Indian Women*. New Delhi: Government of India.

Brailsford, H.N. (1943) *Subject India*. London: Victor Gollancz.

Brandt, Willy (1980) *North–South: a Programme for Survival. The Report of the Independent Commission on International Development Issues*. London: Pan.

Caplan, Ann Patricia (1979) 'Indian Women: Model and Reality. A Review of Recent Books, 1975-1979', *Women's Studies International Quarterly* 2, 4, 461-79.

Census of India (1971). New Delhi: Government of India.

Chand, Gyan (1939) *India's Teeming Millions*. London: George Allen & Unwin.

Chandra, Bipan (1974) 'The Indian Capitalist Class and British Imperialism'. In R.S. Sharma (ed), *Indian Society: Historical Probings*. New Delhi: People's Publishing House.

Cousins, Margaret, E. (1941) *Indian Womanhood Today*. Allahabad: Kitabistan.

Daly, Mary (1978) *Gyn/Ecology*. London: The Women's Press.

Dandekar, Kumudini (1975) 'Why has the Proportion of Women in India's Population been Declining?', *Economic and Political Weekly* 18 Oct, 1663-7.

Das, Kamala 'The Old Playhouse'. Poem reproduced in *Manushi* (1980) 6, p.52.

Das, Veena (1976) 'Indian Women: Work, Power and Status'. In B.R. Nanda (ed), *Indian Women from Purdah to Modernity*. New Delhi: Vikas.

Davies, Miranda (1983) 'Women in Struggle', *Third World Quarterly* 5, 4, 878-9.

de Reuck, Anthony and Knight, Julie (eds), (1967) *Caste and Race: Comparative Approaches*. London: Ciba Foundation.

de Souza, Alfred (ed), (1980) *Women in Contemporary India and South Asia*. New Delhi: Manohar.

Department of Social Welfare (1974) *Towards Equality: Report of the Committee on the Status of Women in India*. New Delhi: Government of India.

Department of Social Welfare (1978) *Women in India: a Statistical Profile*. New Delhi: Government of India.

Desai, A.R. (1959) *The Social Background of Indian Nationalism*. Bombay: Popular Book Depot.

Dhingra, O.P. (1972) *The Career Woman and Her Problems*. New Delhi: Shri Ram Centre for Industrial Relations and Human Resources.

Directorate-General of Employment and Training (1971) *Occupational-Educational Pattern in India (Public Sector)*. New Delhi: Government of India.

Directorate-General of Employment & Training (1973) *Occupational Pattern in India (Private Sector)*. New Delhi: Government of India.

D'Souza, Victor S. (1968) *Social Structure of a Planned City: Chandigarh*. New Delhi: Orient Longman.

D'Souza, Victor S. (1980) 'Family Status and Female Work Participation'. In Alfred de Souza (ed), *Women in Contemporary India and South Asia*. New Delhi: Manohar.

Dubey, Manjulika (1983) 'Interview with Chandralekha', *The Book Review*, VII, 6, May-June.

Dutt, R. Palme (1940) *India Today*. London: Victor Gollancz.

Ehrlich, Carol (1981) 'The Unhappy Marriage of Marxism and Feminism: Can it be saved?' In Lydia Sargent (ed), *Women and Revolution*. London: Pluto.

Eisenstein, Zillah (1979) *Capitalist Patriarchy and the Case for Socialist Feminism*. New York: Monthly Review Press.

Engels, Dagmar (1983) 'The Age of Consent Act of 1891: Colonial Ideology in Bengal', *South Asia Research* 3, 2, Nov.

Everett, Jana Matson (1981) *Women and Social Change in India*. New Delhi: Heritage.

Forbes, Geraldine (1979) 'Votes for Women'. In Vina Mazumdar (ed), *Symbols of Power*. New Delhi: Allied Publishers.

Forbes, Geraldine (1982) 'Caged Tigers: "First Wave" Feminists in India', *Women's Studies International Forum* 5, 6, pp.525-36.

Foreman, Ann (1977) *Femininity as Alienation: Women and the Family in Marxism and Psychoanalysis*. London: Pluto.

Fortes, Meyer (1958) 'Introduction'. In Jack Goody (ed), *The Developmental Cycle in Domestic Groups*. Cambridge: Cambridge University Press.

Frank, Andre Gunder (1977) 'Emergence of Permanent Emergency in India', *Economic and Political Weekly* XII, 11, 12 March.

Friedman, Scarlet and Sarah, Elizabeth (eds), (1982) *On the Problem of Men*. London: The Women's Press.

Frith, Nigel (1975) *The Legend of Krishna*. London: Abacus.

Gage, Matilda (1972) *Woman, Church and State*. New York: Arno Press.

Gandhi, M.K. (1938) *Woman and Social Injustice*. Ahmedabad: Navajivan Publishing House.

Gedge, E.C. and Choksi, M. (eds), (1929) *Women in Modern India*. Bombay: D.B. Taraporewala.

Ghurye, G.S. (1932) *Caste and Race in India*. London: Routledge & Kegan Paul.

Gokhale, B.G. (1959) *Ancient India*. Bombay: Asia Publishing House.

Goody, Jack (1958) *The Developmental Cycle in Domestic Groups*. Cambridge: Cambridge University Press.

Goody, Jack (1976) *Production and Reproduction*. Cambridge: Cambridge University Press.

Gore, M.S. (1968) *Urbanisation and Family Change in India*. Bombay: Popular Prakashan.

Gough, Kathleen (1962) 'Nayar'; 'Tiyyar'; 'Mapilla'. In D. Schneider and K. Gough (eds), *Matrilineal Kinship*. Berkeley: University of California Press. Chapters 6-9.

Gulati, Leela (1975) 'Occupational Distribution of Working Women', *Economic and Political Weekly*, 25 October.

Gupta, Kuntesh (1973) 'Structure and Organization of Indian Family: the Emerging Patterns', *International Journal of Contemporary Sociology* 10, 4, pp.163-82.

Hall, Catherine (1981) 'Gender Divisions and Class Formation in the Birmingham Middle Class, 1780-1850'. In R. Samuel (ed), *People's History and Socialist Theory*. London: Routledge & Kegan Paul.

Hartmann, Heidi (1981) 'The Unhappy Marriage of Marxism and Feminism: Towards a more Progressive Union'. In Lydia Sargent (ed), *Women and*

Revolution. London: Pluto.

Hiro, Dilip (1976) *Inside India Today*. London: Routledge & Kegan Paul.

Hobson, Sarah (1978) *Family Web*. London: John Murray.

Hunt, J. and Adams, S. (1980) *Women, Work and Trade Union Organisation*. London: Workers' Educational Association.

Hutton, J.H. (1963) *Caste in India: its Nature, Function and Origins*, 4th edition. Bombay: Oxford University Press.

Indian Council for Social Science Research (1975) *Status of Women in India*. A synopsis of the report of the National Committee on the status of women. Bombay: Allied Publishers.

Indian Statutory Commission (1930) *Report of the Indian Statutory Commission* (Simon Report) Vol.1 — Survey. London: His Majesty's Stationery Office.

Jacobson, Doranne and Wadley, Susan (1977) *Women in India: Two Perspectives*. New Delhi: Manohar.

Jahan, Roushan (ed. + trans.) (1981) *Inside Seclusion: the Avoradhbasini of Rokeya Sakhawat Hossain*. Dacca: Women for Women.

Jain, Devaki (ed), (1975) *Indian Women*. New Delhi: Government of India.

Joshi, Rama (1978) 'The Status of Female Labour and the Law', *Bulletin of Comparative Labour Relations* 9.

Joynson, R.B. (1970) 'The Breakdown of Modern Psychology'. *Bulletin of the British Psychological Society*, 23, pp.261-9.

Kapadia, K.M. (1968) *Marriage and Family in India*. Calcutta: Oxford University Press.

Kapur, Promilla (1970) *Marriage and the Working Woman in India*. Delhi: Vikas.

Kapur, Promilla (1973) *Love, Marriage and Sex*. Delhi: Vikas.

Kapur, Promilla (1974) *The Changing Status of the Working Woman in India*. Delhi: Vikas.

Kapur, Rama (1969) 'Role Conflict among Employed Housewives', *Indian Journal of Industrial Relations* 5, 1, July.

Karlekar, Malavika (1975) 'Professionalization of Women School Teachers', *Indian Journal of Industrial Relations* 11, 1, pp.53-64.

Karve, Iravati (1953) *Kinship Organisation in India*. Poona: Deccan College.

Kaur, Manmohan (1968) *Role of Women in the Freedom Movement (1857-1947)*. Delhi: Sterling.

Kishwar, Madhu (1983) 'Attenborough's Version of Gandhi', *Manushi* 3, 3, March-April.

Kosambi, D.D. (1965) *The Culture and Civilization of Ancient India in Historical Outline*. London: Routledge & Kegan Paul.

Lambert, R.D. (1963) *Workers, Factories and Social Change in India*. Princeton: Princeton University Press.

Leonard, Diana (1982) 'Male Feminists and Divided Women'. In Scarlet Friedman and Elizabeth Sarah (eds), *On the Problem of Men*. London: The Women's Press.

Liddle, Joanna and Joshi, Rama (In Press) 'Gender and Colonialism: Women's Organisation under the Raj', *Women's Studies International Forum*, 8.

Lipshitz, Susan (ed), (1978) *Tearing the Veil*. London: Routledge & Kegan Paul.

Mackenzie, Midge (1975) *Shoulder to Shoulder.* Harmondsworth: Penguin.

Magdoff, Harry (1978) *Imperialism*. New York: Monthly Review Press.

Mankekar, Kamala, for the Central Institute of Research and Training in Public Cooperation (1975) *Women in India*. New Delhi: Government of India.

Marriott, McKim (1955) 'Little Communities in an Indigenous Civilization'. In McKim Marriott 'Village India: Studies in the Little Community', *The American Anthropologist* 57, pp.171-222.

Marriott, McKim (1955) 'Village India: Studies in the Little Community', *The American Anthropologist*, 57, pp.171-222.

Marx, Karl (1976) *Capital*, vol.1. Harmondsworth: Penguin.

Mathur, Y.B. (1973) *Women's Education in India (1813-1966)*. Delhi: University of Delhi.

Mayo, Katherine (1927) *Mother India*. New York: Harcourt Brace.

Mazumdar, Vina (1976) 'The Social Reform Movement in India'. In B.R. Nanda (ed), *Indian Women: from Purdah to Modernity*. New Delhi: Vikas.

Mazumdar, Vina (ed), (1979) *Symbols of Power: Studies on the Political Status of Women in India*. New Delhi: Allied Publishers.

Mehta, Rama (1970) *The Western Educated Hindu Woman*. Bombay: Asia Publishing House.

Mehta, Sushila (1982) *Revolution and the Status of Women in India*. New Delhi: Metropolitan.

Mencher, Joan (1962) 'Changing Familial Roles among South Malabar Nayars', *South Western Journal of Anthropology* 18, pp.230-45.

Mencher, Joan (1965) 'The Nayars of South Malabar'. In M.F. Nimkoff (ed), *Comparative Family Systems*. Boston: Houghton Mifflin.

Merck, Mandy (1978) 'The City's Achievements: The Patriotic Amazonamachy and Ancient Athens'. In Susan Lipshitz (ed), *Tearing the Veil*. London: Routledge & Kegan Paul.

Mernissi, Fatima (1975) *Beyond the Veil*. New York: Wiley.

Mies, Maria (1980) *Indian Women and Patriarchy*. New Delhi: Concept.

Mirchandani, G.G. (1970) 'Status of Women in India', *India Today*. Delhi: United News of India Research Bureau. Ch.14.

Mills, C. Wright (1959) *The Sociological Imagination*. New York: Oxford University Press.

Misra, B.B. (1961) *The Indian Middle Classes*. London: Oxford University Press.

Mitra, Asok (1979) *Implications of Declining Sex Ratio in India's Population*. Indian Council for Social Science Research: Programme of Women's Studies I.

Moore, W.E. and Feldman, A.S. (eds), (1960) *Labour Commitment and Social Change in Developing Areas*. New York, SSRC.

Morris, M.D. (1960) 'The Labour Market in India'. In W.E. Moore and A.S. Feldman (eds), *Labour Commitment and Social Change in Developing Areas*. New York: SRRC, pp.173-200.

Mukherjee, Prabhati (1978) *Hindu Women: Normative Models*. New Delhi: Orient Longman.

Mukherjee, Prabhati (1983) 'The Image of Women in Hinduism', *Women's Studies International Forum* 6, 4, p.379.

Mukherjee, R. (1969) *Family in India: a Perspective*. Calcutta: Indian Statistical Institute.

Mukherjee, S.N. (1974) 'The Social Implications of the Political Thought of Raja Ram Mohun Roy'. In R.S. Sharma (ed), *Indian Society: Historical Probings*. New Delhi: People's Publishing House.

Namjoshi, Suniti (1981) *Feminist Fables*. London: Sheba.

Nanda, B.R. (ed), (1976) *Indian Women from Purdah to Modernity*. New Delhi: Vikas.

Nath, Kamla (1968) 'Women in the Working Force in India', *Economic and Political Weekly* 3 August.

Nehru, Jawaharlal (1939) *Glimpses of World History*. London: Lindsay Drummond.

Nehru, Jawaharlal (1946) *The Discovery of India*. New York: John Day.

Nichols, Theo and Beynon, Huw (1977) *Living with Capitalism*. London: Routledge & Kegan Paul.

Nimkoff, M.F. (ed), (1965) *Comparative Family Systems*. Boston: Houghton Mifflin.

Nivedita, Sister (Margaret Noble) (1907) *Cradle Tales of Hinduism*. London: Longmans, Green and Co.

Oakley, Ann (1974) *The Sociology of Housework*. Oxford: Martin Robertson.

Oakley, Ann (1981) 'Interviewing Women: a Contradiction in Terms', in Helen Roberts (ed) *Doing Feminist Research*. London: Routledge & Kegan Paul.

Omvedt, Gail (1973) 'Gandhi and the Pacification of the Indian Nationalist Movement', *Bulletin of Concerned Asian Scholars* 5, 1, July.

Omvedt, Gail (1975) 'Caste, Class and Women's Liberation in India', *Bulletin of Concerned Asian Scholars* 7, 1, pp.43-8. Jan-March. Special issue: Asian Women.

Omvedt, Gail (1980) *We Will Smash this Prison*. London: Zed Press.

Orenstein, H. (1961) 'The Recent History of the Extended Family in India', *Local Problems* 8, 4, pp.41-50 Spring.

Ramabai, Pandita (1888) *The High Caste Hindu Woman*. Philadelphia: Jas B. Rodgers.

Rao, M.S.A. (1957) *Social Change in Malabar*. Bombay: Popular Book Depot.

Rawson, Philip (1973) *The Art of Tantra*. London: Thames and Hudson.

Reiter, R.R. (ed), (1975) *Toward an Anthropology of Women*. London: Monthly Review Press.

Roberts, Helen (ed), (1981) *Doing Feminist Research*. London: Routledge & Kegan Paul.

Rosaldo, Michelle Zimbalist and Lamphere, Louise (1974) *Woman, Culture and Society*. Stanford, Calif.: Stanford University Press.

Rosen, George (1966) *Democracy and Economic Change in India*. Berkeley: University of California Press.

Ross, Aileen, D. (1961) *The Hindu Family in its Urban Setting*. Toronto: University of Toronto Press.

Rudra, Ashok (1975) 'Cultural and Religious Influences'. In Devaki Jain (ed), *Indian Women*. New Delhi: Government of India.

Rukhmabai, Dr (1929) 'Purdah — the Need for its Abolition'. In Evelyn Gedge and Mithan Choksi (eds), *Women in Modern India*. Bombay: Taraporewala.

Samuel, Raphael (ed), (1981) *People's History and Socialist Theory*. London: Routledge & Kegan Paul.

Sarah, Elizabeth (1982) 'Towards a Reassessment of Feminist History', *Women's Studies International Forum* 5, 6, pp.519-23.

Sargent, Lydia (ed), (1981) *Women and Revolution: the Unhappy Marriage of Marxism and Feminism*. London: Pluto.

Sarkar, Lotika (1976) 'Jawaharlal Nehru and the Hindu Code Bill'. In B.R. Nanda (ed), *Indian Women from Purdah to Modernity*. Delhi: Vikas.

Sarkar, Lotika and Mazumdar, Vina (1974) 'Note of Dissent'. In Dept. of Social Welfare, *Towards Equality: Report of the Committee on the Status of Women in India*. New Delhi: Government of India, p.355.

Schneider, David (1962) 'The Distinctive Features of Matrilineal Descent Groups'. In D. Schneider and K. Gough (eds), *Matrilineal Kinship*. Berkeley: University of California Press.

Schneider, D.M. and Gough, K.E. (eds), (1962) *Matrilineal Kinship*. Berkeley: University of California Press.

Sen, Anupam (1982) *The State, Industrialization and Class Formations in India: A Neo-Marxist Perspective on Colonialism, Underdevelopment and Development*. London: Routledge & Kegan Paul.

Sengupta, Padmini (1960) *Women Workers of India*. Bombay: Asia Publishing House.

Sharma, Ram Sharan (1966) *Light on Early Indian Society and Economy*. Bombay: Manaktalas.

Sharma, Ram Sharan (ed), (1974) *Indian Society: Historical Probings*. New Dehli: People's Publishing House.

Singh, Andrea Menefee (1976) *Neighbourhood and Social Networks in Urban India: South Indian Voluntary Associations in Delhi*. New Delhi: Marwah.

Singh, Andrea Menefee (1980) 'The Study of Women in South Asia: Some Current Methodological and Research Issues'. In Alfred de Souza (ed), *Women in Contemporary India and South Asia*. New Delhi: Manohar.

Singh, Andrea Menefee and de Souza, Alfred (1976) *The Position of Women in Migrant Bastis in Delhi*. Report prepared for the Department of Social Welfare, Government of India.

Sinha, Surajit (1967) 'Caste in India: its Essential Pattern of Socio-cultural Integration'. In Anthony de Reuck and Julie Knight (eds), *Caste and Race: Comparative Approaches*. London: Ciba Foundation.

Spear, Percival (1970) *A History of India*, vol.2. Harmondsworth: Penguin.

Spender, Dale (1983) *There's Always Been a Women's Movement this Century*. London: Routledge & Kegan Paul.

Srinivas, M.N. (1942) *Marriage and Family in Mysore*. Bombay: New Book Co.

Srinivas, M.N. (1962) *Caste in Modern India and Other Essays*. London: Asia Publishing House.

Srinivas, M.N. (1966) *Social Change in Modern India*. Berkeley: University of California Press.

Srinivas, M.N. (1977) 'The Changing Position of Indian Women', *Man* 12, pp.221-38.

Stacey, Margaret and Price, Marion (1980) 'Women and Power', *Feminist Review* 5.

Stone, Merlin (1976) *The Paradise Papers: The Suppression of Women's Rites*. London: Virago, Quartet.

Taub, R.P. (1969) *Bureaucrats under Stress*. Berkeley: University of California Press.

Thapar, Romila (1963) 'The History of Female Emancipation in Southern Asia'. In Barbara Ward (ed), *Women in the New Asia*. Paris: Unesco, pp.473-95.

Thapar, Romila (1966) *A History of India*, vol.1. Harmondsworth: Penguin.

Thomas, P. (1964) *Indian Women through the Ages*. Bombay: Asia Publishing House.

Wadhera, Kiron (1976) *The New Breadwinners*. New Delhi: Vishwa Yuvak Kendra.

Wadley, Susan (1977) 'Women and the Hindu Tradition', in Doranne Jacobson and Susan Wadley, *Women in India: Two Perspectives*. New Delhi: Manohar.

Ward, Barbara E. (ed), (1963) *Women in the New Asia*. Paris: Unesco.

Weber, Max (1958) *The Religion of India*. New York: The Free Press.

Webster, Paula (1975) 'Matriarchy: a Vision of Power'. in R.R. Reiter (ed), *Toward an Anthropology of Women*. London: Monthly Review Press.

Wolpert, Stanley (1977) *A New History of India*. New York: Oxford University Press.

Yalman, Nur (1968) 'On the Purity of Women in the Castes of Ceylon and Malabar', *Journal of the Royal Anthropological Institute* 93, 1, pp.25-58.

Zaehner, Robert Charles (1966) *Hindu Scriptures*. London: J.M. Dent.

Index

age of sample 8
Age of Consent Act *see* child marriage
agricultural work 89-91
Ambedkar, B.R. 35, 37
Anglo-Indian War 30
Aryans 1, 51-2, 54, 61-2
assemblies, legislative: 35; and sex equality
  37-8

Bentinck, William 27, 31
bhakti 1, 67
birth rates in sample's families 226-7, 251
brahminism *see* Hinduism: 'brahmin
  tradition'
brahmins 1, 51, 54, 58-9, 61, 63-5, 68,
  71-2, 125, 163n51
Buddhism: 62, 64, 94; and tantra 66

caste: 57-76, 87-93; anti-caste movements
  50, 63, 66-7, 95; and class 70-5, 238;
  features of 58-9; and pollution 58, 68;
  and purity 58-61; of sample 125, 245;
  and women's organisations 22-3; and
  women's subordination *see* gender
  relations; and women's work 100-6
child marriage: 19-20, 26, 43n57, 57, 59,
  63-4, 66, 87, 111; and Age of Consent
  Act 20, 26, 42-3n57
child widows 59, 65, 87
Christianity 27
Christians: 8, 244; missionaries 7
civil servants *see* government servants
class: 70-3, 76; and caste 70-5, 238;
  defined 164n53; formation 6, 70-2,
  125; and socialist movement 95;
  and women's organisations 21-3; and
  women's subordination *see* gender
  relations; and women's work 6-7, 72-3,
  106-8, 110-11, 124-56
Code of Manu 65
colonialism: defined 41n8; and underdevelopment 24-5, 70-1; and women
  12, 25-32, 39-40, 49-50, 72-3; and
  World War I 33
constitution, and sex equality 33, 36-9,
  73-4, 81n140

Daly, Mary 31
dependency of women: economic 89, 92,
  106, 111; on employment 247-8;
  social 63
dharma 1, 68
divorce: 37, 39, 57, 59, 74; in Islam 66;
  and lower castes 39, 66, 91; and Nayars
  29; and sample 140, 216, 230n15,
  249, 251
doctors 8, 73, 75, 244
domestic work: 90-2, 142-56; and class
  150-1; and imperialism 151; and men
  149-51, 207-13, 226-7; and seclusion
  89; and waged work 151-4, 198, 250
domesticity *see* gender ideology
dowry 21-2, 62, 64, 74-5, 123, 218
Dravidians 1, 52-3
Dutt, R. Palme 31

East India Company 24-6
education: and economic resources 117-18;
  exclusion of lower castes 63; exclusion
  of women 63; female 19-21, 62, 74,
  117-23; of literate population 246;
  male 117; for marriage 122-3; of
  qualified employees 241; of sample
  241; of sample's parents 226, 246; and
  sex discrimination 121-3; Western 71
employment: and caste 92, 100-6, 109; and
  class 92, 106-8, 154-6; and the family
  151-4; family attitudes to women's
  242; female 37, 50, 62, 89-90, 94,
  104-5, 109, 124-5; and marriage 101,
  103, 107, 110; for marriage 155;
  professional women in 7, 73, 75-6, 92,

116, 124-41, 155-6, 244-5; prohibition
of women's 63, 88-9, 101, 104; of
sample's mothers 226, 230n19; and sex
discrimination 131-6
eve-teasing *see* sexual harassment

family organisation: 142-65; alternative
forms 148-9; and authority structure
145-6, 148, 150; joint 143-7;
matrilineal 26, 28-30, 52-3; nuclear
147-8; patriarchal 29, 52, 61-2, 64, 75;
patrilineal 52-3, 55; of sample 249
franchise: 35-6; universal adult 36, 39;
female 30, 35-7, 74, 81n141

Gandhi, M.K. 22-3, 33-5
gender ideology: and caste 69; and class
186-7; construction of 174-85; context
of 186-90, 192-3; cultural differences
in 89, 94, 187-8; and domesticity 175,
182-7, 192; and imperialism 188-90;
and patriarchy 69; and sexual property
183-4, 193; and women's inferiority
175, 177-80, 188-92; and women's
subservience 175, 180-2, 187-8, 191-2
gender relations: and caste 57-69, 89-93,
100-6, 115-16, 159-60; and class 72-3,
92-3, 105-8, 115-65, 186-7; and control
of women's power 55; and family
structure 50-3; and imperialism 6-7,
24-32, 38-40, 49-50, 235-40; and
Independence movement 20-1, 33-40,
236; and male & female power
principles 51; and mixing with men
105, 107-8, 138-41; and religious
culture 51-5; and social hierarchy 6-8,
11-12, 22-3, 50, 75-6, 95, 109-11,
233-9
Government of India Acts 35-6
government servants 8, 9, 73, 75, 244

Hindu Code: 36-7, 39, 74, 82n143; draft
36-7; five Acts of 45n126; and
matrilineal family 39; and patrilineal
family 39; and sex equality 37-8;
see also law; personal
Hinduism: and 'brahmin tradition' 54-5,
66, 68, 200-1; and control of women
59, 94; and mother goddess 54; and
'non-brahmin tradition' 54-5; and
tantra 66 *see also* shakti; and women's
power 56 *see also* power, female
Hindus 8, 244
honour 70, 106-8

imperialism: 7; defined 41n8; and
education 118-21; and employment
151, 154; and gender ideology 188-90;

and women 22-3, 31-2, 75, 95-6,
239-40
income: of qualified employees 243; of
qualified male employees 242; of
sample's families 242, 245; women's
contribution 164n59, 227
independence, women.s economic 104-5,
110, 126-8
Independence movement: 20, 22, 33-4, 36,
71-2; and arrest of leaders 34; and
Britain 31; and caste 35-6; and civil
disobedience 34; and franchise 36; and
Government of India Act 36; and
Hindu Code 38; leadership 22; and
National Social Conference 20,22; and
non-cooperation campaign 33; and
report on self-rule 36; and salt march
34; and swadeshi 21; and women 33-8,
95-6
Indian Mutiny *see* Anglo-Indian War
Indian National Congress *see* Independence
movement
infanticide, female 26, 29, 43n57
inheritance: 22, 26, 39, 43n57, 89; and
Hindu Code 36-7, 74; Hindu Women's
Right to Property Act 22; matrilineal
28-9; of Muslim women 66; patrilineal
62; and women's sexuality 57, 64-5,
68-9
Islam: 66; and control of women 59, 94;
and female power 51, 56, 66, 188;
and sati 66; and women 66; *see also*
Muslims

Jainism 62, 94
Jains 8, 244
Jallianwala Bagh 33
job segregation 124, 132-3, 135

Kali 54-5, 68
karma 1, 58, 68
kshatriya 1, 58, 61, 63-4, 71-2, 125, 245

Lakshmi 55, 68
land: reform 29; revenue 24-5
law: and the British 26-7, 30; Hindu
Women's Right to Property Act 22;
labour 74-5, 81-2n142; and middle class
38; personal 26, 29, 36-7, 39, 73
see also Hindu Code; Restitution of
Conjugal Rights 17, 40-1n4
lecturers 8, 73, 75, 244
literacy: female 52, 77n11, 117; male 117;
of population 246

Mahabharata Epic 64
managers 8-9, 73, 75, 244
Manu 65, 68

Manushi 1, 17, 40n2&3, 229
marriage: 26, 36-7, 62, 74, 88-9, 198;
    age at in Kerala 52, 77n13; arranged 59,
    209-10, 226; and employment 101, 103,
    107, 110; love 209-10, 226; and mother
    goddess 54-5; and property 65; rate of
    215-16, 227, 230n15, 22&23, 250-1
matriarchal culture 51-6, 67; and Aryans
    61-2; brahminisation of 54, 68; and
    brahminism 58-9, 66-8; defined 52;
    and matriliny 55; and mother goddess
    55; and religious myths 53-5; and
    shakti 52
matriarchy, definition of 52, 77n8
matriliny 26, 28-30, 52-3; and matriarchal
    culture 55
Mayo, Katherine 31-2
men *see* gender relations
middle class *see* class
mobility: physical 89, 104-5, 107-8, 122,
    136-8; social 59, 70, 105-6
monogamy 59, 62-3, 74
mother goddess 54-5, 66-8
Muslims: 7, 104-5, 244; invasions 62, 65,
    90; and Mughal empire 65-6, 70;
    see also Islam

Naidu, Sarojini 34
nationalist movement *see* Independence
    movement
Nayars of Malabar: 28, 52-3, 60; and
    legislation 28-30
Nehru, Jawaharlal 22, 34, 37
'non-brahmin tradition' *see* Hinduism

occupations: of Chandigarh household
    heads 247; of sample's fathers 247;
    traditional for women 8, 107

Partition 76, 95-6
pativrata 1, 64, 66
patriarchy: definition of 52, 77n6; and
    female power principle 51, 56; and
    gender ideology 69; and matriarchal
    culture 51-6; *see also* family
    organisation: patriarchal
patriliny: 52-3, 55; and female inheritance
    62; and male inheritance 62, 68
polygamy: 19, 22, 26, 28, 36-7, 53, 62-3;
    and lower castes 66
power, female: 188; containment 56;
    danger, to men 56-7, 61, 68; incorpora-
    tion into brahminism 66; material
    basis 99
power principle, female *see shakti*
power principle, male: 5, 7; and matriarchal
    culture 53; and patriarchy 52
Prasad, Rajendra 34, 37

property: concept of 29; sexual 92, 122,
    140; *see also* inheritance
purdah 1, 21, 29, 57, 59, 65-6, 88; *see also*
    seclusion

Ramayana Epic 64, 200, 204
region of origin, of sample 249
religion of sample 8, 244
research: method 10-11; objectives 11-12
respectability: 100-1, 104-5, 108, 110;
    criteria of 107
Roy, Ram Mohan 19-20, 22

Sanskritisation 6-7, 60
sati: 1, 19-20, 24, 26-30, 41n11, 42n57,
    57, 59, 64-5, 91, 200; and lower castes
    66; and Muslims 66
scheduled castes 119, 125, 155; *see also*
    sudras
seclusion: 59, 73, 88-93; and caste 66,
    89-92, 105-6; and caste respectability
    90, 110; and cultural differences
    89-90; defined 92; emergence from
    7-8, 12, 76, 87-112; *see also* purdah
sex discrimination: and constitution *see*
    constitution; in education *see* education;
    sample's perception 248; at work *see*
    employment
sex ratio: 29, 77n12; in Kerala 52
sex segregation 8, 73
sexual harassment 121, 137-41
sexuality, female: control of 57, 89,
    91-2, 111, 138, 140, 197, 227; danger
    to men 57, 60-1; and high castes 57,
    92; and property 57, 63-6, 68
shakti: 1, 5, 7, 54, 66; and matriarchal
    culture 52-4; and patriarchy 51
Simon Commission 34, 36
smriti 1, 63
social reform movements: 20; and
    imperialism 95; and women 66, 95-6
sudras 1, 58, 61, 63-4, 68, 71-2, 125,
    163n50, 245; *see also* scheduled castes
suffrage *see* franchise

tantra 1, 66-7, 201

untouchables *see* sudras

vaishya 1, 58, 61, 63-4, 68, 71-2, 125
Vedas 1, 51, 61

Westernisation 6-7: and women's liberation
    7, 12, 24
widow remarriage: 20-2, 26, 30, 42n57,
    57, 59, 62-5, 89, 91-2; and lower castes
    66
widowhood 19, 64, 66, 87-8, 91

witch-burning 27, 43n68
women's consciousness: 99, 167-94;
    contradictions in 169-73, 193-4
women's movement: 5, 7, 21, 49, 73-5, 99,
    198, 229; analysis of 22-3, 31; and
    British women's movement 49-50, 56,
    73, 235; defined 21; distinctiveness 49;
    and Hindu Code 37; and Independence
    movement 21-3, 33, 36; leadership 21;
    men's organisations 19-20; and resistance
    to male domination 49-50, 99, 229,
    235; resurgence 17-18; social composition
    22-3, 39, 75; women's organisations
    20-3, 26, 35-6, 39
women's subordination *see* gender relations
work: domestic *see* domestic work;
    professional *see* employment; unpaid
    family labour *see* agricultural work;
    waged *see* employment

zamindar 1, 25, 71